Retail Marketing

A. SIVAKUMAR

EXCEL BOOKS

ISBN 978-81-7446-575-7

First Edition: New Delhi, 2007

Copyright © 2007, A. Sivakumar
All Rights Reserved

EXCEL BOOKS
A-45, Naraina, Phase I,
New Delhi - 110 028

Published by Anurag Jain for Excel Books, A-45, Naraina, Phase I, New Delhi-110 028
and printed by him at Excel Printers, C-206, Naraina, Phase I, New Delhi - 110 028

Brief Contents

Detailed Contents

Preface

The area of retailing is growing, more jobs are being created, and shopping has become a major leisure activity. Competition across and within retail formats has emerged in a formidable manner. Retail marketing has become a necessity in this situation. There are two specific dimensions to retail marketing, first how to attract customers into the retail environs – shop, restaurant, or the 'virtual' Internet store for instance – and second how to persuade those customers to make a purchase from that outlet. Retailing is one of the most established branches of the Marketing discipline. Indeed most retailing activity predates the concept of Marketing. Retail Marketing begins with understanding of shopping behaviour and its impact on formulating and implementing loyalty programs. It looks at the way marketing principles can address retail industry challenges. Retail Marketing is intended as core reading on specialist Retailing courses, and supplementary reading on courses covering different aspects of marketing. The text has a tactical/operational emphasis and will appeal to retail practitioners as well as students.

The book helps managers and executives how to design and manage successful stores catering to today's sophisticated and demanding shoppers. It helps to analyze your design needs according to your type of store, its location, the product, price-point, and budget. You will find out how to design and organize a store that reinforces a desired image, attract the right kind of shoppers and motivate buying behavior as well as create flexible, timeless and tasteful stores that stimulate today's customers to buy. The psychology of buying and selling as it impacts the various elements of store design including – spatial organization, product display, storefronts, material selection, lighting and systems is covered in detail. Retail is a dynamic and often ruthless world that equally influences and is influenced by the shoppers it exists to serve. New players constantly emerge to better satisfy consumer demands, shopper demands and desires shift with new offerings and existing firms disappear when they can't adapt. Included in the overall retail marketing framework are site selection, advertising, customer analysis, merchandise mix planning, retail price strategy etc.

Food retailers, general merchandise retailers and e-retailers are the three broad retail categories that one finds in the retailing scene. In India, food (grocery) retailing has been dominated by convenience stores all across the country. The penetration of internet in India is minimal and therefore e-retailing in India is confined to a small minority in the affluent urban areas. Therefore, the types of retailers who have a great scope of expansion in the near future are the general merchandise retailers. Retailing classification in India is absent unlike the precise data available on each type of store in the American context through syndicated data and is traceable to the type of store with the help of the NAICS classification. The churn happening in the retail sector in India triggers one to look at ways of managing the onslaught of competition in the not so distant future from multinational retailers. Of specific interest would be the best management practices and innovations that are seen in the USA. USA represents a country with a saturated and developed marketplace for retailers prompting many to expand overseas. In the domestic market, many of the US retailers would have obviously tried several methods to be successful in business. This look at the US retailers presents an opportunity for Indian retailers to see if some of the strategies could be applied in the Indian context. Moreover, comparison and contrast of the American and Indian retail scenarios on history, growth and development would provide an insight into future developments that we may anticipate in India.

Absence of large area for retail stores necessitates development of specialty retailers. Excessive competition in the food-retailing sector would drive prospective retailing sector investors to choose specialty retailing. Greater margins possible in the specialty store sector and rapid development and entry of new product categories enable specialization. Moreover, retailing entities tend to specialize, as the wheel of retailing theory gets operational. Therefore, in the future we can see a rise in specialty retailing in India. A significant section on specialty retailing is a major constituent of the book.

This book fills in major gaps in the present business education scenario in India. Several business schools in India have started an exclusive MBA program on retail management targeted at the retail sector. In these programs, there is obviously a dearth of books that deal with Indian retailing. As retailing becomes a sectoral specialization and as more and more detailed examination of retailing in India takes place, there is a need for a textbook that caters to specific understanding of the nuances of the Indian retail scenario. The focus of this book therefore helps bridge a void in the literature in the Indian context.

DR. A. SIVAKUMAR

Acknowledgements

I wrote an article on Retailing in one of the leading business dailies in 1996 fresh into my academic career. I had been curious about how retail stores and retailers function in an industry dominated by marketers. However, given the performance of a company like Walmart in the international context, I felt that the biggest battleground of marketing would be retailing in the not so distant future in India. Within a matter of about 5 years, retailing has been hitting the business headlines and a new breed of retail entities has taken shape. The traditional Indian retailers have slowly started changing with the changing contours of the sector and the shoppers. Retailers and the way they manage their business have been my inspiration for my interest in retailing as a discipline as well as this book.

I would like to acknowledge our Director Prof. Nagabrahmam for providing wise counsel guidance and encouragement all through my academic career. The academic freedom available at TAPMI has been one of the major contributors to my specialization in the retail arena and one of the outcomes is this book. I would like to thank my marketing area colleagues for their support and other faculty colleagues who have provided encouragement.

Excel Books has been very fast in processing the requirements for publishing the book. Mr Anurag Jain and his team need to be thanked for the sheer pace in their efforts.

I would like to gratefully acknowledge my wife for her constant support. My thanks to all my other family members for their encouragement.

About the Author

Dr. A. Sivakumar is a doctorate in marketing. He is a faculty member teaching marketing at TAPMI for more than 12 years. He introduced Retail Marketing as a course at TAPMI and has since been offering the course for the past more than 5 years. His first offering of the course had senior executives from RPG retail take sessions on different topics. He had been a long serving academic contributor for the premier B2B retail magazine RetailBiz. His efforts in all his writings have been to refer to academic contribution in the field of retailing, understand the best practices in the American or developed country context and then suggest implementable ideas (from a retail practitioner's perspective) in the Indian context. The author offers an executive education course on retail marketing. He has been a resource person in several executive education/management development programmes for various organizations like Ashok Leyland, Jindal Vijaynagar Steel, Corporation Bank, HP, Oracle etc. In addition to retailing, his interest areas are in Agribusiness Marketing (where he has consulted), Written Analysis & Communication and Case Teaching.

CHAPTER ONE

Retail Marketing – An Introduction

Retailing is one the oldest businesses of mankind and almost close to settled agriculture, as its origins can be traced back to the time when exchange of goods started taking place. Any exchange (even barter) as in prehistoric times represent retailing as there was a direct interaction with the consumer. As the development of human civilization took place and business as an entity took birth, the direct producer-to-the-consumer interaction gave way to a business-to-consumer interaction. Any business to consumer interaction in the present context can be termed as retailing. Retailing, therefore, encompasses all forms of direct marketing too, in its broader sense.

Retailing can be dealt with in different perspectives. One of the long standing ways in which retailing was dealt with was that the retailer was one of the channel members in distribution. This from a marketer as well as a marketing perspective meant that they represent last mile connectivity for the marketers to the final consumers. In this perspective, the inherent assumption was that the marketer dictates what happens to the product or the brand or the service till it reaches the consumer. Moreover, the retailer in this case is intended to serve as a postman for the products/services of the marketer. The role of retailer was limited to execution of all the requirements of the marketer. The deep rooted assumption was that the marketer wields the power in the channel and therefore the marketer's writ runs.

The supply chain management dimension of retailing helps make the distinction between traditional retailing and professional/organised retailing. In traditional retailing as in the case of local provision stores (*kirana*) in India, the power in the supply chain still rests with the marketer and therefore, decisions on retailing cannot be independent of this position. Therefore, the nature of relationship with the marketer/supplier/vendor decides what would be stocked and sold by the traditional retailer. One way of defining professional or organised retailing is that it represents control of the supply chain by the retailer. The control of supply chain by the retailer could be due to the uniqueness of the products or services the retailer provides or due to the enormous clout enjoyed by the retailer on account of its presence across a region or country through a chain of stores. The number of stores implies the number of consumers with whom the retailer interacts with and has information about as well as the huge volumes of purchase that is possible with a large chain.

The business of retail management could be analogous to the media or specifically the newspaper business. Space selling is one of the greatest requirements of the newspaper or the print media business. Space selling also means that one has to balance space allocation for content and other uses like advertising. The promoters need to do a fine balancing act within the content as well as the nature of the remaining space. Retail management business is also about space management. One can gauge the importance of space from the efficiency parameter used for evaluating retail entities. The gross or net margins per square feet are one of the most important indicators of the nature of functioning of the store along with being a standard for comparison across stores of the same format or different formats. Real estate management could, therefore, be a proxy for retail management. In a country like India where the population is high and space is at a premium, management of this dimension of retailing assumes a larger proportion of the total activities in a retail set-up. The understanding of space from movement of consumers to future developments as envisaged by plans of the government as well as the commercial development of real estate is one of the major requirements to be successful as a retailer.

Retail management is a business in itself as it embodies all the functional areas in business. Successful running of a retail business is not possible without understanding all the major sub-disciplines of management namely operations management, financial management, information technology/systems management, human resources management and marketing management. Operations management forms one of the key functions of retailing as the supply chain view dominates. Interactions and transactions between suppliers/vendors and the chain store corporate headquarters or the individual stores, inventory management and logistics and the specific activities that take place from the production of the product/service to the consumption and feedbacks from the consumers are to be managed by the retailer. The term "Retail is in the Detail" aptly sums up the significance of each of the operations involved from the vendor to the consumer as well as the feedback loop back to the vendor.

As retailing is a consumer interfacing activity and acts as a last link in the supply chain, it is where data generated about the consumers and about products and services could be of immense help for members across the supply chain. As product and service categories as well as products and services proliferate, the data that could be collected increases by leaps and bounds. If the number of consumers that retailers interact with increases, the need for a mechanism to track all the customers and transactions increases in order to make meaningful inferences from the same. Traditional retailers depended on personal memory to record consumer and product information, but as retailing became a professional and widespread enterprise, personal memory started to fail and therefore, a need for technology to record data for analysis emerged. Information technology, therefore, is one of the greatest enablers of efficient and effective retailing. In addition to data that is captured at the consumer end all the individual transactions as part of the supply chain are also amenable for capture of data and analysis. This results in greater transparency and professionalism in dealing with supply chain issues dealing with operations management.

One of the first customers for software enterprises for outsourcing were retailers. This was because a major requirement was for the automation of individual transactions. Once the transactions were automated and data was generated, there was a need to store and analyse data that was gathered in large volumes. Technologies for data warehousing and data mining and development of expert systems were the initial developments that later developed into a full-fledged retail ERP that integrated all the components of the retail business and helped to provide a seamless view of the impact of changes of parameters to the entire retail business. Thus in view of the data intensive and operations oriented nature of the business, retailing involves a strong complement of information technology management, both of the hardware as well as the software.

The retail marketing dimension is the face of retail management that is visible to the consumers. All the efforts of the retailer to manage his retail business is to finally attract consumers to his store and make them buy more and stay with him. While the components of business-to-business marketing are involved in the supplier/vendor relationship, the major forms of marketing that the retailer involves him are in services marketing. Broadly, retailing can be physical products retailing and services retailing. Even in the case of services retailing the add-on services that the retailer provides and represents marketing of services other than the actual service that is marketed. In the case of products retailing other than store labels, products/brands belong to different types of marketers/suppliers/vendors. These products or brands are marketed by the respective producer/marketing companies. Therefore, product marketing like in the case of a typical fast moving consumer goods marketer or a consumer durable marketer does not happen at the retailer's end. Thus a retailer is in the business of services marketing.

In services marketing, we deal with 7Ps instead of the normal 4 Ps in product marketing. The additional 3 Ps that make the difference are people, physical evidence and process. Human resources management forms the bedrock of services management and is, therefore, no different in retail marketing. The retail counter sales-person is the representative of the retail marketing organisation that interacts with the prospective consumer. The ambience in which service is produced and delivered is a crucial differentiation point for a service. In the case of retailing too, marketing success is to a great extent a direct effect of the shopping ambience that is provided. The process of service provision impacts consumer psychology – his attitude and perception towards the marketer. Retail image is greatly dependent on the process of the shopping experience that the shopper undergoes in the store. Thus, the additional dimensions of service marketing are directly relevant in retail marketing and therefore retail management could be akin to retail marketing management.

Marketing management for products and services starts with an understanding of consumer behaviour. Retail marketing needs to start with an understanding of shopping behaviour. Shopping behaviour needs to be distinguished from consumer behaviour. The study of consumer behaviour is generally product or service centric. For example, we study consumer buying behaviour for soaps or banking services. However, one aspect of the buying behaviour which is not stressed upon is the place where one buys. This represents the retail business. A product or brand or service could be available through multiple channels or outlets but a consumer or a group of consumers buy them in deference to their preference of outlet.

Depending on the nature of the product/service, the time and nature of shopping varies. The consumer here turns a shopper and the shopper dimension of the consumer needs to be studied. Thus study of shopping behaviour helps answer questions like how many shops does the consumer go to before he makes a decision to buy a product, why does he choose a retailer compared to others etc. The other aspect that would be of great relevance to retailers is the reason for the shopper to shop. Shoppers could have different intentions for shopping. These could range from socialising to therapy to information seeking. Collection of information of shopping intentions along with factors that impact shopping provides a strong basis for the retailers to formulate their own marketing strategies.

Just as in marketing as grouping of homogeneous set of consumers would help in segmentation, targeting and positioning, in retail marketing, shopper segmentation, targeting and positioning helps in a focused effort in marketing. Segmentation efforts in marketing are to bring in a product/service market fit. In the case of retail marketing, shopper segments have to relate to various retail formats. While retail formats could be developed on the basis of the dimensions of the retail marketing mix, market fit of the format is achieved by shopper segmentation. Another actionable part of shopper understanding is shopper's store loyalty. Store loyalty has implications in introduction of store brands as part of merchandise management.

Product as a marketing mix element plays a significant role in retailing. Its manifestation is in the form of formats that specialise in specific product/category. Variety and assortment of product and service could be used to bring a range of formats from category killer to general merchandisers. Another aspect of product is merchandise management. This encompasses a range of activities from vendor search for new product introductions to vendor recruitment, selection, appraisal, management and retrenchment to inventory management as well as visual merchandising. This aspect of the retail marketing mix forms the lifeline of retailing. The nature of merchandise management and the decision on merchandise are crucial in the formation of the store image among shoppers. Category management is a refined form of merchandise management that also takes into account human resource management as well as financial management simultaneously. This new concept is marketing-oriented as categories at the retailer level are defined on the basis of the analysis of consumer shopping pattern for products through tools like market basket analysis. The different brands to include and delete as part of brand management are part of a marketer's decision. A retailer needs to decide on variety and assortment based on the understanding of the shopper's requirement as well as store loyalty.

Distribution in retailing has a different connotation compared to the marketer. It relates to the option of make and buy in expansion. The decisions on going in for own-store versus franchisee store are strategic decisions requiring the weighing of pros and cons of ownership. Another major decision that needs to be taken is the location of the outlet. Co-location of outlets as in a mall has its benefits in capitalising on incidental footfalls which otherwise is not possible in independent locations. Distribution has an impact in designing the right organisational structure in managing a chain of stores. As the number of stores in a chain increase, the span of control goes beyond the influence of the corporate office. Issues of centralisation and decentralisation crop up in organisational design. Transportation and inventory management are crucial elements in managing successfully the operations of a chain of stores. In this context, the development of centralised distribution centres to cater to a region as well as methods like direct store delivery make the logistics the life line of retailing.

Pricing is not a decision that could be taken independently by a retailer. In the US, the resale price maintenance act is a major measure that curbs retail pricing power. In the Indian context, the MRP regime is a significant dampener in the pricing flexibility available to the retailer. In view of this, the nature of vendor-retailer relationship dictates the extent to which pricing can be influenced. Wherever market pricing is possible, all the pricing tactics followed by any marketer are equally applicable to the retailer. In the case of product and price bundling, concerns about the image of the national brands used may result in contentious decisions.

The various promotional tools used by the marketer are equally applicable for retailers. One of the characteristics of promotion by retailers is that individual store promotion has a strong local orientation. Moreover, cooperative advertising is a common technique followed by the retailers to reduce the extent of investment on advertising. As shopping in a same store repeatedly would result in shopper fatigue, all formats of retailers need to think of innovative ways of creating excitement in shopping. Thus, surprises in the form of in-store promotion are a major requirement of promotion. Community relations and participation in the activities of the local community that coincides with the primary trading area of the store becomes crucial in building long-term relationships with prospective target shoppers.

Physical evidence is a component of retail (services) marketing that relates to ambience or store atmospherics. At a macro level, store location and layout have a significant influence on the shoppers. Inside the store, the ambience is a combination of effects of the response to stimulation of the five senses of the shopper. The use of colour, lighting, fragrance and the various elements of design determine the positive or negative perceptions of the consumers. Retail ambience is a manifestation of the image that the store wants to portray to the target segment. Shoppers may be attracted to one store over the other, based on ambience if the format of the two stores are the same. The types of signboards, nature of flooring and the ambient air are the kinds of aspects that could influence shoppers. Therefore, in-store experience from a store atmospherics perspective is a crucial determinant of the satisfaction of the consumer's shopping experience.

Retailing is one of the largest employers even in a not very highly populated country like the USA. All the direct and indirect activities related to retailing need the help of a skilled work force. The corporate functions in a retail chain require candidates with skills in management and strategy. At the distribution centre, prospective employees must be comfortable with an operations management orientation. At the store level, if much of the aspects of running the store are mandated or standardised at the corporate level, then skills in human resource management would be important. Thus, at different levels in the organisation, the nature of skills required and the expectation on knowledge and attitude are also different. However, one of the significant impact of employees on the shoppers is when the interaction takes place between the shopper and the counter salesperson. As it is true in every service marketing encounters in retailing, this interactive marketing to be effective, must be backed by sufficient internal marketing and external marketing efforts. The pride about the organisation as well as the confidence with which the customer facing employees relate to shoppers can also be enhanced by training.

Process represents the pre-store, in-store and post-store activities that the consumer undergoes as part of his retail service experience. In a blue printing service experience, the individual acts which the shopper puts forth does during each of the stages of the experience, are important. In this context, moments-of-truth like each of the touch points with the service provider, would be crucial in determining consumer perception of the store or its corporate image. In pre-store processes, the place for parking and the ease with which parking can be done and how a shopper is able to access the store lets say in a mall through appropriate signage, help in inducing a sense of efficiency and effectiveness to the process. Inside the store, ease of locating departments as well as merchandise helps with understanding pricing and offers as well as use and demonstration of merchandise, reduced waiting time at the billing section and ease of reaching the parking lot from the exit of the store, are processes that would significantly impact shopper perception of an in-store shopping experience. Post store, shopper's queries on return/exchange of merchandise and information on new arrivals etc. are some of the processes that have to be comforting and fast from the shoppers' side.

Retail marketing efforts to bear fruit need to have a strong element of support from all the other functional areas in a retail organisation like Financial Management, IT Systems management, Human resources management and Operations management. The nature of cost structure of the retailing business is such that fixed costs tend to dominate. Therefore, financial management would need to work on reducing these costs on a constant basis through innovative means. This would be in addition to a decrease in variable costs. Maintenance of an error free database with minimum downtime and use of sophisticated tools to mine and decipher shopper behaviour data would be a significant contribution of the IT systems group. Motivating, selecting, recruiting, appraising and rewarding the right employees go a great way in helping to retain them and at the same time helping provides a conducive environment for them to contribute towards the betterment of this organisation. Retailing thrives in its details. One of the foremost competitive advantages for any retail entity is the prowess it has in managing the supply chain. The need is to look for efficiency and effectiveness in operations management almost on a daily basis. This aspect of retailing has a profound effect on service levels for the consumers.

Shopper/Shopping Behaviour

THE GROCERY SHOPPER

The three top categories of products for which global retail sales are the highest are grocery, apparel and furniture. Grocery retailing has the highest sales because of its crucial position in satisfying one of the basic needs of any human being-food. The Indian grocery-retailing scenario has changed since the 90's. There are about 6.5 million grocery outlets in India in various formats. In value terms, an estimate of total grocery retail sales is $90 billion. Grocery constitutes over 50% of the Indian retail market.

Though it is an extremely large market, the organised sector's share of this market is very small. Grocery has three components, branded products including packaged foods, soaps and detergents and toiletries and household items; dry unprocessed grocery including grains and cereals; and fresh grocery including fruits and vegetables, meat, dairy and daily products. The sheer increase in the number of categories from instant to ready-to-cook to ready-to-eat has made the job of the consumers as well as the retail marketers quite tough.

Grocery retail in India has an array of players ranging from the *kirana store*; city-based chain stores, regional chains as well as reasonably priced national chains like Food World, though we cannot term any single grocery chain in the Indian context as a typical national chain. Grocery as a category has the greatest advantage of high purchase frequency and it makes the retail managers of these outlets dig deep into consumer behaviour in order to market themselves better. While the data generated is enormous at present—thanks to the advent of information technology, interpretation of the data is still a complex affair given the nature of consumer behaviour. Understanding and interpreting consumer behaviour, therefore, the crucial challenge faced by grocery retailers.

The grocery retail chain faces some of the following issues concerning consumer behaviour:

- Should there be a reduction in number of SKUs in a particular category
- How should sale of non promoted categories be looked at in judging promotional effectiveness
- Is there a need to classify variety seeking behaviour
- How should one monitor consumption rates for packaged goods
- What are the long-term effects of promotion on consumer behaviour

SKU Reduction

In the early 1990s in the US, traditional-format grocery retailers began losing sales to "alternative format retailers" (e.g. Wal-Mart) whose superior operating systems provided a major cost advantage. Industry studies suggested that retailers should decrease the cost associated with carrying large assortments. These studies advised retailers to adopt "Efficient Assortment", whereby, low-selling stock keeping units (SKUs) are eliminated from a category's offering. However, retailers resisted the idea with the opinion that a decrease in number of SKUs in a category badly affects the attitude of customers towards the store. This could be the thinking among Indian grocery retailers too.

Retailers assume that there is a one-to-one correspondence between consumer perception of the stimulus of assortment and the cue of the total number of SKUs offered in that category. However, if we observe closely most choices made in grocery stores are very low in involvement; and consumers do not actively process information about choice alternatives. You do not make comparisons across different categories of edible oils, brands and SKUs to decide what to buy. Psychophysics shows that individuals are able to detect a change in the environment only when it surpasses a certain threshold or "Just Noticeable Difference". Therefore, even consumers (very rare!) who use the total number of SKUs cue might not be able to detect small or moderate changes in the number of items offered. Hence, a retailer has to decide on two things: (1) which SKUs to eliminate and (2) what to do with the empty space in the category display.

In the face of SKU reduction, consumers will be less likely to lower their assortment perceptions if retailers remove low rather than high-preference SKUs. They could be national or local brands based on the brand franchise. Consumers will be less likely to lower their assortment perceptions if stores hold the amount of space devoted to the category constant. Consumer will lower their likelihood of choosing a store only if their assortment perceptions are lowered. When favourite SKUs are available, consumer assortment perceptions are unaffected by a reduction in the number of SKUs offered or changes in the category space. When retailers eliminate SKUs and favourite items are not available, consumers' assortment perceptions fall.

The impact of the SKU count, Favourite Available, and Category Space cues on assortment perceptions affect store choice even though the Favourite Available cue also has a direct link to store choice. Moderate reductions of 25% SKUs do not affect consumer assortment perceptions or store choice negatively. Cues of Favourite Available and Category Space can attenuate the impact of SKU reduction and raises the level of threshold at which consumers notice a difference. However, the most important issue is the nature of purchase timing and therefore the impact on consumer behaviour.

Timing

The economic assumption underlying the analysis of brand switching and purchase timing for a single product category are the separability of consumers' utilities across the different product categories that constitute the basket of goods purchased by consumers. Casual empiricism, however, suggests that such an assumption would not be appropriate in category pairs such as ice-cream and ice-cream toppings. Most grocers generally store these related categories together. This is with an assumption that a household's choice in one category is dependent of its choice in the other. In other words, the decision of when to purchase in one product category might depend on the decision for a related category.

Such an understanding is useful for the retailer because it helps him by giving him an idea about what kind of promotions will click with the consumers. A critical issue when studying household purchases of multiple categories is being able to identify the related product categories. This requires characterisation of the purchase/non-purchase behaviour of households in several different categories. Retailers need to monitor Inter-purchase time of consumers. There are several sources of the observed correlation in the inter-purchase times across households. Consumers typically consume certain products together and therefore purchase them together for example dhoopsticks and camphor. The main source of relationship is this nature of consumption. Other sources of the estimated correlation across categories are due to:

- Consumers visiting the store only on few occasions and therefore making purchases for all categories at the same time like the monthly grocery purchase.

- The retailer promoting "unrelated" categories together, which results in joint purchase of products in different categories like for example deodorant free or toothbrush.

- The household exhausting its supply of both products and at the same time prompting joint purchase.

The variety-seeking behaviour of the consumer can greatly affect purchase timing.

Variety-Seeking

Variety-seeking as a consumer motive has generated considerable research attention. This can be attributed in part to interest in non-purposeful behaviour (e.g. variety seeking or exploratory purchase behaviour, vicarious exploration, use innovativeness), which cannot be accounted for by the traditional information-processing perspective.

There are two behavioural phenomena to study variety-seeking behaviour of consumers - True variety-seeking versus derived varied behaviour and product category differences in true variety seeking behaviour. The distinction between true variety seeking behaviour and derived variety-seeking behaviour depends on whether observed switching, is motivated intrinsically or extrinsically. True variety-seeking of consumers takes place only when variation is rewarding in itself. In these instances, consumers seek variety and the stimulation it brings to the situation. This is as if I want to change my *atta* (wheat) brand to see if the new brand gives me better *chappathis* (Indian bread)! Each consumer needs a certain level of stimulation to function effectively and this preferred level of stimulation varies across people. There are times, however, when the level of stimulation is too low (e.g. boredom, satiation), and variety-seeking is one active way of increasing stimulation and restoring it to the preferred level.

Companies need to differentiate true variety-seeking behaviour, repeat purchasing and derived switching behaviour. People who engage in variety-seeking behaviour have a higher need for variety than those who engage in repeat purchases and extrinsically motivated switches. Variety-seeking behaviour is more likely to occur for products that evoke lower rather than high levels of involvement e.g. purchase of salt. Variety-seeking behaviour is more likely to occur for products that have higher rather than lower purchase frequencies e.g. purchase of toothpaste. Variety-seeking behaviour is more likely to occur in situations in which perceived differences among the alternatives are smaller rather than larger e.g. edible oil brands. Variety-seeking behaviour is more likely to occur for products that are higher rather than lower in hedonic characteristics e.g. branded *dal* (pulse).

Variety-seeking behaviour does not occur for all products to the same extent and there are several product category-level determinants of variety-seeking behaviour. The controlling influence of product category-level variable plays a more important role in distinguishing variety-seeking behaviour from repeat purchasing than in discriminating variety-seeking behaviour from derived switching. In terms of effect sizes, product category-level variables in general and the behavioural variables, in particular (i.e. purchase frequency and purchase history) make a more important contribution than need for variety in determining variety-seeking intensity.

The distinction between intrinsically and extrinsically motivated brand switching has important implications for practitioners. Insight into the underlying motivation for brand switching is central to decisions regarding the suitability of various marketing strategies for either stimulating or reducing brand switching. Product category-level characteristics determine when a marketing strategy might be successful in attracting consumers high in need for variety to an alternative brand. Products such as packaged snacks are lower in involvement, more frequently purchases, less preference-driven, and characterised by small-perceived differences among brands. In these cases, a viable strategy might be to encourage consumers to "put spice into their lives" and "try something different." Alternatively, in product categories in which variety seeking is less likely to occur, strategies aimed at extrinsic factors might be more appropriate (e.g., coupons, price promotions). One of the most commonly used extrinsic factor in motivating variety seeking is price promotion. Price promotion promotes purchase acceleration and therefore it would be appropriate to look at its significance.

Early Purchase

Promotion's effect on consumption stems from its fundamental ability to increase grocery inventory levels. Higher inventory in turn can increase consumption through two mechanisms: Fewer stock outs and an increase in the consumer's usage rate of the category. The first of these is simple – fewer stock outs mean the household has more opportunities to consume the products. Economic and behavioural theory supports the argument that households increase their usage rate when they have high inventory. Consumption should increase with inventory, not only because of the stock pressure from inventory holding costs, but also because higher inventories give consumers greater flexibility in consuming the product without having to worry about replacing it at high prices.

Scarcity theory suggests that consumers curb consumption of products when supply is limited because they perceive smaller quantities as more valuable. Faster usage rate occurs if products are perishable; are more versatile in terms of potential usage occasions (e.g., snack foods), need refrigeration, or occupy a prominent place in the pantry. Retailers can categorise goods under the flexible usage rate phenomenon and therefore use these categories effectively for promotion. In this context, it would be useful to study the stock piling behaviour of consumers.

Consumer Inventory

Over the years, there has been constant increase in the promotion budget of companies. Companies in all areas have been giving increasing importance to promotions. This is because of a constant increase in competition and demands of consumers. Competing products are essentially similar in terms of their product attributes and marketers are using promotions largely to influence the sale of their products. Sales promotions generally have a large, measurable and immediate effect on the brand's sales.

In spite of the substantial, albeit temporary increase in household purchases attributable to the use of promotions, there are concerns that such promotions might have a differing long-term effect. For example, in categories in which promotions have become frequent, consumers might learn to anticipate future deals. This particular scenario suggests that a particular promotional event induces a household to stockpile on a given purchase occasion (short-term effect), followed by the promotion's long-term negative effect, which is manifested as an increased probability that the household waits for another promotion before buying on subsequent purchase occasions.

Precisely, a short-term promotional effect is an immediate response to a promotion on a particular shopping visit (single point in time), while a long-term effect refers to the cumulative effect of previous promotional exposures (over Quarters or years) on a consumer's current, or short-term decision of whether and how much to buy. The effect of past exposures on current purchases also suggests a carryover effect; a promotion in the current period will affect behaviour in subsequent periods.

Households develop price expectations based on their prior exposure to promotions over a long period, such as months or years. These expectations, coupled with the costs of inventorying product, affect consumer purchase timing and purchase quantity decisions. Increasing expectations of future promotion lead to a reduced likelihood of purchase incidence on a given shopping trip and an increase in the quantity bought during a purchase. This strategy is consistent with a consumer learning to wait for especially good deals and then stockpiling when those deals occur. Promotions lead to higher price sensitivities, reduced promotional efficacy, greater inventories, and higher demand volatility. These effects all conspire to hurt category profits. Therefore, promotion and stockpiling by consumers together create a bad effect on the retail outlet.

The job of grocery retailing would get tougher as organised retailing in this category gathers momentum. The only way in which organised retailers can hold their ground is to study in-depth consumer behaviour at their stores and make changes in their marketing strategies effectively. In terms of consumer behaviour, some of the crucial challenges that can critically affect success are the ability of a grocery retailer to undertake item reduction to optimise category space without affecting the consumer and at the same time to manage higher sales by catering to variety seeking behaviour. To ensure stability of sales, retailer has to monitor promotion and its effect on consumers' future purchases.

LOYALTY CARDS

High degree of uncertainty and complexity characterise modern retail markets. In this context, micromarketing actions relating to consumer's loyalty are becoming significantly important. The main activity in which micromarketing gets down to facts is the realisation and management of the loyalty programme through which these companies aim to take advantage of behavioural heterogeneity of customers. Loyalty programmes have undergone many innovations. The original idea of loyalty programmes was restricted to only a reduction in price to the consumer. Presently outlets offer consumers, loyalty programmes that have features like prizes brochure, greater coherence of the programme with the company position, change in the duration of promotional sales and having a retail partner's network. The latter is the most interesting among these innovations. It consists of an integration or coordination of the loyalty programmes of the chain store with one or more loyalty programmes which other companies that had already developed as a stand-alone.

Information safety

A customer "loyalty card" is in common parlance a means of providing discounts on specific items, in exchange for consumer information that will aid in better tailoring the company's marketing efforts. Combining the data from one's loyalty card application with data from other commercial databases or public records (for examples, mortgage records, or court filings) can often allow a very specific profile of each consumer. Some states in the United States limit the types of information that a grocery store can collect from you when you register for a loyalty card. For example, California state law prohibits a grocery store from requiring that you provide your social security or your driver's license number. This kind of sensitiveness to the invasion of privacy has become a major movement in the US. The protagonists of this movement have substantial evidence to claim that even the government uses loyalty card data for several purposes without the knowledge of its citizens.

Privacy-sensitive consumers complain that loyalty cards result in improper use and sale of customers' private information to third parties. Even if customer contracts do not allow third-party sales of data, government authorities can always access data compiled with a warrant and use it against the customer in court proceedings. Meanwhile, consumer advocates claim that certain loyalty cards do not really offer savings that they promise. Nevertheless, numerous stores employ loyalty cards. Consumers can take defensive measures. Retailers cannot force consumers to join a loyalty programme. It is easy to set one's browser to reject cookies or to erase them after a session is over. One can even use a variety of credit cards or anonymous payment technologies to make purchases hard to trace. In short, with today's technology, sellers can post prices, observe choices, and condition future prices on observed behaviour. However, buyers can also hide the fact that they bought previously. Hence, it is likely that sellers will have to offer buyers some benefits in order to induce them to reveal their identity. The seller can induce such a change in value by offering enhanced services to prior users, such as discount coupons (common in supermarket loyalty clubs), prizes or awards (common with airlines and credit cards), lowered transactions costs (such as one-click shopping), or personalised services (such as recommendations).

Performance measurement

The need to monitor the performance of loyalty cards leads to the need for looking at effectiveness measures for measurement. Consumers often buy from different retailers and hold different competitive loyalty programme memberships. Usage of competitive information is important for a correct assessment of loyalty programme effectiveness. Loyalty programmes differ on several dimensions like the degree to which, they give discounts; have a saving programme, and the extent of cooperation with other companies. The exact design of the loyalty programme might be an important determinant of its success. The study on the relation between loyalty programme design and behavioural loyalty in a real market setting is important to understand effectiveness. Share of the wallet is one of the most comprehensive measure of effectiveness and an understanding of behavioural loyalty. Share of wallet measures the percentage of total amount spent on purchases at a particular retailer. Share of wallet integrates choice behaviour and transaction sizes.

A saving programme gives customers saving points, dependent on the monetary amount spent at the company. A programme member can redeem his points for a reward, such as a free product, after s/he has reached the minimal redeeming threshold. This threshold is such that the customer must repatronage for some time. Hence, a saving component offers incentives to spend a high share-of-wallet at the retail entity during some period. Many loyalty programmes give price discounts on promoted items. The consumers appreciate core product discounts that represent direct rewards. Most retailers print the consumer's received discounts on the receipt, and loyalty programme members may evaluate these discounts as a reward of their loyalty. This provides a visible exposition of the saving.

Multiple loyalties

Some companies have a loyalty programme cooperating with companies from other industries using non-overlapping product offerings. In general, companies cooperate to exchange resources for mutual benefit, such as enhanced product value and market reputations, and access to new markets and information. If a consumer becomes a member of a multi-vendor loyalty programme, s/he benefits from the programme at all participating companies, e.g., at each company a consumer receives saving points, and members can potentially save credit points quicker. Because the programme has a wider application than single-vendor programmes, a consumer is likely to be more involved with the programme and more aware of the incentives and benefits provided. Further, participating companies can benefit from each other's reputation, especially if a consumer is loyal to one of the companies, but not yet to another. A loyalty programme provides the company with full information of customers' buying behaviour. Juxtaposing, socio-demographics and causal information such as price promotions would enrich this information. This could result in target marketing, e.g. providing coupons to certain customer groups. Retailers can spend marketing money efficiently with this strategy of target marketing. At the same time, it fulfils customer needs more specifically.

Both a saving component and a multi-vendor structure enhance the effectiveness of a loyalty programme, but high discounts do not lead to higher share-of-wallets. Further, if households have multiple loyalty cards, the effectiveness of an individual loyalty programme is much smaller. The positive loyalty programme effects on share-of-wallet entail substantial additional customer revenues. However, given the high number of loyalty programmes already available in the market, a new loyalty programmes introduction will only lead to small effects on share-of-wallet.

Location effect

Gravitation areas or attraction's poles are aggregations of elementary territorial units, as Boroughs, which show systematic commuting phenomena from an origin zone – usually the residential area, to a destination area that exerts attraction force on the first one. Therefore, gravitation areas aggregate social groups travelling daily for job, entertainment, and so on. The zones that attract these groups are cities, districts, extra city areas where goods and services are particularly concentrated and characterised by high qualitative standards, more convenient prices, and so on. If gravitation areas hypothesis is correct, the greater part of the outlet in those boroughs, which exert an attraction force on the other boroughs belonging to the same gravitational area. In this way, chain stores are potentially able to intercept consumers of its own city and consumers of the zones, which compose the gravitation area. This could be a useful mechanism for deciding on the stores to collaborate with for a loyalty programme.

Information technology impact

In 1988, the cost of a gigabyte of hard disk storage was about $11,500. By 2000 that cost was $13, roughly 900 times cheaper. Today, a gigabyte of storage costs about a dollar. This remarkable reduction of the cost of storing information has led firms to capture, save, and analyse much more information about transactions with their customers. Supermarkets, airlines, credit cards and other industries have compiled vast databases of individual consumer transactions. Sellers in these industries routinely offer price promotions, prizes, and other sorts of inducements to individual customers based on their analyses of purchase behaviour. Collecting and analysing such information are even easier in the online world. Though the HTTP protocol used by Web servers is stateless. Browsers typically accept "cookies" from servers that contain information about the current transaction. These cookies persist after the session has ended. The next time the user accesses the server (using the same account) the server can retrieve identification to match with details of past interactions. Service providers can identify individual users even without cookies with static IP addresses, credit card numbers, direct user authentication, and a variety of other mechanisms. Since more and more transactions are mediated by computers, both online and offline, sellers can easily condition the price offers that they make today on past behaviour. With computer-mediated transactions, price discrimination on an individual basis becomes quite feasible.

Several organisations in the US reportedly deploy more than over 21 million smart cards. However, consumers still have little opportunity to use the technology, due to the lack of smart card acceptance devices at retail and merchant locations. Target, the first major retailer to implement smart card acceptance devices in their stores, has the unique position of being the issuer and retailer. With a reported more than 7 million cards issued, Target has upgraded 37,000 POS terminals in 1,000 stores to use the smart card chip and offer electronic couponing as its first chip-linked application. Target terminals are Euro pay Master Card Visa (EMV) compliant and thus capable of engaging in EMV transactions based upon payment software installed in the device.

Smart card-ready POS devices are making their way into additional retail and merchant locations. In 2001, approximately 25% of the over 1.3 million POS devices shipped by the three largest terminal providers in the United States were smart card ready. With the aging of the POS installed base, IT hardware marketers expect US retailers to upgrade increasingly their existing terminals with smart card-ready devices. Additional retailers have also made recent investments in smart card-ready POS terminals, including: CVS, the leading pharmacy and health service retailer, will install smart card readers in 450 of its stores to provide support for credit, debit, electronic benefits transfer (EBT), gift card transactions, and electronic signatures. Virgin Mega Store, the entertainment retail chain, has installed 320 payment devices with smart card reader attachments at all U.S. Virgin Mega Store locations. Rite-Aid, one of the nation's leading drugstore chains, has installed smart card-capable terminals in 4,000 stores to handle the store's closed system, chip-based gift (stored value) card. ShopRite, the largest retailer-owned supermarket cooperative in the United States, is setting up smart card-ready POS terminals at 200 stores to implement a loyalty programme.

Smart card technology

Smart card payment at physical retailers requires the following components:

- Consumer smart cards and smart card applications.
- Retailer POS hardware and software that can accept and process smart cards.
- Acquirer/processor infrastructure to authorise and settle smart card transactions and manage the terminal base, terminal applications and keys.
- Issuer systems that support the transaction process and manage the issued card base.

  The Internet retailer smart card infrastructure includes the following components:

- Consumer smart cards and smart card applications.
- A smart card reader for the consumer's personal computer (PC).
- PC client software to support smart card applications.
- Internet retailer server support for smart card applications.
- Acquirer/processor infrastructure for authorisation and settlement of smart card transactions.
- Issuer systems supporting the authentication and transaction process and managing the issuer card base.

Contactless technology is particularly well-suited to the retail environment. The pass-by method of card presentation is convenient. This method helps the retailer to allow multiple form factors for using the payment device. The shopper can accomplish a fast, secure transaction simply by presenting a card, key fob, or other contactless device to the reader. One of the most compelling uses for contactless cards is at drive-through retail establishments, where long read ranges are required for a good user experience. Devices such as the ExxonMobil Speed Pass are usable outdoors, even in inclement weather or a dirty environment. Contactless readers have no slots, switches, or pins, significantly lowering the cost of ownership and maintenance. Finally, ISO international standards specify contactless systems, supporting straightforward extensibility and interoperability. Contactless technology can be an excellent complement to contact technology in appropriate situations.

The arena of loyalty cards is getting complex with the infusion of technology and the use of the mechanism by more and more retailers. This would mean that the primary and preliminary benefits of loyalty cards might not necessarily attract consumers. Data mining, data warehousing and development of the philosophy of customerisation would be the key in implementing loyalty programmes effectively. Retailers in India can afford to invest in IT and use the knowledge gained in serving retailers abroad as vendors in increasing the effectiveness of loyalty cards operated domestically.

LOYALTY PROGRAMMES

Social identity research has shown that consumers feel a sense of group identification. Loyalty programmes generally use loyalty cards that members carry with them and have to show at each transaction with the company. This explicit token of membership will strengthen their sense of belonging to the company and thus enhance the identification effect. Loyalty programmes give rewards to members, varying from saving for items and targeted offers, to special shopping nights and preferred service treatment. The marketing activities within the loyalty programmes reward stimulates customer loyalty by providing either social or economic value. For example, a members' relational magazine hardly provides economic value, but it stimulates customers' feelings of belonging and special treatment by the store. In this sense, social value may far outweigh economic value in terms of the influence on prospective consumers to go in for a loyalty card.

Loyalty programmes are popular with customers: in the United States, 53% of grocery customers are enrolled in them, to say nothing of 21% of customers of casual-apparel retailers. Of those who join grocery programmes, McKinsey research indicates that 48% spend more than they would otherwise. Loyalty programmes have gained as a major marketing tool in the retailing sector after the early adoption of the concept in the airline and the hotel sector. Loyal shoppers are the targets for such programmes. It would be necessary to understand the need for loyalty programmes in the context of shopping behaviour. Trips to stores involve time and financial outlay and in addition, place natural constraints on the product and price assortment which the consumer will encounter. One might, therefore, expect shoppers to deliberate carefully, before developing allegiances and remain somewhat faithful. Consumers appear to habituate to store environments over time. For most shoppers, consideration sets for stores are relatively small. Furthermore, shoppers derive benefits from the accumulation of store-specific knowledge and are in effect willing to pay higher prices to shop in stores that they know well. A re-evaluation of the preferred store may only occur when the shopper perceives a substantial change in the marketing environment. In view of this observed behaviour of the consumers with regard to retail outlets, it makes business sense to develop store loyalty.

One of the basic motivations behind all loyalty programmes is cost effective retention of existing customers. Consider the following illustration. The customer-lifetime-value table below shows the benefits of a loyalty programme. The following were the parameters considered for the calculation for the period of four years. It clearly shows the benefits of customer retention through a loyalty programme.

- One lakh customers with retention rates increasing from 75% to 85%

- Purchase per customer increasing from Rs. 210 to Rs 280

- Referrals increasing from 8% to 10%

- Costs of acquisition @ Rs. 40/customer

- Advertising costs to retain Rs. 6/customer/year

- Record keeping costs/customer/year Rs. 5

- Service costs per loyal customer Rs. 20/year

- Referral incentive per customer referred Rs. 20

- A discount rate of 20% to account for time value for money

Customer Lifetime Value

	Year 1	Year 2	Year 3	Year 4
Before Programme	Rs. 34	Rs. 71.50	Rs. 97.75	Rs. 111.16
With Programme	Rs. 9	Rs. 72.68	Rs. 135.33	Rs. 185.88
Difference	Rs. (25)	Rs. 1.18	Rs. 37.58	Rs. 74.76

Source: Paul Gray and Jong Bokbyun Customer Relationship Management, March 2001

Understanding consumer behaviour at an individual level is also another great benefit of the loyalty programme. Tesco, the leading UK grocery chain, for instance, uses club card (loyalty programme) data to tailor 80,000 variations of a letter offer (based on each member's profile) and the magazine it sends to club card members. This reflects the concept of mass customisation. Individualised attention to personal consumer needs greatly impacts upon the shopping behaviour and therefore helps develop loyalty towards a store. Consequently, frequent purchases and greater customer spending (of the total budget for retail expenditure) in a store constitute broadly the indicators of loyalty.

The fast-paced growth of organised retailing in the Indian context and the shorter life cycle of retail formats entail different marketing strategies to be competitive on a sustainable basis. Loyalty programmes is one such strategy that Indian retailers can embrace effectively. The comprehensive use as well as the uniqueness of the programmes would decide the success of loyalty programmes in the Indian organised retailing scene.

Some of the examples of loyalty programmes in place in the Indian context are:

- Bharat Petroleum Corporation Ltd.'s - *Petro Card*
- Lifestyle retailer Globus's, - *Globus Elite*
- 'First Citizen Club', - *Shopper's stop*
- Consumer durable retailer Viveks - *Loyalty Card Akshaya*

Loyalty segments

Competition among stores would mean segmentation of store customers and differentiation of the store offering to individual customers. The scope for differentiation of the store offering to the customers exists in any retailing entity. The retailing strategy dimensions like product assortment provide the scope for differentiation- Category killers like the Kancheepuram silk sari showrooms vs. Big Bazaar and Giant type hypermarkets, price - discount store Subiksha or other aspects like the quality of service. However, in large multi-outlet retailing chains are not currently fulfilling the consumer information requirements for differentiating the offering to individual shopper. Loyalty stems from this customised offering to the individual customer or a customer segment. Therefore, the utilisation of information technology (using tools like data mining/warehousing) in the success of a loyalty programme attains paramount importance.

Large-scale multi-outlet retail chains through a successful use of loyalty programme try to recreate personal relationships that exist between the *kirana* shop owner and his customers by obtaining personal preferences of the customers. If an apparel retailer (like say Raymond's) can track the preferences of the consumer in terms of brand, colour, design, material (cotton vs. others), accessories and occasion, it represents an enormous opportunity for the retailer to tailor make (literally) or target marketing efforts directed at the individual. Rewards for consumer loyalty to the apparel retailer in exchange for information and frequency thus form the bedrock of loyalty programmes.

Exclusive outlets like Sony World, LG Shops or Philips Arena give much more flexibility in terms of implementing loyalty programmes and modifying customer service to increase customer brand loyalty. In a multi-brand outlet, one is constrained by other factors like, layout, staff and store management etc. The customers who come to exclusive outlets are loyal to a particular brand. Moreover, it gives a complete feel about the company, its brand and its products. With better service to the customer, the loyalty chart can go up. Thus, multi-product brand marketers can reap great benefit by vertical integration through retailing forays and the use of loyalty programmes effectively.

Programme Cycle

Loyalty programmes in retailing follow a cycle. The innovating (pioneering/first mover) company starts a programme and other chains could easily replicate the same. This happened in the retail grocery sector in the UK. The proliferation of loyalty programmes by not only the retailers but also marketers of products and services who have made the job of differentiation is difficult. Therefore, the significant aspect of loyalty programmes is the data that stores generate about consumers and the effective use of the same for targeted marketing. For example, CVS a leading drug retail chain in the US introduced its Extra Care loyalty card programme chain wide in February 2001. To date, the company has signed up more than 27 million card-holders (far exceeding initial expectations) for the programme, which combines discounts, rewards and information for consumers. Based on the information they gather, as shoppers use the card, retailers send customised information to customers with an educational focus. For example, if a shopper is buying formula and diapers, the store manager understands the customer by segment. He sends the shopper a newsletter on parenting tips.

The advantages of loyalty programmes are greater in the "low-value high-frequency" and "high number of transaction situations" as it happens in the retail grocery sector. Here, consumer information collection and analysis has been a difficult proposition until now. Information technology has made this job easier. Nearly half of the American population belongs to at least one frequency (loyalty) programme and such programmes are growing at a rate of about 11% a year. Moreover, new technologies (e.g., smart cards and the Internet) facilitate the proliferation of such programmes by providing cheaper and more powerful solutions for managing customer relationships. The greatest penetration of loyalty programmes in the retailing sector in the US and the UK has been in the grocery and the gasoline categories. In these categories, more than half of the top 10 retailers in the US and the UK have loyalty programmes in place and all of them have exploited the power of IT effectively.

Requirements

The presence of distinct market segment and the absence of instant gratification among consumers are some of the prerequisites of an effective loyalty programme implementation. The customisation of the offering of the store, either as "mass customisation" or as a segment that is price sensitive, is the product of a successful loyalty programme. For example, in a music store like Planet M, we should be able to distinguish a segment that would prefer any new album release and a segment that would always go for classics. Retailers can target different incentives at these segments for the loyalty programme without giving scope for any comparison on a monetary or non-monetary basis.

Loyalty programmes in general, are deferred rewards for the loyalty to a store. The time of deferment depends on the objectives of the store. In this respect, catering to instant gratification would result in the loyalty programme degenerating into a sales promotion programme. The case in point could be Co-optex as a retailer offering round-the-year discount and additional discounts during anniversaries of great political leaders. This results in the consumer looking at additional incentives as a sales promotion. There has been no effort to derive loyalty by postponing rewards to a future date based on purchases in this chain of stores. Therefore, the (presently) loyal customers of Co-optex do not feel happy. This deferred rewards dimension thus affects the other dimensions of the retail marketing mix in terms of the product assortment, service level and price positioning.

Measurement

Financial indicators of evaluating a loyalty programme are a difficult measure of its success as factors such as objectives, life cycle position, nature of markets and the nature of service across outlets may differ. Therefore, the better way to assess the impact of loyalty programmes would be to monitor the following indicators:

- Level of take up among customers
- Redemption rates
- Level of dialogue with customers
- Longevity of the programme
- Contribution to knowledge base
- Ability to segment customers

Despite the tremendous popularity of loyalty programmes in the developed countries, the factors that influence consumer perception/response to such programmes are still in the nascent stages of research. Researchers have looked at the match between the promised reward and the level and type of required effort. Consider this - The Chart House (a US based restaurant chain) *Aloha Club* programme (a loyalty programme) rewarded customers who dined at all the 64 Chart House restaurants in 21 States around the country with a trip for two around the world. The surprisingly high number of eligible winners made the restaurant chain to drop subsequently this reward from the programme. This at the end resulted in the learning that there could be an extremely high level of motivation among consumers depending on the nature of the reward.

As the level of programme requirement increases, marketers should enhance the relative share of luxury rewards in their reward mix. For example, a supermarket (like Food World) loyalty programme might offer Rs. 50 in supermarket vouchers for consumers who spend a total of Rs. 2,000, whereas consumers who spend Rs. 20,000 could be given the option of earning a three-day trip to Colombo, Sri Lanka. Marketers can also offer simultaneously two or more programmes with different levels of required efforts (frequencies/quantities/value) and reward types (monetary/non monetary). This is in a way segmenting customers based on the shopping efforts.

One of the unique issues in retailing that can affect loyalty programmes is the nature of the industry in itself. While loyalty programmes in sectors like airlines and hotels can benefit due to high fixed cost and high-unused capacity during certain periods, the variable cost component is the higher in retailing. This in addition to the modest per-customer sales and low margins make the loyalty programmes a big drain on the income. In most of the retail entities in the US, experts report that the total cost of the loyalty programme has been underestimated. They found that retailers overlooked the magnitude of database maintenance costs and efficient servicing of the programme. Polygamous loyalty i.e. loyalty across several schemes and promiscuity i.e. early switching to other (store loyalty) programmes by the customers is a fact that retailers have to contend with in a competitive situation. This would result in a situation where the question of loyalty itself may not arise.

Cooperation

The solution to the increasing cost of loyalty programmes is teaming up. Loyalty management specialists, who team up interested retailers and manufacturers in a programme, now manage Loyalty management programmes on/offline. They perform the job of business process outsourcing for loyalty programmes. Air Miles, a Canadian alliance is one such alliance. In India, Club Mahindra, TNG Apparels, Maruti, LG, Dominos and Wimpy's have joined hands to reap the benefits of customer loyalty for each other's brands through Netcarrots, a loyalty-management programme. SurfGold is another loyalty management specialist that has Indian retailers like Music World, Bharat Petroleum, Bombay Store, AMF Bowling and Archies as its clients. Tesco-the UK grocery retailer, solved the cost problem differently by deploying a two-tier Club card programme.

Loyalty programmes must reflect the value of the retailing entity. Target the famous U.S. based retailer, has a loyalty programme offered through its Target guest card. It appeals to the emotions of the customers by donating benefits of the loyalty programme towards developing schools in the locality of the retail outlet. Target describes the programme as "school fund-raising made simple" and as "a cornerstone of our commitment to the communities we serve." This is an effective use of a loyalty programme to reinforce the values of Target. Moreover, as retailing in itself has a major influence in the trading area of the location of the outlet, it makes more sense to appeal to the local (primary trading/catchment area) community. Two insights drive Neiman Marcus's InCircle Rewards loyalty programme: first, a small percentage of customers generate a majority of the company's sales and, second, the brand connotes exclusive merchandise and excellent service. Therefore, the loyalty programme is an exclusive club of the customers and the rewards to them.

The success of loyalty programmes lies in the strong linkage that it brings about between the strategy of the retailer and the positioning and perception in the minds of the consumer. Value-added and consistent interaction can earn True loyalty. Offer based 'bribery' brings in only Ephemeral loyalty. Retail marketers must realise that sustaining the customer-brand-franchise for a retailing entity would mean developing emotional bondage through a loyalty programme rather than converting them into a series of sales promotions for the store.

CASH STARVED CONSUMER

Every retailer needs to make efforts towards catering to different consumer requirements. One of the ways in which you could look at this difference across the consumers is the way in which they would want to buy. Specifically, the retailer can look at the ways in which the consumer wants to pay. Some of the options available are pay cash, pay through a debit card, and pay by availing a loan from the retailer, financier or the marketer. One of the other forms of buying could be to layaway the product chosen, then pay for the same over a period, and then get the product. A layaway plan is an easy way to buy something when your cash is running low. You do not want to use credit. When a consumer buys a product on layaway, the seller agrees to put the purchase aside and keep it for him until he pays for it in full. In the Indian context, this may happen in the form of an informal arrangement with the retailer in the case of select customer known personally to the retailer proprietor. However, an implementable policy needs to be in place if one looks at a professional chain of stores.

Components

The crucial components of the layaway plan are:

- Amount of the down payment to be made

- Length of time the goods will be held for the consumer

- Amount of each payment and when it is due

- Description of goods

- Total price of goods

- Separate listing of any special costs, any terms or conditions of the layaway agreement

- Seller's refund policy

Until the consumer finishes paying for his layaway, the store has his money and the layaway item. If the store goes out of business while he is still paying, his money and the item may be lost. Therefore, there is a need to check out the store's reputation before the consumer buys on layaway. Among the big discount chains in the US, Wal-Mart and K-Mart offer layaway, but Target does not. Consumers can find layaway at many US stores selling clothing, electronics, jewelry, musical instruments or antiques and collectibles, though not always advertised. Nowhere is layaway more popular than at Wal-Mart. By paying a 10% deposit, customers can put almost anything on layaway other than clearance items and hazardous materials. Hundreds of bicycles with layaway tags hang suspended above the shelves at Wal-Mart's. The layaway counter at the back of the store attracts a line of shoppers with carts loaded with toys and games. The store boxes and stores them until redemption. Many Wal-Mart customers use layaway year-round for big-ticket items such as televisions, bicycles and diamond rings. The service is also popular for back-to-school items such as uniforms, clothing and school supplies. Normally Wal-Mart offers a 60-day layaway, but for the holidays, the layaway period starts in September and ends by mid-December, allowing goods that aren't picked up to be returned to the shopping floor well before Christmas.

Reaction

Customers who do not finish paying for their layaway items get their money back minus a service charge. Some stores restrict the use of layaway. Obsolescence is a big concern. Some stores have a service charge up front for layaway, while others charge a fee only if a customer fails to complete the purchase and wants a refund. Layaway appeals to people who like to do their holiday shopping early but do not have the cash in hand to pay for it. They can snap up this year's most popular toys while a good selection is still available. Because customers have to pay for their goods in full, layaway imposes the kind of spending discipline that financial experts applaud. Consumer complaints are rare in the US where layaway is a common phenomenon. The consumers need to be aware of aspects like the options in case the layaway item has been misplaced or lost. Different rules may apply during the holiday season. He needs to be also aware of what happens if he does not complete his payments - Can he get a cash refund or just a store credit? Is there a service charge?

Store needs

If a retailer provides layaway as an option to buy merchandise, it would be worthwhile to look at the aspects that he needs to concentrate on. He needs to help assure that customers understand their payment obligations. The retailer needs to give notice to customers of his layaway policies. In addition, prior information can help prevent misunderstandings and disputes. It is always a good business practice to inform customers about the retailers' cancellation and refund policies because the absence of cancellation and refund information can be a great source of customer dissatisfaction. By disclosing these policies in writing, the retailer may significantly reduce customer complaints. It would also lead to the possibility of dissatisfied customers taking their business elsewhere. Retailers can use a number of different refund policies for layaway transactions. Some can provide full or partial cash refunds if layaways are not completed. Others could give credit toward future purchases. By disclosing refund information, a retailer's customers will know what to expect if they do not complete the layaway purchase.

If a retailer requires a specific amount of money to be paid at set intervals (for example, every two weeks), or require payments to be completed within a set period (for example, within 60 days of the start of the layaway), it will help the layaway customers to know the exact requirements. This disclosure might include the required payment amounts; the dates when payments are due; and the date when the consumer must make the final payment, if applicable. While the amount, the number, and sometimes the frequency of payments may vary with the cost of the purchase, it would be useful to develop a standard payment disclosure format. Vague descriptions of payment terms will not help customers understand policy. A retailer may have a policy of cancelling the layaway if the customer does not make a payment by a certain date or does not complete the transaction within a specified period. If a retailer has such a policy, it should inform its customers in writing to avoid misunderstandings. Some other retailers will let a layaway completion date go by, particularly if the payments are almost complete. As a reminder, such retailers send notices to their customers giving them a new date for completing all payments.

If you add a service or layaway charge to the purchase price, customers would want to know this before they begin the layaway. If stores impose any other charges, like shipping, then informing customers with a similar statement is very important. In addition, customers who buy merchandise on layaway may expect that the item will actually be "laid away"— physically separated from stock available for sale. Many US retailers remove layaway articles from the sales floor; others keep large items, such as furniture or major appliances, on the sales floor but mark them "sold." If a retailer does not separate the layaway purchase from store merchandise, telling customers about the practice, may avoid future complaints. Similarly, customers would want to know when and under what circumstances a store would have to order merchandise from the vendor in advance. Because several months may lapse, between the time, a consumer initiates a layaway purchase and the time the merchandise is picked-up. A retailer's customers may not always remember all the details about the merchandise they purchased. To help avoid potential confusion about the particular merchandise selected, a retailer may want to identify the layaway item on the layaway sales slip. Clearly describing the items identifying characteristics, such as colour, size, stock number, model number and trade name or manufacturer, may prevent misunderstandings when the customer makes the final payment and is ready to claim the layaway merchandise.

Applications in India

There is a great opportunity available to introduce layaway as a strategy in the Indian context in view of the strong trust that brick and mortar Indian retailers enjoy with respect to Indian consumers. This could be one of the mechanisms of developing customer relationship management, as there is constant interaction between the consumer and the retailer regarding the payment. Moreover, the concept of chit funds, where prospective buyers accumulate small amounts of money for buying products especially in jewelry and utensils outlets is quite common. The concept of layaway is a slight variation over this concept. In addition, in retailing entities where there are more unique products that are displayed, chances of a consumer liking a product and not being able to buy it and therefore be dissatisfied can be avoided with the provision of a formal layaway plan.

CHAPTER THREE

Merchandise Management

BRAND WARS

Store Brands constitute about 20% of unit sales and are among the top three Brands in 70% of supermarket product categories in the USA. The development of organised Retailing in the Indian marketing scene, in the not so distant future, is going to bring up issues associated with the emergence of strong Store Brands and its attendant impact on National Brands of manufacturer/marketers not in Retailing business. Already Retail Entities like Shoppers Stop, Food World & Ebony have taken their first steps towards challenging the supremacy of the National Brands through their own Brands of products. One of the alternatives for the national brand marketers and manufacturers could be to make a foray into Retailing. This may not happen in a big way, as there are already established retailers who have created a brand identity for themselves. The other alternative is to establish exclusive retail Outlets. In this case, stores deny the choice of comparison to the consumers though it may not succeed as well. In view of this, the Threat of store brand for National Brands is here to stay.

Store Brands are the only Brands for which the Retailer is responsible, for not only promotion, shelf placement and Pricing but also for defining the very nature of the product. In particular, retailers decide on the exact positioning of Store Brands in product space. This includes the size, shape, colour, lettering and art of a store brand's packaging as well as precise quality and taste specifications. For National Brands, in contrast, these are core strategic decisions made by their respective manufacturers. Store Brands are the only brand for which the Retailer must take on all responsibilities in the business value chain — from development, sourcing, and warehousing to merchandising and marketing. Unlike National Brands, where manufacturers' actions drive retailers' decisions, retailers play the key role in the success or failure of their own labels.

Marketers' Brands

Retailers especially the large multi-brand Outlets often use National Brands to draw customers to their stores. Retailers who pursue this traffic-building strategy usually carry more National Brands, deeper assortments, and offer promotional prices on National Brands. This takes place in both the FMCG as well as consumer durable Retailer segments. Each of these actions works against the retailer's own Brands, highlighting the important balancing act which the Retailer must perform in profitably managing sales revenue and Margin Mix across categories. Adding a higher quality, premium store-brand programme may mitigate this trade-off. However, this would involve a great amount involvement in the development of the product and brand. National brand/private label Price differential boosts store brand performance. If the Price of Food World jam is significantly different from the national marketers, we can expect Price consumers to notice and switch. It could be the case with a Vasant (brand of Vasant & Co - an MBO in consumer durables) mixie. When retailers obtain more than their fair share of a category i.e. lets say pickles, they also do much better with Store Brands. For example, in this case, pickles branded in the store's name have a great probability to succeed.

From the national brand's perspective, encouraging the Retailer to carry more Brands and deeper assortments may be the most effective way to keep Store Brands in check. The importance of these aspects, however, may depend on the national brand's market position. A category leader may be glad to see a rise in store brand share if it comes at the expense of one of its secondary national Brand Competitors.

The exact impact of most of the Variables depends on the underlying quality of Store Brands in a category. When store brand quality is high, competitions at the retail and brand level are more important, as are Variables capturing economies of scale and scope enjoyed by the Retailer. This means that a national multi-store chain with a large presence in strategic markets could be a big Threat to established National Brands of marketers. In contrast, when store brand quality is low, demographics associated with consumer Price -sensitivity, matter more i.e. the Store Brands might have limited presence based on historical association of the Store Brands with the locality.

Finally, premium Store Brands offer the Retailer an avenue for responding to the national brand's ability to cater to heterogeneous preferences. This appears more likely in categories where Store Brands already offer high quality comparable to the National Brands.

Leading manufacturers must be alert to these changing practices, but in general, they will get their fair share of category sales irrespective of which Retailer makes the sale. On the other hand, Retailer imitation of successful store brand programmes is more threatening for national manufacturers' cannot easily make up within-store loss of share to the retailer's store brand (or for that matter another national brand) with a sale at a different Retailer. The national brand marketers in the U.S. have observed this. As European retailers with high-powered corporate branding programmes, such as Sainsbury, continue to acquire regional chains in the U.S., the Threat to National Brands becomes immediate. This implies that national manufacturers need to identify which of their products are most vulnerable to Retailer investments in private labels, and understand what actions they can take to limit store brand encroachment in key retail accounts.

Threat level

National Brands are most vulnerable in product categories where there is a high variation in private label share across retailers. It is here that imitation of best practices could result in substantial increase in store brand share. When average private label share is high, these categories pose "big current threats" if low share retailers start doing as well as the best performers.

When average private label share is low, categories pose a "future Threat," mainly because poor performers are starting from scratch and will imitate in the high Threat categories before allocating resources here. National Brands should spend less time worrying about how retailers manage their Store Brands in categories where there is less variation across retailers.

Retailers can easily observe each other's actions, assess the impact of those actions, and quickly imitate successful strategies. For retailers, arguably the most important practices are those that successfully build store traffic and produce significant shifts in market share, such as new store formats, store appearance, Perimeter Departments and Advertising. It seems that Store Brands succeed in product categories with high margins, less intensive brand Advertising, and presence of high quality Store Brands. The introduction of Store Brands is likely to increase retailer's profits in product categories in which cross-Price elasticity between National Brands is low, but cross-Price elasticity between national and Store Brands is high. Retailers who introduce Store Brands perform better, when they commit to Store Brands with high quality (even premium Store Brands), when they sell a large variety of products with the store brand name, and when they use their own name.

Positioning issues

Store Brands (SBs) or private labels are created and controlled by retailers. As is true for any brand, positioning of the store brand can have an important influence on its performance. Unlike manufacturers of the National Brands (NBs), however, the downstream Retailer has a different objective function. Whereas national brand manufacturers position their products to maximise the profits from their own products, the Retailer focuses on maximising profits from the entire product category, including profit from store and National Brands.

The Retailer should position the store brand to maximise category profits within the context of a category with two National Brands, one of which will be stronger. The perceptual distance between two Brands is operational positioning. Brands positioned closer, exhibit a higher cross-Price elasticity. Retail chains should focus on whether the store brand should target a specific national brand or follow an "in the middle" positioning and compete to a lesser degree with both NBs; and if targeting is better, which NB to target. A better understanding of store brand positioning strategy is also important to NB manufacturers who must coexist with Store Brands.

Store Brands often imitate the category leader, presumably to signal comparable quality at a lower Price. Although the demand for the store brand may increase, the downside is that demand for the targeted leading national brand may also decrease. Since the Retailer also makes money by selling National Brands, it may not be optimal to have the store brand specifically compete against the national brand with the largest customer base and higher margins. Instead of targeting a national brand that generates substantial profit, adopting a mid-point position where the store brand competes to a lesser extent with both NBs may be better. Yet, we often observe retailers targeting leading National Brands.

SB positioning essentially involves choosing the appropriate perceptual distance between the SB and the NBs. This distance in turn determines the degree of Price competition between the store brand and each of the National Brands. As such, positioning the store brand closer to one national brand results in higher cross Price sensitivity between the two. The Retailer should position the store brand close to the stronger national brand unless the cost of doing so is beyond a critical level. Further, compared to other prospective strategies, this strategy is more profitable in categories where the leading national brand is stronger. SB targeting of the leading national brand leads to

- Lower wholesale prices from both the leading national brand and to a lesser extent the secondary brand

- Higher margins for the Retailer on National Brands

- Higher profits from the store brand

- Increased category demand - all of which adds up to increased category profit, relative to other positioning strategies.

Retailers should be interested in category profits rather than the profit from any specific brand. The retailer's objective function reveals itself in the optimal positioning strategy of the Store Brands. The retailer's positioning decision is choosing the degree of competition between the store brand(s) and each of the National Brands in the product category. The Retailer should position the store brand closer to the stronger national brand. Targeting is relatively more profitable in categories where the leading national brand is stronger. Differential positioning leads to greater competition between the store brand and the leading national brand but only for categories with high quality SB alternatives. Consumers can readily detect retailers' efforts to use extrinsic cues to position against the leading national brand. This does not necessarily translate into consumer perceptions that the SB offers comparable intrinsic quality.

The Retailer prefers to have a store brand, which competes heavily with the National Brands. The basic premise here is that it cannot increase both cross Price sensitivities at the same time. Hence, there is a rationale for the tendency of Store Brands to imitate the category leader. There is empirical evidence to show that Store Brands do particularly well in categories with high concentration. Store Brands do better in concentrated national brand categories because it is easier for consumers to compare the store brand when there is a distinct category leader. Store brand can pursue a focused positioning strategy in a concentrated market characterised by less heterogeneity in tastes, and offer an attractive alternative with a lower Price. The focus of that positioning strategy should be the leading national brand.

Targeting the category leader may not be the optimal strategy always. For example, if the secondary national brand provides a much lower margin than the leader, the Retailer may be better of by diverting sales of the secondary national brand to the store brand. Alternatively, in some categories, targeting strategy may lead to negative inferences; consumers may prefer to buy the "real thing" rather than the "lower quality copycat". In this case, the Retailer may elect to make its brand as distinct as possible. Being closer to the customer, may help the Retailer identify the unfulfilled needs or a niche market, thus leading to a differentiated product strategy.

Vendor deals

That retailers control store brand positioning is one of the reasons that makes Store Brands so valuable to them. Moreover, professional retailers can be better than national brand manufacturers at positioning Brands because of their skill in precisely identifying consumers' preferences. Retailers also value control over store brand positioning because they could never source a national brand with their desired product positioning. The value to retailers of controlling the positioning of their Store Brands arises when retailers negotiate supply terms for National Brands that they stock. In negotiations with national brand manufacturers, one of the key determinants of the supply terms manufacturers can bargain for with retailers, is the value that their national brand adds to the Retailer. Since this added value is related to how differentiated the national brand is relative to other offerings of the Retailer, the Retailer benefits from carrying close substitutes to key leading National Brands.

Substitute Brands to key National Brands improve the retailer's "disagreement pay off," thus allowing the Retailer to improve its supply terms with national brand manufacturers. A Retailer will not be able to club those Substitute Brands among the ranks of National Brands because their manufacturers do not benefit from the positioning the Retailer would like to see. This is because the ability of manufacturers of National Brands to negotiate favourable supply terms with the Retailer is lower, the more substitutable their Brands are with other Brands that the Retailer carries. Hence, it is the retailer's control of brand positioning that enables a Retailer to carry Substitute Brands –in form of Store Brands – to key National Brands.

Retailers survive in organised Retailing as a business, due to their superior Supply Chain management skills. This felicity in Supply Chain management is one that helps retailers get into Outsourcing for developing Store Brands. Retailers in their efforts at drawing customers are involved in marketing efforts akin to national brand marketers. Thus, the two main ingredients of success in a national brand manufacturer/marketer's efforts are already available as resources to utilise in managing Store Brands. Therefore, the emergence of Store Brands and their competition with national brand marketers is inevitable in the future. The critical dimensions that would determine the success of retailers and their Brands are the overall chain strategy and the place of Store Brands in the same, commitment to quality, breadth of store brand offerings, a premium brand offering and a greater number of stores. These would consistently enhance the retailer's private label share performance in all categories. In addition, Retailer promotional support can significantly enhance store brand performance.

CATEGORY MANAGEMENT

In a few years' time we as consumers might be bewildered by the variety of products that would be available. The Indian retail scene will have no option but to manage this increase in the volume of categories that are cropping up in each product. The traditional role played now by the independent Retailer as well as the chain retailers in dealing with individual Brands and companies need to give way to new ways of handling product category proliferation. Category Management as is being practiced now in the west, could be the answer.

Retailers developed Category Management as a strategy to successfully compete with each retail category for the shopper's loyalty and rupees. As a cornerstone of the Efficient Consumer Response (ECR) initiatives, the industry formulated Category Management to help retailers provide consumers the right mix of products, at the right Price, with the right promotions, at the right time, and at the right place. Category Management insists that the retailers' categories, rather than the manufacturers' Brands, become the focus of management resources. A category is defined as a distinct manageable group of products that consumers perceive to be related and/or substitutable in meeting a consumer need.

Category Management must be viewed from the marketing dyad - the Retailer and manufacturer. The role of a category manager being responsible for the following:

- Category managers (at both sides) must have full responsibility for a range of related products and perform like business managers or entrepreneurs with full P&L responsibility and enough clout in their own and the other organisation.

- Category managers (at both sides) must be assigned a team of experts and support personnel in some kind of working relationship to make sure that all topics and issues arising in the business relationship can be covered with vigour.

What is logical to the consumer, what is easy to manage (routing, layout, suppliers) and other factors like buying moments could be the basis for the retailer's choice of classification of categories. Another way to classify could also be the nature of products like Specialist (soft drinks, wine, fresh), Traffic builder (beer, dairy products, canned food), Service (paper, coffee/tea), High margin (snacks, detergents, tobacco, sauces). A third way could be to base on market share and market growth of a set of products.

Influencing factors

Though Category Management holds great potential, it has several inherent barriers that can impede Category Performance. Two central factors that can have critical impact on Category Management are category plan objectivity and implementation. Category Management theory posits that retailers can maximise their sales in the category through:

- An optimal mix of Brands, SKUs
- Pricing that is determined from the consumer's perspective and on historical sales data.

The operating assumption of Category Management implies that performance improvements in a category at the retail level will result in improvements in the suppliers' performance. Supplier Brands constitute that category. It is clear to retailers, wholesalers, and suppliers alike therefore that effective Category Management practices are critical to retailer's Competitive Strategy. However, these partners in the Supply Chain need to work together, to effectively, develop and implement Category Management. The competing interests of the suppliers (who seek to increase share of their products in the category) with those of the retailers (who seek to increase the performance of the overall category) creates tension that can hinder the development and implementation of Category Management plans. A natural tension exists between manufacturers' brand focus and retailers' category focus. Internally, manufacturer companies' Brand Management is likely to pressure their sales organisation to favour their Brands in Category Planning. Retailers may not be able to recognise opportunism by the supplier in Category Management relationships. Moreover, marketers/suppliers that commit resources to Category Planning are vulnerable to Retailer inaction.

Category Management should be free from prejudices of the respective manufacturer' brands' interest and from retailers' interest in their private label offerings. Supplier as well as Retailer can consider a category plan objective when it fairly considers the store and market-level data, so that the interest of the consumer is fully taken care of.

The incentive to maintain objectivity of category plans is that by using actual sales data and by incorporating knowledge of the consumer's needs and wants, the plan should deliver the assortment, placement, promotion, and Pricing of the SKUs in a manner that enhances the performance of the category. The Retailer benefits through category volume and revenue growth as well as enhanced category profitability. The supplier benefits from Category Management to the extent that the category plan that has the potential to grow the most, will simultaneously grow within that category.

Measurement of success

Assessing a retailer's performance in a category is important to both retailers as well as manufacturers. There is need to understand the factors that determine across Retailer variation in Category Performance and Category Development Index (CDI) can be a tool to measure it. The ratio of its share in the category compared to its market share across all categories represents Retailers' CDI for a category.

Category Management involves both front-end activities to enhance category demand and back door activities to improve supply management and Logistics coordination with vendors. Retailers influence category volume by taking marketing actions that either increase store traffic and/or increase probability of category purchase by consumers who already are in the store. The role category plays in both consumer and retailer's portfolio groups includes: staples (high penetration/high frequency); niches (low penetration/high frequency); variety enhancers (high penetration/low frequency) and (4) fill-ins (low penetration/low frequency) which is a significant influencer.

Merchandising Variables as a group plays a significant role in affecting CDI. Reductions in the breadth (number of Brands) and depth (number of SKUs in terms of size, type of package, flavour) of assortment may meet with resistance in many product categories. This could be due to their positive impact on Category Performance. Retailers should be more accepting of reductions in assortment in staples categories where shoppers are unlikely to notice reductions, as much as in niches, variety enhancers and fill-ins.

Visual merchandising impact

Feature Advertising helps build the store and hence category traffic, while display influences category volume by leading to opportunistic in-store purchasing. Feature-based promotions are more effective in increasing CDI in traffic-building staple categories and to some extent in niches and variety enhancers too, while display promotions enhance category volumes, more so in low-visibility fill-in categories in which displays help to significantly enhance shelf space relative to the regular shelf-set. Price promotions, without any display or feature support, are mainly effective in high-traffic staples and variety enhancers where they can increase volume by causing opportunistic in-store purchasing.

Store Brand Programme

A strong Store Brand Programme which leads to higher unit CDI's for a Retailer can happen. A retailer's store brand can play a great role in increasing primary demand for the category, even to the extent of overcoming lower revenues that may arise from intra-category switching of consumers from higher priced National Brands to lower priced Store Brands. This role of private labels in building store-traffic and hence category volume is much more likely to matter in staple categories which have both a broad-based appeal and constitute an important part of a consumer's shopping budget. A lower category Price plays an important role in increasing Retailer unit-category sales and to some extent revenues, too, in variety enhancer and niche categories. Regular Price elasticities are low in staples, as competing retailers seem to have similar prices in these important traffic-building categories.

Store Brands obtain higher share under certain conditions like:

- Quality relative to National Brands was high

- Quality variability of Store Brands was low

- Product category was large in absolute terms (rupee sales)

- Per cent gross margins were high

- There were fewer national manufacturers operating in the category

- National Advertising expenditures were low

The first two Variables show that everything else being equal, consumers are more likely to buy private labels that provide parity quality. The middle two factors reflect the retailer's scarce resource allocation problem. Because retailers must draw on internal funds for branding, packaging, production, and Advertising of their Store Brands, they invest more heavily in large categories offering high profit margins to maximise their return. The last two Variables demonstrate the influence of manufacturers and show that private labels can be crowded out of the market when national brand competition is high and when those Brands invest Advertising resources into the consumer franchise.

Three parties influence the performance of Store Brands consumers, national brand manufacturers and retailers. Although store brand Pricing has a substantial impact on store brand market share, it plays a key role in a successful and profitable private label programme. If the Retailer maintains a large Price gap between the two, then they will sell more store brand units than if the gap is smaller. The optimal gap in that case should be in terms of maximising category profitability.

Outsourcing Category Management

Outsourcing is expanding from parts and components to include services and process management. The question is no more just about who designs and manufactures the goods, but also who manages the logistical processes along the Supply Chain. Outsourcing provides new opportunities for those Retailing and Grocery sectors that traditionally have not considered Outsourcing as a strategic option to develop their operations. Retailers, especially Supermarkets, are managing an increasing number of product categories and stock keeping units (SKU) that have forced them to develop their replenishment practices in order to minimise out-of-stock problems.

The goal of Category Management is to optimise assortments, promotions and product introductions, as well as consumer value creation. Category Management is known to improve revenue creation, but it also aims to reduce costs. Professional storeowners carry out Category Management process through a multistage process, which consists of defining the category and its role and establishing measures for performance of the category.

Vendor Managed Inventory (VMI) is an operating model in which the supplier takes responsibility for the inventory of its customer. In a VMI-partnership, the supplier makes the main inventory replenishment decisions for the customer. The supplier, which may be a manufacturer, reseller or a distributor, monitors the buyer's inventory levels and makes supply decisions regarding order quantities, shipping and timing. For suppliers, the major attraction of VMI is in understanding demand. Large, infrequent orders from customers force suppliers to maintain inventories that enable them to respond to uneven demand. In VMI, the supplier is able to smooth the peaks and valleys in the flow of goods, and therefore to keep smaller buffers of capacity and inventory. The supplier has better opportunities to coordinate shipments to different customers. It can schedule in that either postpone or advance shipments according to production schedules, customer inventory situations and transportation.

In the Grocery sector, VMI is adopted successfully, for example between Procter & Gamble and Wal-Mart. The Retailing industry does not have an Outsourcing trend similar to manufacturing industry. Retailers are still trying to manage by themselves an ever increasing product range. The Outsourcing scope is confined to warehousing and shipment.

Any company in any sector should identify its core competencies, maintain and build on them. The Outsourcing strategy should be based on the strategic risk of Outsourcing and the potential for gaining a competitive edge. Companies take up activities that have high Outsourcing risk and high potential for competitive edge internally. Those activities in which both the risk and potential for competitive edge are moderate, need moderate control. The company can outsource these activities. Even though there is a globalisation trend in Retailing, it is still a relatively local business. However, suppliers to the retailers are in many product categories globally operating companies and the competition is global. The retailers could better utilise capabilities and big resources of global vendors. When the Outsourcing approach is applied, the company has to open up and analyse business processes and service concepts. Retailers should identify activities that the supplier performs more efficiently than the Retailer does. In addition, these suppliers may be able to offer services that add value for retailers' customers.

Retail orders or distributor's replenishment decisions or deliveries from distribution centres or directly from suppliers form the basis for the current Retailer-demand-fulfillment model in many retail chains. Distributors or suppliers (who try to fulfil the need in the best possible way) obtain Communication on Retailer demand. The present model may appear to be efficient from the point of view of the Retailer; the typical supermarket gets deliveries from a supplier several times a week, large hypermarkets even delivery twice daily, and the order to delivery lead-time is short.

There are several serious problems hidden in this demand fulfillment model. The actual item level replenishment cycle is far slower than the order fulfillment cycle. With up to 200,000 items in the range, the Retailer may have difficulties in managing the ordering process. A Retailer may place an order too late, when he has sold out the product or will be out of stock before the delivery arrives. On the other hand, forecasting errors or Price reductions connected to minimum lot sizes may lead to high inventory levels and best-before problems in the store. Moreover, in view of the short delivery lead-times and high service level requirement, the distributor keeps the inventory levels high. Typically, there exists accurate information neither about retail sales, nor about out-of-stocks along the chain, due to lack of visibility. Therefore, the supplier is not aware of the lost sales. This means that the real trade-off between providing a good Logistics service level and cost level remains hidden from the supplier.

An illustrative situation

Take the case of a product category which comprises mostly school and office supplies and drawing equipment. This is a non-core category for the Grocery Retailing. If the Retailer would take care of the management of this kind of category, it would have to decide on the assortment, deal with a number of suppliers concerning orders, invoicing and payments and plan the shelf layout. The store personnel would have to place the products in the shelves and follow and react to the trend changes and seasonal changes in the category. There is a possibility that the management of the category would fail, and the store personnel would concentrate on the more important categories generating more sales. The result would be that the sales and profits of the category would sink, and when reallocating the limited space in the store, products that are more profitable occupy this Category Space.

When the supplier takes care of the category, the assortment contains the right products, which allows for the latest trends. The Retailer gets more sales and profits in the limited retail space. The supplier in this case develops the operations in the Supply Chain further and ensures the competitiveness of its products and service offerings. The store can use the time consumed in the Supply Chain (in the stores and by the distributor) through better information sharing and a collaborative planning process. The Supply Chain realises the economics of Collaboration in the form of lower inventories and accurate planning results. Using better information-sharing capabilities of electronic commerce, participants in the Supply Chain can use POS-data to drive the whole chain. The supplier takes care of deliveries, ordering and stocking, and above all Category Management.

This outsourced model of Category Management would cover category sales forecast, order forecast and logistical forecast. The Retailer gives all the responsibility to the supplier and the supplier has the knowledge, ability and resources to perform all of these functions. The supplier also is motivated to develop the functions further to remove inefficiencies in the Supply Chain, to improve the relationship with the manufacturer by efficient information sharing and a quicker replenishment cycle.

Category Management is a potential tool in moving forward to efficient Retailing practices. However, the path to this form of management at the retail level is not strewn with roses. It requires the Collaboration of all members of the Supply Chain. The level of understanding among competing suppliers should be high in order to make it an orderly happening. This requires professional understanding of the impediments to effective Category Management.

VENDOR COLLABORATION

Thomson, the global electronic durable giant, boasts of awards (Wal-Mart Canada's Vendor of the Year Award 2002, Best Buy BRAVO Award, OfficeMax Strategic Vendor Partnership Award, Aaron's Sales & Lease Vendor of the Year Award 2002) from four major retailers in the North America for the year 2002. This shows the extent of importance that vendors accord to retailers. This is also a clear reflection of the power of retailers. At the same time, retailers also reward vendors, acknowledging the key role played by the good vendors that help them in managing their businesses efficiently. However, the situation is not as simple as imagining a single vendor like Thomson and few retailers like Wal-Mart, Best Buy, Office Max and Aaron's Sale and Lease. Imagine a Multi-departmental Store that has to deal with thousands of vendors, for lakhs of SKUs on a daily basis. In this context, strategic marketing Collaboration with vendors assumes greater prominence.

There are important dimensions of the Collaboration deal with the product related aspects. The supplier can tailor product quality, product design, pack design and nature of the product to suit the needs of the Retailer. If the sales of the product from a store are a significant portion of the total sales of the vendor, there is a possibility of co-branding as it increases credibility of the brand. Moreover, quality of the product itself may be different from the quality of the same product being available in other Outlets. Depending on the need of the Retailer, the design of the packaging can also vary. Retailers significantly facilitate new product development experimentation and control. In a strategic marketing Collaboration between the Marketer and national Retailer, specification of the stores where the new product might be placed and a set of control stores could be done in order to study the differences and obtain appropriate inferences for the launch of the product. Thus, one of the greatest benefits is the availability of flexibility to vendor/supplier/Marketer for test marketing. From the Retailer point of view, this acts as an opportunity to test and provides variety in product categories. It also reduces the boredom of consumers involved in shopping and therefore helps sustain interest in the store.

Organisational characteristics

The organisational characteristics of both the vendor and Retailer play an important role in determination of the strategic marketing Collaboration. While both the vendors as well as the Retailer reap marketing benefits, the hidden part of the alliance to the consumer is the smooth working/operational relationship.

Operations Management in the retail sector can make or mar business. The smooth relationship between the vendor and Retailer depends on the following factors:

- *Size of the company:* Relative difference in size of vendor and Retailer in terms of the people employed, turnover etc., each of which has an impact on the relationship.

- **Client service:** Nature of client servicing expected by the Retailer as compared to the actual. The Marketer providing all the help versus a situation where the Retailer also takes up equal responsibility in servicing the ultimate customers.

- **Sales policy:** Terms and conditions of sale that are strategically decided.

- **Company organisation:** The nature of delegation of authority in the vendor as well as the retail company ends. If decentralised decision-making is encouraged, then there are bound to be conflicts if the regional/unit level decision-makers in both the companies do not cooperate. In centralised decision-making, responsibility is to ensure that the Collaboration works at all cost. The situation is similar to an arranged marriage by the parents versus a love marriage.

- **Supply strategy:** The two major supply strategies of the vendor are supplying through the existing distribution system or direct store distribution. In the case of a large retail chain, the supply strategy needs to align with the distribution system of the Retailer. If the Retailer owns a central distribution centre catering to a region for some key product categories and asks the supplier to ship direct to store certain other categories, a great deal of understanding is required in operational terms.

- **Geographic scope:** The Home Depot which is an international Retailer has established a strategic relationship with Phillips for lighting products for its entire stores in the US. In this case, the geographic scope or implication of the alliance is mutually beneficial. As The Home Depot increases its presence internationally, its international presence and an assured customer base would benefit Phillips. This decision however of the domestic or the international level of cooperation reflects also on the nature of delegation of power within the organisation.

- **Store access:** The physical as well as virtual access to the store makes a huge difference to the nature of relationship between the vendor and Retailer. In terms of distribution, it plays a crucial role. At the same time, access to store data provides a clear evidence of performance of the various SKUs of different product categories to all vendors. A competitive perspective is also possible if the Retailer has a Multi-brand Outlet.

- **Price strategy:** Product Price to the consumer is a marketing strategy decision of the Marketer. In the same way Price is a crucial dimension in the positioning of any retail entity. There needs to be perfect harmony in the Pricing strategies of both organisations. The relationship needs to synchronise the understanding about consumer shift in preferences, based on Price points and act collaboratively in fine-tuning strategies on a dynamic basis.

- **Reordering:** Logistics comprises of a significant component of marketing efforts of both the vendor and Retailer. With the Outsourcing of this function, the Retailer needs to tackle another organisational entity to have a strong marketing Collaboration between the vendor and Retailer. Concepts like collaborative planning, forecasting and supply-chain-management need to work in practice. The key activity of reordering has a ripple effect on the channel system.

Space Management

Space Management in a different dimension is the job of a Retailer. Retailers can view vendors as those who would obtain the space for rent. In this view, the Retailer needs to take space-related decisions very carefully. Some of the decisions that have an impact on marketing are:

- *Space configuration:* While the retail chain would be interested in a standardised and replicable space configuration of the stores to preserve its identity, the vendors would be interested in a special space provision for its products in order to enhance visibility. This means a compromise required on both sides. The introduction of concepts like "Shop-in-shop" is a step in that direction. Food World accommodating the growing importance of MTR as a major ready-to-eat products vendor in Bangalore and providing a corner for MTR in their Outlets is a good example of this kind.

- *Shelf position:* The way in which the outlet positions shelves in a store determine the effect of visual merchandising on consumers. Design interaction with the product category and shelf position has an impact on sales. Therefore, a clear understanding of the store shelf positions with the prospective vendors makes sense.

- *Shelf allocation:* There are varying pressures towards allocation of shelves. One of the key dimensions could be the margin from the product category or brand. Other important determinants are remuneration paid for a favourable shelf allocation in the case of a large retail outlet. In addition, introduction of a new category requires special shelf allocation. The vendor - Retailer relationship helps in sorting out the multiple pressures on shelf allocation effectively.

- *Special store needs:* This point is especially true in the case of a Heterogeneous Market like India as well as the absence of a standardised store concept. Special store needs in terms of highlighting product categories, makes the job of Space Management very difficult. Moreover, space itself may be a constraint in the case of locations like the central business district of metros. Here an appreciation of the space constraint by the vendor makes the job of Space Management much more effective.

Problem areas

Some of the key problem areas that have an effect on strategic marketing Collaboration between vendors and retailers are:

- Manufacturers and suppliers giving discount allowances to retailers in exchange for their products getting more-prominent display and promotion. This may sometimes be a violation of the general perception among the other manufacturers and suppliers that display and promotion are not a function of the discount on the product but are directly dependent on the margins offered to these activities exclusively and separately. There is a sense of non-transparent dealing in this case.

- Retailers assessing manufacturers and suppliers with charge backs pay them less than what they are billed for. This happens due to mistimed deliveries, shortages, mislabelling and mistakes in product coding. Charge backs if agreed as per terms and conditions of the contract are fine. However, if charge backs on suppliers are without Communication to them and are directly reflected only in billing, then the relationship between the vendor and Retailer takes on an adversarial position.

- Vendors intentionally over ship merchandise to stores, so they can report that they have exceeded sales goals. In a highly competitive scenario, there is tremendous pressure on the salesmen of vendors interacting with stores for achieving higher targets year after year. Overshipping is a result of this achievement of an over-enthusiastic target. Here again in the absence of the right Communication, relationships get affected and one which has a bearing too on marketing efforts.

Role of information technology

Information technology is one of the greatest enablers of the Collaboration between the vendor and Retailer. Wal-Mart, the largest company in the world with more than 2,700 stores and $217 billion in revenue last year, gets a major competitive advantage from the efficiency of its electronic product information, ordering, supply-chain management, and delivery systems. It possesses the influence to get manufacturers into collaborative E-business, because it can represent 5% to 30% of a manufacturer's total business. Wal-Mart requires every manufacturer to manage its own in-store inventory and uses EDI networks and its private collaborative trading hub, SupplierLink, to consolidate global purchasing. It brings 10,000 suppliers online to bid on contracts and communicate sales and inventory data. Wal-Mart also uses its networks to manage its Supply Chain and Logistics. In this kind of an environment, greater data transparency and information sharing as well the speed of response cement the supplier - Retailer relationship. The same is the case with 7-Eleven Inc., with over 30,000 suppliers in all-different sizes.

Even in the fashion conscious sectors of Retailing, the use of IT helps. Payless' sources nearly 80% of the 250 million pairs of shoes sold through its 5,000 stores from Asia. This represents challenges in a style- oriented business. The shoe business is very fashion driven. Many products have short lifecycles like 13 weeks. Payless is concentrating on a core vendor/ core factory programme to achieve production efficiencies and stay ahead of fashion trends. The speed of interacting, enabled by IT helps in competing with similar stores in the shoe business.

IT enablement is not without attendant technical glitches. TruServ's independently owned hardware and garden stores presents unique challenges for sharing information. The IT Infrastructure needs to support 27 different point of sale platforms. This means heavy Dependence on technological and highly skilled workforce support that would make information sharing a smooth affair. However, despite these challenges, TruServ have been one of the biggest proponents of Retailer-supplier Collaboration. Among all of TruServ's collaborative partners, one of the most valuable has been Black & Decker. This Collaboration includes vendor-managed data and vendor managed inventory. Black and Decker executives get to see POS movement through a statistical sample of 650 stores. One of the most interesting benefits of collaborative data is the ability for TruServ at the store level to learn about new product changes at Black & Decker within hours of their registration. Chevron Retailer Alliance (CRA) is another great application of the use of IT effectively in strategic marketing Collaboration. CRA simplifies business processes for Chevron Retailers. Utilising the Internet, Chevron electronically deploys business transactional data and many of its programmes, products and promotions through the Retailers Market Exchange Web site. In addition, their Retail Marketing Centre provides a single point of telephone contact to support retailers in managing their daily business with Chevron.

Information

In developed countries like the USA, there is a clear link between performance of the relationship and stock prices of the suppliers and retailers. For example, Retailer sales announcements have an effect on the security prices of suppliers. Moreover, there is greater transparency in information sharing as mandated by law. In the discussion of business section in the 10K reports, there is need for retailers to mention names of suppliers who have more than 10% sales in total sales of the Retailer. In spite of this mercantile relationship between the vendor and Retailer, competing sources of firm specific information are the ones that have an impact on the stock market. These include purchase record, complementarity of future expectations, and cooperation and adaptation between both the parties. Both the Retailer as well as the vendor would find it difficult to measure these qualitative factors objectively.

Qualitative factors

The nature of qualitative factors that determine the strength of the relationship are many. The ones that are most quoted are trust and commitment. General understanding assumes that trust and commitment will emerge when bilateral convergence characterises the relationship between the suppliers and retailers. That is when the interdependence structure is such that interests of both parties are convergent. Additionally, as the relationship becomes more asymmetric, interests of the parties diverge. Increasing asymmetry in interdependence reduces structural impediments inhibiting the more powerful firm's opportunistic behaviour, self-serving exercise of power and punitive actions. Supplier-Retailer relationships with high symmetric Dependence are likely to generate benefits, such as more favourable performance, for both parties. Although perfect symmetry is an elusive objective and one which is rarely achieved, reducing asymmetry is a more realistic goal for collaborators.

Trust in collaborator's honesty reflects in the acceptance of a reasonable explanation, accurate information and advice (sharing its best judgement) on business operations and sincerity.

Trust in the collaborator's benevolence should be reflective in readiness and willingness to offer assistance and support, concern about each other's welfare, response with understanding, and a clear idea of how his decisions and actions will affect the other party as well as the other party's support.

Retailer's affective commitment is the ability not to drop the relationship, remain a member of the supplier's network and enjoy the relationship. There is a sharing of positive feelings and the expectation of continuity. The renewal of the relationship is virtually automatic. In addition, commitment relates to the willingness to invest and specifically invest in supporting the supplier's line. It also means more effort and investment in building the retailer's business in the manufacturer's product and collaboratively in the customer's mind.

Dependence

The Retailer/supplier enjoys relative power in Collaboration. Dependence is a key dimension of this Collaboration. The first aspect of Dependence is Retailer Dependence. Other retailers can provide the supplier with comparable distribution. The supplier could incur minimal costs in replacing an existing Retailer with another Retailer. In both the above cases, the Retailer Dependence would be high. In strategic Collaboration, it would be difficult for the supplier to replace the sales and profits which the Retailer generates and therefore the Collaboration is mutually beneficial.

The other factor in Dependence is supplier Dependence. Other suppliers could provide retailers with a comparable product line. If strategic Collaboration exists, the total costs of switching to a competing supplier's line would be prohibitive. In the latter case, supplier Dependence is less and therefore Collaboration persists.

Net based Collaboration

Some of the examples below explain how the spread of the Internet access has helped in strategic marketing Collaboration. Yahoo and Softbank Venture Capital announced an agreement with Kmart to create a co-branded free Internet access service. Microsoft cut a deal with Tandy-owned Radio Shack stores to promote its MSN services, pumping $100 million into the electronics store and featuring it on the MSN portal. AOL has also been busy pursuing this strategy. Computer retail chain Circuit City will promote AOL's products and services and in return get prominent placement on AOL's site. AOL has signed a marketing deal with Seagram's Universal Studios that will bring AOL kiosks to Universal's new Island of Adventure theme park in Orlando. A co-branded Wal-Mart/AOL ISP will be a customised version of the CompuServe service. This Retailer uses this service to target customers wanting lower prices. The service provides Wal-Mart customers, software they can use to quickly and easily, create an online account with the new Internet service offering local access. In addition to distributing the co-branded Wal-Mart/AOL ISP, Wal-Mart will also distribute AOL 5.0 software that will have an automatic link to Wal-Mart's Internet shopping site.

Strategic marketing Collaboration between vendors and retailers is a multifaceted effort. It needs to look at possible benefits from both sides. Collaboration needs to emphasise in addition to quantifiable benefits, an inherent qualitative relationship between retailers and vendors. The advent of new tools of information technology can greatly synergise collaborative efforts of marketing. In sum, a combination of professional attitude, an emotional attachment and enabling technology make for a successful marketing Collaboration.

ASSORTMENT PLANNING

The Indian Retailing scene is increasingly seeing a surge in product turnover and proliferation rates in all product categories. There is intense competition brewing domestically for retailers, leave alone the potential foreign competition on the retail format front. The ever-dynamic consumer tastes have also left retailers gasping. Thus, three Cs-competition, congestion (proliferation of categories) and consumerism have created a huge challenge for the Retail Managers in their decision-making efforts on assortment and Category Management. The 4th C - Cost has also an important role to play given the inventory obsolescence cost or higher buffer stock requirement costs because of the 3Cs above. Assortment (the number of different items to be carried in a merchandise category represents the assortment) decision as a component of Category Management which has acquired relevance in the present Retailing context.

Assortment variety is one of the obvious first stimuli that have an impact on consumers and competition. In the West, fashion/apparel retailers, dedicate up to 10% of the open-to-buy budget to experimenting with assortment variety. The question of assortment variety acquires a complex dimension when the retail chain views the twin objectives of category profit maximisation as well as providing variety to consumers at the same time. The shelf space available in a retail store is limited. Therefore, the store manager has to undertake all the experiments with assortment variety with caution. This would involve category-space-allocation decision as well as merchandise arrangement and location. For example if a local consumer durables dealer wants to establish assortment variety as his competitive strength, then one of the categories of durables he can think of is washing machines. If he decides to have one of each type in semi-automatic, automatic, and similar decisions for the individual attributes of the washing machines like brand, colour etc, then he would probably need to allocate the entire store space to only washing machines. Therefore, the Retailer needs to decide the right method of stocking the right assortment-variety factoring in all the competing objectives.

Methodology for choosing assortment

The standard mark-up bestsellers' approach is one of the most common methodologies followed in assortment planning. For example, if we go ahead with the same category as described above i.e. washing machines, then the normal practice in most retail Outlets is to look at space as a constraint and look for the number of washing machines that could be accommodated. A retail chain can conduct experiments across stores based on the variety available. Let us say the chain can choose the top three performing models based on all the attributes. These should also represent a constant mark up. However, retailers need to plan assortments scientifically with much more sophisticated mathematical modelling. The cost and benefit analysis needs to be done. The major costs associated with assortment decisions are cost of display space and the indirect costs of stock out and overstocking. Thus, Inventory Management, too, plays a crucial role.

Any Retailer can use retail assortment as an instrument for store differentiation and competitive advantage. Some of them use consumption occasions during the day, to be used to club product categories. In extreme cases in Europe, where retail saturation has set in, stores use day of the week and time of the day for assortment change. Just imagine a store changing the assortment by the day, based on the requirements of the customers who shop during that time! Efficient Assortment composition and display also require commensurate change in back office operations. The coordination of the supplies of different SKUs, which are larger in number from the same vendor or small number of SKUs from different vendors, increases complexity of transactions. The question that would immediately arise is whether Outlets have to add more functions to existing departments or create more departments. In this situation, use of benchmarked competitive processes is more important than functions and departments in managing retail assortment. Retail assortment decisions based on a sustainable and robust process rather than multi-level Hierarchical Process (cutting across functional and departmental boundaries) can help.

Assortment reduction

One of the crucial decisions that store managers need to take in Retailing is also assortment reduction. With increase in the breadth and width of assortment, consumers face a clutter with regard to choice. Therefore, consumer clutter reduction becomes relevant in the face of diminishing marginal value attached to additional variety in assortment. However, storeowners need to see this against the background of consumer segments that look to shopping for noting trends, variety, activity and pleasure. The importance of providing sizable selections for consumers with uncertain preferences and for those who tend to seek variety cannot be underestimated. One of the possible options for the Retailer to get out of this dilemma is to provide more services and reduce the assortment. One of the other issues that retail chains could look at is whether any item in the assortment available in the store supports any of the following:

- *Store patronage* - increase in loyalty towards the store

- *Store sales Stimulation* - increase store sales in general

- *Company image* - maintain the image of the store in spite of reduced margin

- *Exemplars of the category* - required for the category to be recognised in the store e.g. National Brands of soaps

One of the ideas of effective assortment reduction could be to see how the store manager can use effectively the effect on sales resulting from different types of SKU reductions (i.e. cuts based on product characteristics) other than being low- or non-selling. Not every product cut will lead to elimination of a brand, size, or flavour. Merchandise managers might eliminate purposefully or inadvertently, entire Brands and sizes from a selection. They might just trim a number of specific brand-size combinations. For example, if sachet packs of Kissan Jam are eliminated but the consumer can still get sachet packs of alternative jams and other sizes of Kissan (e.g. 200g pack), then only a specific *brand-size combination* was cut; the brand and size themselves are still available. The retail outlet can view the total number of brand-size combinations cut, as indicative of a reduction in *redundant* items as long as it does not eliminate all Brands or sizes. Consequently, we expect these types of cuts to have a positive effect on sales, as eliminating clutter makes it easier for the consumer to find what he or she is looking for. If too much choice is truly demotivating, then eliminating redundant items should help boost category sales (a simple positive relationship).

Consumer Perception of assortment

The perception of variety among a selection affects consumer choice. This has a direct implication on assortment decisions. This means that variety depends on more than just the number of distinct products on the shelves. Space devoted to the category can influence consumer's perception of variety - more space allocated to a category would create an impression of variety. The presence or absence of the consumer's favourite item, the arrangement of an assortment and the presence of repeated items and the number of acceptable alternatives can also create such perceptions. Therefore, a thorough analysis of consumer requirements at least as far as the Primary Trading Area served by the store on these counts is important in making decisions. Retailers could look at three important components that determine an assortment's structure in order to influence consumers. These are its assortment organisation i.e. organised /disorganised classification and layout, size i.e. the shelf facings that each variety in the assortment obtains and entropy i.e. alternatives and frequency of the displayed assortment. These can directly influence perceptions of variety and consumption quantities, even when actual variety is unchanged.

The Filtering or screening method that the Retailer provides for examination of the assortment is an important constituent of perception creation. Filtering refers to how much the consumer views an assortment. For instance, the entire assortment can be presented all at once where every product is visible at once (no filter), or it can be filtered and presented in sections, where ultimately the whole assortment need not be viewed. For example, on a Web site links might filter the assortment. A consumer clicks on specific hyperlinks and then views only those sub-sections of the assortment. In a physical retail store, guided maps or store sales persons who lead consumers directly to items of interest might filter the overall assortment. Physical retail stores follow shelving configurations that force consumers to view more of the assortment.

Consumer mind map and the physical assortment fit

In spite of the discussion above on creating perception through different components of assortment, it is still a difficult task to assess Consumer Behaviour as exhibited towards assortment. There could be internal processes in the consumer's mind that determine perception. These could relate to how the consumer's existing category scheme i.e. his thinking of clubbing of products under a category works or as a function of his/her shopping goals.

For familiar categories like say for example breakfast foods, for which consumers have a strong internal category scheme, congruency between his/her categorisation (e.g., by brand or by attribute) and the retailer's layout of the assortment will result in higher perceptions of variety. It would also result in higher satisfaction with the assortment offering and choices from the assortment. For unfamiliar categories like say ready to eat foods, or categories without a single internal categorisation, consumers will have higher perceptions of variety. This will also go along with higher satisfaction with the assortment and with their choices from the assortment. Such experiences could be more impressionable if they have a specific Goal-driven Shopping task rather than a general one. If the external Filtering mechanism (a guide to exactly locate an item in a large Multi-departmental Store) of the assortment matches a consumer's shopping goal (i.e. a consumer wants to buy a particular brand of baby food), then it allows the consumer to avoid observing items in the assortment. This would result in consumers having lower perceptions of variety and lower satisfaction with the assortment offering and choices from the assortment. Thus, the nature of Filtering is very important.

Use of information technology

The advent of information technology has made the job of assortment planning easier, given the exponential and spiralling combination of various SKUs. One of the technologies that have recently facilitated the same is Data Mining. For example, the Retailer first does a market basket analysis for the representative customer of the store. Then "association rules" as a Data Mining technique for assortment planning can be undertaken. The association could be in the form of complementarity, conditional independence and substitutability. These rules establish the association between Consumer Behaviour as well as the assortment available. In this way, the store can achieve greater synchronisation between display or selling of items and consumer requirements. Information technology tools thus act as facilitating entities in the efficient planning of assortments. In fact, customisation of the assortment at the individual customer level is possible, given the tracking of the consumer, over a period of time. This can actually result in customer delight. A Retailer can find out from typical Buying Behaviour of a customer, his level of experimentation with regard to the inclusion of new product categories or forms through market basket analysis and thus ensure a proportion of the same in all future purchases. This could be a suggested assortment to every customer.

Assortment planning features the primary level of decisions with regard to a Category Management and therefore reflects category profits. In the case of Category Management, the approach towards stocking products or items in stores has undergone a metamorphosis from vendor/supplier-driven to product/brand-driven to customer-driven approach. Assortment has to reflect consumer tastes and preferences and hence marks as the true test of implementation of the marketing concept. Consumer Behaviour is both on rational and perceived counts. Therefore, assortment needs to take both the real and tangible factors of number as well as perception, to satisfy consumer needs. This would become central to all decisions in order to have an impact on marketing. In the case of national chain stores, assortment has also to take into account regional sensibilities.

Assortment has implications on other aspects of store management like operations, in the sense that the greater the variety and number of items, the greater the need to tightly monitor Supply Chain management. Store assortment is not at the cost of efficient Financial Management. Therefore, cost and profitability considerations have to be inherent in the decisions. In the age of enterprise wide systems, infotech support must be the maximum for experimentation with variety and in complementing efforts at analysing outputs. If variety and speed of change of assortment become the hallmark of a Retailer, the corporate culture in the organisation as reflected by human resources must believe in the credo - "variety and change are the spice of life!"

Marketing has a crucial role to play in highlighting characteristics of the assortment. In the case of competition from stores with similar assortment, outlet has to emphasise on services. Assortment variety and speed of change require the help of helpful retail sales persons in order to orient consumers. Internal marketing and internal customer satisfaction as in typical services marketing, then attains greater significance. The elements of the Retail Marketing mix have to work in tandem in order to present a cohesive picture about the Retailer. In this respect, adaptation of the marketing mix and specifically the use of appropriate Communication, become relevant.

You go to a sweet shop and are bewildered by the variety of sweets. One of the obvious choices available to you as a consumer, is to ask for an "assortment", that to some extent solves your problem of choosing which one to buy. On the other side of the business, could you imagine a category manager taking a decision like this? This predicament really makes assortment planning as a part of Category Management rather interesting and challenging.

CHAPTER FOUR

Retail Pricing and Communication

PRICE PROMOTIONS

"Your saving today from a store is Rs. 50 on a purchase of Rs 500"- You stare at this printed statement at the end of the bill you receive from a retail outlet. There are two columns mentioned while calculating your bill - the column showing the maximum retail price (MRP) and the column showing the actual price charged. At the end, the retailer calculates between the totals of the MRP and actual price columns and the statement above is printed automatically through the billing software. Price promotion in one of the ways above is a common phenomenon in the retailing scene in India. It may be justified in the context of the stage of India as per the wheel of retailing theory. Organised retailing starts in this manner and then graduates as saturation sets in so that there is a constant effort towards differentiation.

Reasons for price promotion

Theories of why retail firms may find it rational to periodically reduce prices, and then raise them again shortly thereafter, revolve around a few key assumptions regarding either the structure of the market, firm behaviour, or consumer behaviour. Consumers differ in the cost of search. This means that there are consumers who would go to any length to find out a bargain price for even frequently purchased commodities. Price promotion can easily lure these consumers. The degree of price-information they possess also determines why retailers indulge in price promotions. In the case of a segment of customers who are loyal to brands, the only price information that may matter is the difference in the price of the brand over the previous purchase, if any, and not any other information. In these cases, price promotion does not make much sense as long as it is not for the brand that the shopper buys often. Salaried class that gets salary every month and does grocery purchase once a month, does not care about the cost of holding inventory of groceries for a month or two. Same is the case with some among the salaried class who go in for a yearly purchase of groceries like chillies, *toor dhal* etc., during the peak arrival season of these commodities to save on price fluctuations and do not take into account the cost of inventory holding. In these cases, their cost of inventory holding and the perception of the same have an impact on price promotion. Consumer's loyalty to a particular store increases the chances of price promotion to retain the existing set of customers. Similarly, to increase their intensity of demand, the store can provide offers on regular purchases on products, whose consumption of quantity, the store can increase (like soft drinks). In the case of retail chain, lower costs of procurement and distribution may result in the ability to offer lower prices.

Advertised vs. unadvertised brands

One of the first and visible dimensions of price promotions is the decision on which brands to promote. Several studies have proved that price promotions work best on well-advertised brands than unadvertised brands. The retail mark-ups for these products are lower but higher volumes make up for the revenue. The traffic generating power of the heavily promoted national brand facilitates the phenomenon of loss leaders. That is why you always find the competitive ones among the super markets advertising *Horlicks* now at Rs. 90 compared to the original price of Rs. 105 etc. and not a price reduction on the new *Vinayaka ragi malt mix!*

Retailer efforts

Sales can result if supermarket retailers behave as price-discriminating monopolists maximising revenue by allocating goods among high-value and low-value consumers either at one point in time or over time as low-valuation consumers accumulate prior to a sale. Promotions may arise if retailers are uncertain regarding the level of demand, so they reduce prices in order to attract enough customers to clear their inventory. In the case of apparel and furniture purchases, where the demand uncertainty is high, as soon as the retailer senses, a decrease in the rate of sale of goods, there is a possibility of price promotion to clear stocks. Retailers may conduct sales for strategic reasons. Trigger strategies designed to support implicitly a collusive oligopoly or a recognition that low prices now will invite relatively benign punishments from rivals would propel store managers to undertake sales. The efforts of many consumer durable exclusive dealers in promoting a brand by reducing prices, amply reflect this phenomenon. They are sure that dealers of other brands may not be able to do so. Managers often regard price promotion as an essential part of introducing a new product. This has also to do with the diffusion of innovation as a process. Therefore new products/brands/services are initially price promoted at retail outlets in order to induce trial and then have the good experience of the product/brand spread among the consumers through word of mouth.

Consequences of price promotion

Retailers need to concentrate on effects of price promotion on consumers. Frequent promotions tend to reduce consumers' sensitivity of price-response as they come to expect and anticipate periodic price reductions. This is the case with CO-optex the retail chain of the handloom industry in Tamil Nadu where there is a periodic regular price reduction, thus reducing the sensitivity as well as credibility of the organisation. While looking at price promotion as a device to increase category demand, it is pertinent to be careful about the ultimate, bottomline effects of price promotions on store traffic and profit. The outlets have to monitor the impact of promotions at both a product and store-level. There is a need to separate promotion strategies that merely reallocate store-share among different products from those that truly generate incremental store traffic. This means that if blazers are on discount in an apparel shop does it also result in more than usual sales of ties or rather it shifts the demand from ready-made shirts to blazers. Retail price promotion needs to measure impact of sales on some types of contemporaneous consumer choice – what brand to choose, how much or when to buy. The store manager can detect the effect on consumer choice from the proportion of brand switching, purchase acceleration and stockpiling that takes place during price promotion. Price promotions are likely to have significant dynamic components arising from both adjustment effects and permanent impacts. There is a need to track the long-run consumer response to a price promotion in order to plan better for the future.

Dimensions of price promotion

The dimensions of price promotion also have an effect on the response of the same. Frequency as was discussed earlier may have a negative impact on consumer price sensitivity. On the other hand, the depth of price promotions - both in terms of the number of promoted products and the size of the discount may have a significant positive impact on the consumer. The number of products on promotion must be a judicious mix of the frequently purchased items of the typical consumer segments visiting the store as well as slow moving items. This will have an effect on the primary demand of these slow moving items. Retailers in India have used the size of discount as a weapon very wisely (deceptively!). The advertisements of retail outlets offering discount up to 75% on premium non-moving items during a sale represent such use. The communication of the size of discount based on the nature of the product also makes a difference in the perception of the discount by the consumers. This is where the deft handling of the copy of advertising comes into play.

Communication

The communication component of price promotion has a great significance in the consumer perception of the store. It also creates a different image of the store. Retailers can communicate price promotions in the following three forms (a) former price comparisons, (b) other retail price comparisons and (c) advertised retail prices suggested by manufacturers' comparisons. Each one of these has a different connotation. A loyal store customer has his credibility reinforced in the store when he sees that the prices are lower as compared to the normal price. On the other hand, a new customer would be tempted to visit a store as the store is inviting him with an offering that is enticing as compared to what he has seen in another store. In the Indian context, however it is rare to see an advertisement that states that we offer a price that is less than the suggested retail price by the manufacturer/marketer. This is a risky option as it has repercussions on the manufacturer/marketer as well as other retailers in a geographical area selling the same brand. However in reality, whenever negotiation takes place with a buyer, (for example in automobile dealerships) it is generally the practice by the dealer to show the retail price (list price as suggested by the manufacturer/marketer with the signature of the responsible person) from the marketer to affect a price cut.

All advertisements on price promotion provide a cue to the consumers about the nature of promotion. However these cues may not be concrete. Cue concreteness is the degree of detail and specificity about the price comparison, which the retailer provides. A cue such as "Regular Price/Sale Price" can be considered as concrete because it is very specific about the nature of the price comparison. The "Regular Price/Sale Price" cue clearly indicates the product's customary price and the current offer price. It is quite likely that consumers feel confident about understanding the price implications of these words. Comparatively, a cue such as "A Rs. 5000 value product now at a sale price of Rs. 500" is more abstract in nature and the price implications may be less well understood. Such a cue does not provide any information as to who is assessing the "value" or whether the value is a price that existed previously or not.

Retail Pass-through

Internals to the store are aspects of price promotion that have to be analysed on a regular basis. There are several types of trade deals - off invoice, bill back, free goods, display allowances, inventory financing. Retailers have to understand the financial implication of each of these deals and then decide on retail pass through. Retail pass through refers to the amount of these deals that are converted into price promotion for various products and are passed to the ultimate consumers. The store needs to look at it from the backdrop of "over shifting" of sales tax - increase in prices which are much more than increase in the sales tax. In both these cases, while the decisions are internal, the answers lie externally. Retail "pass through" and "over shifting" of sales tax depend on consumer acceptance and response. With the rise in consumer awareness and consumer organisations in India, retail outlets or chains have to take these decisions of discretion judiciously as their reputation may otherwise get a beating.

Promotional calendar

Price promotion is one of the components of the promotional calendar of a retail outlet. The promotional calendar of a retail outlet spreads almost across the entire year and therefore, offers scope for price promotion for various brands during different parts of the year. In this era of category management, one of the objectives of a category manager would also be to manage the price promotion calendar for his category's brands efficiently. In this context, the nature of retailer manufacturer/marketer/supplier relationship comes into play. This could also be a serious point of decision-making for a marketer who supplies to the national retail chain. If two big national brands cooperate with the help of a marketing calendar of price promotion, it would greatly limit the threat from other competitors. This could help benefit both the retailer as well as the marketers.

Quantity surcharge

In the case of the store brand, one of the techniques that a store can adopt for price promotion is the quantity surcharge. Quantity surcharge is charging a premium for a bigger packaging or a higher unit volume. If the retailer uses this premium charged for price reduction, then it would either be revenue neutral or result in a reduced margin. However, this is subject to factors like surcharge magnitude i.e. the extent of premium charged, quantity discount beliefs i.e. the intensity of the belief that larger quantity would entail reduction in price per unit as well the gender difference in the perception of quantity surcharge.

Price promotion as a component of the marketing mix has serious repercussions on the positioning as well as the image of a retail outlet. Stores in different localities (in the case of a chain), nature of suppliers and characteristics of customer segment must relate to these considerations. Internally financial considerations become crucial in addition to category management considerations. It requires very astute decision-making to see that the fine balance of all these requirements are satisfied in making price promotion a successful proposition.

PRICE PERCEPTION

Retail pricing is one of the crucial points in retail marketing as retailing represents the step closest to the consumer. While in marketing, various methods of pricing are discussed, in retail marketing, pricing needs to reflect greatly consumer's behaviour in a geographical span that is within the primary trading area. The use of reference price is beginning to provide a foundation for optimal price strategies at the retail level. While there are different points of reference for price, the study of reference for pricing deals with the relevant reference price used by the shopper. One of the key components of reference price is latitude of acceptance.

Latitude of acceptance as a concept accepts the fact that market response to price changes involves a reference range of prices rather than a single reference price. This latitude of acceptance may not be the same for all the categories of customers for a retail chain and therefore there is a possibility that there is heterogeneity in latitude of acceptance. Optimal pricing at the retail level is sensitive to both latitude of acceptance and heterogeneity. Under the latitude of acceptance model, cyclical pricing patterns can be optimal even if losses are more heavily weighted than gains. In addition, if only a portion of the market exhibits latitude of acceptance, then a large enough proportion must do so for cyclical pricing to be optimal.

Pricing contexts

Suppose that a retailer, such as Viveks, carries water heaters Racold, Johnson, V-Guard and suppose the manufacturer of the V-Guard offers a trade promotion (essentially, a decrease in the retailer's cost). The existing marketing literature suggests that Viveks should lower the retail price of V-Guard. The retailer has to decide on whether or how to change the prices of the rest of the brands. This kind of a situation typically requires decision-making on pricing that straddles across areas of consumer reference pricing as well as the elasticity of demand–cross elasticity of demand for a brand, to be precise.

Consider a computer retailer carrying a laptop line consisting of low-quality laptops with nickel-cadmium batteries and high-quality laptops with manganese-lithium batteries. For simplicity, suppose there are two types of potential customers: low-end buyers and high-end buyers. The laptops with the lithium batteries provide performance features demanded by high-end buyers who pay a premium price to obtain these products. The low-end buyers are more price-sensitive—they buy the high-quality product variants if the price is low enough; otherwise, they relinquish the lithium features for the lower priced laptops. Now suppose the cost of Nickel decreases so that the cost of the low-quality laptop decreases. Clearly, the price of the low-quality laptops should decrease, but it is unclear how to adjust the price of the higher quality laptops. Analogously, if the cost of Lithium increases, the cost of the higher quality laptops should increase leading to higher prices. Should lower quality laptops' prices increase or decrease? - This kind of situation is something that consumer durable retailers would face for products with changes in the price of components. While trying to address the price issue would it also mean that the retailer look at the cost of ownership for the consumer. In many cases, solution selling may be required at the consumer level and therefore the understanding of the individual consumer and his choice vis-à-vis features as well as price for components will make a difference. Here again qualitative dimensions of the individual consumer characteristics gain prominence as compared to the price itself.

Another example of a common problem facing food retailers is as follows. Suppose a sudden cost increase or shortage of foodstuffs (e.g. a fruit) leads to the discontinuation of some food products containing this ingredient. How should the retailer adjust the price of other food variants (e.g., bakery goods, jams, and jellies) when some variants are removed from the line?

Quality tier competition

The answer to many of the situations above may lie in the understanding of a concept called Quality tier competition. Quality tier competition refers to the response to price changes in terms of the consumer's brand buying behaviour. It is asymmetric in the retailing context. This means that although lower quality brands were vulnerable to higher quality brand's price reductions, high-quality brands did not show this vulnerability. This in practice would mean that many consumers "switch up" to higher quality brands rather than "switch down" to lower quality brands. Retailers to be effective in pricing, must check whether this phenomenon really operates in their stores through constant price related response analysis so that they could work on the pricing strategies accordingly.

Every Day Low Pricing is a strategy that is common, especially in the United States. Instances in the Indian context, of using this pricing strategy have been very few. Experts observe that in the U.S., this strategy may be appropriate for supply chains that produce and sell items with stable demand, but it cedes most control over demand. Therefore, an EDLP strategy may be less profitable than a high low pricing strategy, when the demand is seasonal. However, other environmental factors (demand elasticity, promotion cost, production change costs etc.) may favour one pricing strategy over another. This is assuming the performance criterion is total supply chain profit. In the Indian context, retailers are yet to understand supply chain and the context of supply chain profit in its entirety. Therefore, it will be some time before we see the actual use of several pricing strategies.

Zone pricing

Another interesting dimension of pricing is zone pricing. In practice, independent category managers tend to make supermarket-pricing decisions weekly on a category-by-category basis. As a result, most supermarket pricing studies consist of the category in question, rather than a broader model of the storewide pricing decisions and their implications for inter-store competition. Consumer losses within a category may be small from the category manager's perspective. From a store manager's perspective, aggregating the impact of zone pricing across categories could generate non-trivial consumer welfare losses that, in the end, could translate into losses in store traffic as consumers switch to other stores. This possibility generates a strategic motivation for identifying categories in which zone pricing generates substantial additional profits without extracting too much consumer surplus. The primary trading area of the store, the non-overlapping nature of these areas and therefore the feasibility of zone pricing must be the crucial factor in deciding the effect of zone pricing. This is one form of price discrimination that relies on consumers' non-accessibility of information in different stores and goes against "the anywhere, any store same price", kind of concept.

The explanation for why consumers in some stores gain value while others lose value from these more flexible pricing policies relates to the ability of the store to realign its product line pricing according to local demand. For instance, store A raises most laundry-detergent-powder prices on average of about 2-3%. At the same time, the price of the category leader (lets say Surf) in the store with roughly 15%, more share than the 2nd-ranked alternative is lowered by 1%. As a result, the conditional share of, lets say, Mr. White detergent powder rises almost 16%, while the conditional shares of most of the other brands fall by 1-3%. The situation is that the store is in one of the high-price zones in which consumers have high search costs. As a result, demand is inelastic which explains why the store would want to raise its price level.

In contrast, in another store, let us say that the Mr. White detergent powder has a much smaller lead, dominating the 2nd-ranked alternative by only 4% in category share. In this store, the prices of its top three products are almost fixed, while it lowers the prices of the remaining brands in the category 1-2%. As a result, shares become much more equalised with shares of the two largest-share goods falling 2-3%. At the same time, the conditional share of, lets say, Ghadi detergent powder rises almost 9%, making it (by a narrow margin) the new category leader. This store caters to households with relatively low incomes and house values. The area also caters to a higher proportion of ethnic households with larger families. As a result, demand is much more elastic, which explains why the store reduces most prices, allowing a better-value brand to gain relative share. Thus, value and pricing as derived by consumers are dependent on product line pricing as well as its perception by consumers.

Retail Pass-through

Storeowners need to study retail pass-through as a significant dimension in the context of pricing. It has implications for retailers as well as consumers. Wholesale prices are determined at the market level. Retail managers should know how retailers alter pricing strategies and what extent pass-through of changes in wholesale prices to consumers takes place. Retail pass-through rates are high, especially for large-share items. Pass-through rates may vary across stores based on similar store characteristics. Therefore, extent of retail pass-through again depends on the understanding of the consumer behaviour in the store. This has a direct impact on profitability as lesser the retail pass-through and a simultaneous increase in sales, means higher profitability.

Consumers may use multiple reference points—including cost of goods, past prices, and competitive prices—to judge price fairness. Thus, reference pricing and perception of fairness of price have a complex linkage. Consumers are inclined to overestimate profits of the retailer, often to an extreme extent. Consumers perceive prices to be unfair because they fail to take into account vendor costs. They also underestimate the effects of inflation and attribute competitive price difference to profits. Potential corrective intervention by marketers—such as cueing costs, providing historical price information, and explaining price differences have been insufficient to eliminate unfairness perceptions. In addition, prices for goods are stickier than prices for services and therefore are especially susceptible to these systematic perceptions of unfairness.

Given that consumer knowledge of explicit and unambiguous retail price information can be depressingly low, it seems reasonable to expect poor appreciation of closely guarded cost and profit information. In most country, environments in which inflation exists above nominal levels, sticker shock (consumer feeling shocked at looking at increased price of the product on the sticker) and perceptions of unfairness should be anticipated. In terms of an attribution hierarchy, profit attributions dominate store cost attributions. From a consumers' perspective, price differences appear fair(est) only if they can attribute it to quality differences. Therefore, actual/perceived quality differences provide real value to consumers, when they analyse retail-pricing policy.

Retail pricing strategy can synergistically act along with marketers pricing strategy. Retailers, however, can exclusively use category level pricing, zone pricing and reference pricing. In all these different methodologies, consumer understanding and perception play a major role. As retailing becomes competitive, retail-pricing methodologies need to be consumer- oriented.

RETAIL PROMOTION

."Free advice on the right stone on your ring to match your birth chart - famous astrologer in town - offer valid till 31st December", an advertisement of a jewelry store messages. "The author of the book would sign on limited copies of his book at our book store today evening - rush to get a unique possession for lifetime", this is an advt. of a book-store.

As competition heats up among India's retail arena, the latest marketing tool employed by major retailers is to attract more customers through quirky "event packages"/attractions or price promotions. Customers are encouraged to celebrate a special occasion with a celebrity with the intention of getting them as well as to spend money in the stores. Retail promotion has gained significantly with the growth of organised retail sector in India and the need to attract and retain customers. Retail promotion comprises specifications for a marketing operation. This operation is limited in time. Drawing increased attention of consumers to the enterprise (the retail outlet or the retail chain) in its sales market or the influencing trading area is the major aim of this operation. Resultantly, it increases sales.

Types of promotion

Various types of promotions that a retail chain/ independent store can undertake include:

- *Chain-wide sweepstakes -* Sweepstakes promotion offered in all stores through a retail chain.

- *Co-op media -* Promotional advertising for a manufacturer's product that appears on a retailers' television or radio advertisement and is funded by the manufacturer.

- *Frequent shopper programmes -* Support by manufacturers of promotions offered by retailer through its loyalty card programme (i.e., discounts - paperless coupons, etc.)

- *In-ad coupons -* Coupons for manufacturers' products that appear in the print ad of one retail company and are redeemable only through that one company.

- *In-store advertising -* Point of sale advertising in the retail store; on shopping carts, aisle markers, in-store radio or TV, etc.

- *In-store coupons* - Coupons that are distributed in the retail store.

- *In-store demos/sampling* - Sampling of products in the retail store.

- *Instant redeemable coupons (IRC)* - Coupons that are attached to products in the retail store.

- *Internet programmes* - Promotional programmes that are offered to consumers through the retailer's web page.

- *Manufacturer purchased display space* - Special displays that are built in the retail store in a space that is paid for by the manufacturer.

- *National sweepstakes* - Sweepstakes promotion advertised, promoted by a national organisation, and available through various types of retail stores throughout the country.

- *Near pack offers* - Premiums that are offered by manufacturers as an incentive for purchasing a product and are available in the store.

- *Paperless coupons* - Coupons that are made available to consumers through a frequent shopper programme or some type of card marketing programme.

- *Premium giveaways* - Any promotion that offers a premium to consumers as an incentive for purchase of a product, often a mail-in offer. This promotion can also be one that offers a premium to a store or department manager.

- *Promotion tied to local organisation or charity* - Special promotion where the retailer and manufacturer agree to contribute a portion of the sales to a local group.

- *Retailer crossruff* – Promotions or coupons delivered on one product (national brand) that are good on another product (retailer brand).

Objectives

The launch of a promotional activity for a store requires creative handling of one of the above ways of handling retail promotions. The objective for a promotion should be the most important consideration for retail promotion. If Food World advertises that it has the IR 8/20 rice at one of the lowest prices in town, the objective is to use the destination category of the retail grocery store to attract greater store traffic. Promotions that increase footfalls and therefore improve store traffic, may result in competing store loyal customers to visit the store and even try non-promoted merchandise. At the same time, it would increase store inter-visit time for the regular loyal store customers. Retail promotion objectives can be store specific or product specific but the intended result of the promotion is something that has to be explicitly borne in mind while formulating a promotion plan. The retailer needs to review the same after the promotion to see if he has achieved the stated objectives.

Shopper reaction

The consumer perspective of retail promotion is also crucial in formulating promotions. Purchase event feedback is one of the crucial elements of the understanding of retail promotion. This concept means monitoring if the promotion enhances or detracts consumers from future brand-purchase probabilities compared to non-promotion. In order to understand this concept, it is important to look at one major theory in psychology as applied to consumer behaviour, namely the self-perception theory. Self-perception theory as attributed to the deal prone consumer results in questioning by the consumer - Did I buy the product because of brand preference/ promotion? The answer to this question by a majority of the consumers of your store determines the store's nature of promotion. If for example Shoppers Stop has through its customer relationship management software a clear idea of the nature of customers especially on deal proneness, it can decide what to emphasise on, in its promotion. The store manager should take a decision on whether the primary reinforcement is the store/brand or the promotion/ deal. The nature of promotion needs to adapt according to the understanding of consumer behaviour. In this effort, we would also be able to clearly track brand loyal as well as store loyal consumers.

Effects of retail promotion

The nature of buying reflects the behavioural mannerisms of the consumer, especially when a promotion is on. This has implications for the retail outlet. Category purchase timing, brand choice, and purchase quantity are the three major dimensions that one has to track in order to see the effect of sales promotion. Category purchase timing refers to the decision by the consumer to alter the regular purchase cycle for the product. If *Atta* is bought once in a fortnight, does she buy *Atta* earlier because of promotion? Brand choice refers to the decision on being brand loyal in spite of a promotion on a comparable competitive substitute brand. Would a consumer change from say Captain Cook to Tata salt because of promotion? Purchase quantity is a very important variable to monitor, for it relates to the nature of consumption. Stockpiling reflects this common effect of a promotion on a product or a brand. For example, buying five-litre edible oil can at a lower price and storing the same for longer future use.

Let us take the example of a specialty coffee outlet selling different brands of coffee. If we decompose the effect of sales promotion we may look at, lets say, contribution of the three dimensions in the following manner - brand switching (84%), purchase acceleration (14%), and stockpiling (2%). This decomposition may be used to compare the effectiveness of alternative promotional offerings and to determine the most suitable and effective promotion. Putting together the facts that sales promotions generate dramatic immediate sales increases and that brand switching accounts for a large percentage of this increase, we can conclude that sales promotions are strongly associated with brand switching. If promotion increases a brand's sales by 100 units, how many units come from other brands and how many units are due to category expansion, i.e. shifts in the timing and/or amounts of purchase?

If three-fourths of the sales effect were due to other brands, retailers might conclude that promotional activities provide little benefit. That is, unless promoted, items provide higher margins, the vast majority of the effect would simply be a reallocation of expenditures by households across items within a category. Manufacturers/national brand marketers might conclude that most of the effect increases competition between brands and would not support promotions. Therefore, stockpiling and/or consumption increases appear to be the dominant sources to look for sales effects due to temporary price cuts. Cannibalisation of future sales through stockpiling is an important consideration in the assessment of the effectiveness of sales promotions. In some product categories like beverages (e.g. soft drinks), a substantial component of the primary demand increase may represent enhanced consumption. I might drink more of Coke/Pepsi because of a price cut. However, in other categories (like house cleaning liquids); households are unlikely to accelerate consumption. I would not buy more of toilet, cleaning liquid and drain it down the toilet, because of a price cut. In these cases, effect of sales promotion may just represent inventory management by households.

Price/brand promotion

Extensive research in the west suggests that price promotions are detrimental whereas non-price promotions are neutral/positive. Price promotion of national brands erodes the loyalty of the national brands and therefore helps private labels/store labels to gain market share. While looking at from the point of benefit for the store, the chain of causation could be - price promotion which would lead to loss of national brand loyalty, which in turn would trigger greater trade allowances and therefore increase in store profit. However, the question of store image and loyalty are important. Discount stores like Margin Free shops can afford to involve continuously in price promotion whereas others cannot. Stores need to guard against reaction by competitors. It is important to realise that increase in market share through weak brand franchise may undermine both the marketer and the retailer.

The conflict of promotion of store brands as compared to national brands would become a matter of great concern in the years to come in India. Many retailers in India now see great benefit in developing store loyalty as the opportunity exists to extend this loyalty to store brands. We still have few store brands in multi brand outlets of specialty category that can compete with national/regional brands. However, even in the case of store brands, studies in US have found that non-price promotions have a more favourable long-term effect on store profit as compared to price promotion.

IT in Retail Promotion Management

Several IT companies in the west have comprehensive solutions that increase productivity and sales from promotions. They allow supply chain participants to communicate more effectively throughout the various stages in the design, implementation and evaluation of retail promotions.

The significance of retail promotion has triggered several comprehensive IT-based retail promotion solutions. Experts estimate that promotions constitute 60% of all retail activities and up to 40% of these promotions fail to meet expectations. Estimates suggest that the industry loses €80 billion a year in retail promotions alone in Europe. Inefficiencies in available management information, monitoring and auditing of promotions result in:

- Time losses i.e. delay in communication from the suppliers to retailers

- Communication errors in planning and execution among various departments

- Real costs at the end of the promotion i.e. lack of clear cost identification

- Lack of evaluation and management information

    "Live" access through an internet enabled retail promotion software and communication between all those involved in the promotion cycle can greatly enhance efficiency of the promotion while dealing with a large number of formats & stores. In a large retail chain, a number of individuals like the brand/category manager, promotions specialist and the individual store manager are involved. A good understanding of the systems and an efficient IT backbone would eliminate inefficiencies involved in planning, implementation, and evaluation of promotions. It can reduce the number of communications between the brand sponsor, retailer, and supplier involved in any single promotion - traditionally by telephone, fax, or e-mail - by upto 30%. In addition to effective tracking of planning and implementation of a promotion, it can also dramatically reduce current industry booking costs, by as much as 60% through efficient document generation and promotion auditing. Time and labour saved through inefficient document management and communication is another great plus point. An easy-to-use online design and presentation ensures a seamless flow of communications between staff at all levels.

Cause related promotion

Imagine spending Valentine's Day 2008 in a store that sells kiss-shaped badges for charity, made from a lip imprint of a local supermodel and limited edition pins bearing the supermodel's signature. Only 1,000 are available and all proceeds go to the Foundation for mentally handicapped children. A "Lips for Love" campaign during the week of the Valentine's Day with the first 20 couples who purchased Rs. 10000 worth of products winning dinner at the store's Cafe. A "lipstick kiss marks" campaign featuring female guests including high-society figures and celebrities whose lipstick kiss marks would be engraved on T-shirts and "In the Mood of Red" campaign featuring a multitude of Valentine's novelties from heart-shaped plants to teddy bears in red colour. These are different options to attract the consumer. Depending on the consumer profile of the primary zone of influence of the outlet, promotion needs to be location specific and unique. However, now with increased interest in cause-related marketing, cause related retail promotion especially those who serve sponsor the local social organisation, can have greater draw.

Retail promotion in practice is akin to sales promotion by marketers. However, by the very nature of business, retailers need to create excitement round outlets in order to sustain themselves. Therefore, retail promotion has both short-term as well as long-term implications. A good mix of promotions to serve both the objectives and a continuous effort to test promotions through control stores and monitor store profitability will help in sustaining any retail organisation. Sales, traffic and profit need to be compared as measures with base line sales/traffic in control stores in order to study the effects on brand share, chain share, market share. These measures would provide feedback on future promotions. Cost effective non-price promotions, unique promotion campaigns that differentiate and position your outlet, coordination of the complex transactions using good information technology are the backbone of corporate strategy oriented objectives. A constant eye on consumer feedback is ingredients of a successful recipe called retail promotion.

RETAIL SALESPERSON

The LPG of retailing location, people and goodwill is the important fuel that propels retailing. The crucial and central aspect of this fuel is people. From a service marketing perspective, other than the traditional four Ps in marketing, three other Ps are also emphasised. They are People, Process and Physical evidence. This translated in the retail marketing context means that design of the outlet–an expression of physical evidence and visual merchandising are important. However, enhanced value of these two aspects entirely depends on the nature of people who retailers employ. Retail salespersons perform a crucial boundary spanning activity translating consumer needs into future changes in the organisation and at the same time marketing the product/services and the retail entity in itself through their actions. Therefore, both the people and process which are the other two Ps of marketing has great relevance in influencing retail marketing. More than the structured process, delivery of the process by the counter salesperson makes a difference to the effectiveness of the process. Therefore, the store manager has to look carefully at the various critical dimensions of the retail salespersons.

Hiring salespersons

One of the first issues that a retail entity faces is the question who should it hire as a salesperson. For example, when a music retail outlet hires a person, he must have a passion for music and one in a sports good outlet must have an interest in sports. This is one of the fundamental requirements as this basic requirement reflects in the involvement shown by the salesperson in his job. Moreover, it reduces the training regimen load that may be required to make the salesperson literate on the basis of music/sports.

Psychosociological literature suggests that similarity in salesperson and customers make a big impact on sales. Similarity can be across the following dimensions. Objective characteristics like height or visible characteristics like nationality, race and sex. Physical appearance of people creates a bias that is natural. The expectation of appearance is set either by a pioneer in the field of retailing or as a normal expectation in the outlet. Consumers expect salespeople to possess normal height. Too tall or too short, a too fair/too dark complexioned salesperson creates its own bias in the mind of the consumer. Grooming makes a big difference in presentation by salespeople. Heavily soiled uniform, unkempt hair, and a drooping eyes indicating an exhausted look can put off the consumer. Therefore, the store should take care of visible dimensions carefully. Several restaurants insist on washing the face, applying talcum powder and religious marks neatly to make waiters presentable. These are clear efforts at heightening the favourable disposition at the moment-of-truth experienced by the consumer in any retail outlet. The store can look at this aspect in the context of decision-making for product categories.

It is important to consider gender of salespersons employed for specific departments. For example, selection of innerwear by women in an outlet, unless manned by a woman would be a big deterrent in purchase. However, dissimilarity between the salesperson and consumer may also work. For example, in the case in selecting clothing for middle aged/older men/women, the adolescent in the family in many cases is involved in decision-making. Therefore, when in the garment outlet while buying individually, an adolescent salesperson suggesting the elderly person on the design/colour of the garment makes a favourable impact on purchase. It has, however, to be specifically understood if this happens in the target segment of the store/not.

Service encounter characteristics

Encounter characteristics like education, religious preferences, and political preferences are also very important. The interactive/external marketing involved in a typical service-marketing encounter like retailing means that encounter characteristics have to be carefully analysed. This can make a difference, especially if the similarity increases the favourable influence in turning the transaction into sales. Imagine an incidental conversation based on any of the encounter characteristics like education. Let us say the salesperson is knowledgeable enough to provide some interesting information about the school in which the daughter of the consumer studies, then this familiarity increases the probability of buying due to favourable influence.

Mood congruent information and credibility of the salesperson are two factors that enhance the shopping experience. The store can provide several cues since that would enhance the mood of the consumer. With the development of a competitive retail scenario, stores are not just vending products/services, they are also a place for entertainment. In this context, consumer's mood is a crucial aspect to monitor. Atmospherics in the store are getting prominence in the store due to this development. The use of proper lighting, colour, kind of background music have all been researched in the west for different product categories so that the mood is enhanced and it results in increased buying/sales. There is an enhanced awareness also in the Indian retailing scene on the need to invest in visual merchandising. In spite of all these cues, the salesperson as an entity has tremendous potential to convert walk-ins and undecided customers into final sales for the store. Imagine a consumer with his family in a bad mood due to factors totally unrelated to the store, then the salesperson would need to gauge the mood and present the product based on a clear understanding of the tone of the communication of the customer and by observing his shopping behaviour. Research suggests that the credibility of the salesperson increases with the presentation of mood congruent information.

All counter salespersons need to exhibit the quality of patient buying assistance. Let us suppose that there is an argument in the consumer durable shop between the husband and wife on the type of fan to buy. Either one of them has not clearly understood the needs or there is a paucity of cash to go in for a better brand with better features. The salesperson needs to communicate tactfully that they could take some more time to decide on their purchase. If the store policy allows (and given the understanding of the consumer through relevant unoffending questions) she can offer to give the two brands (in debate) a free trial and thus help them take a decision.

Product competence/product merchandise knowledge is the key to consumer susceptibility to salesperson influence in the case of those customers who can be termed informationals i.e., those who depend more on information on the core product and peripheral benefits and competitive offerings. The core product details include industry awards for the product, performance and safety specification, satisfaction ratings etc., and peripheral benefits like financing schemes which add to the credibility of the salesperson. The retailer can enhance trustworthiness of the salesperson through trust transference techniques.

Consumer search characteristics and salesperson number

Assisted/unassisted search of information/goods and services of the target consumer has a direct implication on the strategy of the retail outlet. This gives an idea of the nature of service available in a continuum, ranging from full service to low service retail outlet. This strategic decision has direct bearing on the salesperson numbers. Take the example of a footwear outlet, which has an open display and imagine a few days before Durga Puja in any of the prominent footwear outlets in Kolkata. Customer congestion in the outlet is a clear picture that you can visualise. In this kind of situation, there is need to apply the queuing model (as applied to typical service marketing situations like banks) to determine the number of salesperson who would be required. Incidentally, during festival season when some of the stores in Chennai offer goods at a discount, there is literally a queue that forms in front of the stores in order to buy the products. The estimation of the probability of consumers who would need search assistance and the number who would seek assistance after an unassisted search is important here. There is need to make a distinction that assisted search typically takes more time than unassisted search. If this is the case, waiting time is directly proportional to the number of salespersons employed in the outlet. This kind of specific scientific estimation of salesperson requirement would greatly reduce the burden on the existing salespersons to service a disproportionately large customer size.

Post purchase effect

Positive post purchase psychological state of the consumer, specifically the feelings of satisfaction and equity i.e. fairness of transaction increases favourable word of mouth recommendation for the store as well as the salesperson. It influences the evaluative dimension of post purchase communication. Positivity/negativity of word of mouth, specific recommendations/warning as part of inter-personal advice, consumer feedback in the form of not only complaints but also praise are three points to look for while enhancing post purchase positive communication. It also helps in reducing cognitive dissonance between the expected and actual service levels. They have a correlation with effective consumer - salesperson interaction. Here, the salesperson acts as an ambassador of the store, helping create a positive feeling about the store. Many of us have faced situations where we do not go to a store to avoid a particular salesperson in a department!

Adaptive selling skills i.e. ability to tailor the product/services as per customer needs, quick service and a personable style, are key attributes expected of an effective salesperson.

Evaluation

The sales outcome of the department decides generally the evaluation of a salesperson's performance. However, for a fair and just effort of appraisal, there is need to look at subjective, objective and behavioural aspects of the salesperson. In outlets where cross selling is possible due to presence of various departments, team selling/cooperation should be greatly encouraged. This helps in overall sales of the store rather than looking at individual targets. This typically happens in a garment outlet. The various department salespersons need to have a clear link across all departments so that they are able to direct the consumers well. Rotation of the salespersons across departments also helps in building cooperation. It boosts the morale of those department salespersons whose sales are not as large as others are. This is especially true of incentive-driven salesperson compensation for salespersons.

Knowledge of merchandise procedures is a crucial component of evaluation, as any slip up on this front would greatly affect the store profitability. This point starkly affects merchandise in the case of offers where the store offers other merchandise free. Most grocery stores follow the system of availability of the free/complimentary product at the cash counter. Stacking, counting and ensuring complimentary supplies of the free merchandise on offer need clear coordination and good understanding of merchandise procedure.

Customer service ability is one dimension of the salesperson that shows the "down to earth" nature of the salesperson. Empathising with consumer especially when she carries a baby and is unable to do her shopping conveniently is a clear instance of where a salesperson can service customer requests. In the case of consumer durable outlets, one of the interesting observations is that the consumer is more comfortable to meet the counter salesperson the next day after his purchase for any problems that he faces with say his refrigerator, TV or washing machine. In fact, some of the stores may not be directly involved in servicing, however the consumer needs to be directed properly by the salesperson herself rather than she directing her to the store manager. This would be a clear demonstration of customer service. Customer service ability should be evaluated using mystery shopping and praises of service by specific salesperson by consumers.

Sales ability especially in converting customers preferring low-end products to high-end products and from low-margin to high-margin brands ethically would mean a lot in terms of the turnover of the store. Store owners can encourage and evaluate sales ability by having meetings of salespersons every fortnight/month and ask them to demonstrate and explain instances of sales ability that resulted in tangible benefit to the store. The retailer can use this to develop best practices and avoid unethical practices.

Product merchandise knowledge needs to be tested/evaluated, using the understanding of two types of customers - the sophisticated customer and the ignorant customer. In the case of a retail store selling PCs or even consumer durables, salesperson training needs to incorporate this expectation. This is also true of drug stores. The use of qualified technical professionals from the marketing/manufacturing company probably is the right person to evaluate the specialised knowledge of the salesperson, whereas a first time customer randomly selected is the right person to evaluate the ignorant customer. This evaluation on an unannounced basis would ensure that the salespersons are competent in answering queries of different types of consumers.

Knowledge of store policy reflects professionalism of a retail entity during the interaction with the salesperson. How often have we faced situations where the counter salesperson is not sure on how she should react to a stain in a sari or a broken handle of a refrigerator in transit from the store to your house? In many cases, the store might have levels of hierarchy to deal with such issues or have no policy at all. In professional retail entities, here is empowerment that flows up to the counter salesperson in answering queries of customers on store policy. Store manager has to test store policy knowledge on a routine basis, as there may not be many instances experienced and therefore the tendency to forget policies. The retailer can test store policy understanding through hypothetical situations also.

The most important aspect of the LPG of retailing is people. When actual LPG leak takes place there is smell and danger of fire, similarly in retailing when the retail salespeople fail, the customer feels psychologically amiss and fears danger of poor service. As a retailing entity, one must guard against generating this feeling in the mind of the consumer.

FESTIVE OR SEASON SHOPPING

The peak or the most awaited quarter for every FMCG and consumer durable company is fast approaching. Consumers are ready to look for bargain deals during the Diwali sales that happen every year. Retailers brace up for their peak season too. In this context, we should definitely be looking at what happens because of all this frenzy. The use of heavily-advertised sales events, with their ability to generate excitement, attract shoppers, clear out time-sensitive merchandise, and sell complementary, high-margin items, is deeply ingrained in retail strategy. Therefore, the need is to understand factors that have an impact on season sales of retailers.

Supply chain impact

Retailers are at the end of the supply chain downstream in direct contact with the consumers. Their geographical proximity to the consumers and their understanding of consumer behaviour make them take a favourable position in the supply chain. In view of this, marketers and manufacturers in the upstream of the supply chain greatly rely on the insights from retailers. Retail chains similarly rely on store managers in order to obtain a view of the prospects of the season ahead. Increase in consumer demand and a grossly different pattern of buying make for a perfect situation for players in the supply chain to experience the whiplash/bull whip effect. This effect is attributed to four factors - Demand forecast updating, Order batching, Price fluctuation and Rationing and Shortage gaming.

Store managers/independent retailers plan season sales based on last year's performance, the perception of the economy and the anticipation of higher demand. However, when the transmission of demand takes place in the supply chain, lead-time as well as safety-stock considerations related to stock-out fears for time-sensitive merchandise colour the nature of demand forecast updating. These result in heavy build up of inventory at the manufacturer/marketer level. In case of a coordinated forecasting mechanism, supply chain participants can avoid this situation. The consumer may benefit from this situation after the end of the season as marketers along with retailers may end up selling merchandise at throw away prices to liquidate the stocks if the stock build up was for the specific season.

Some retailers may batch orders to take advantage of juicy offers from the vendors. While this results in inflated demand, unless the retailer is aggressive he may not be able to sell his stock during the season. If these are all season goods, then it results in a reduced demand in the subsequent reordering by the retailer. Price fluctuation is one of the biggest issues that create bigger spikes in the supply chain. This goes back to the basics of retailer philosophy of high-low pricing and the understanding that price sensitive shoppers react favourably to offers of price reductions during the season. It is difficult to estimate price sensitiveness of shoppers in different areas where retailers operate. As a result, demand is mostly overstated resulting in higher amplitude of the bullwhip effect. Here again, the consumers may gain the process post the season sales. However, the burden of inventory costs should have to be borne by some member of the supply chain. Invariably, we would find that the consumer bears after the sale has happened for his regular purchases.

If the vendor makes a consumer demand estimate on his own and finds that the retailer is demanding higher quantities ahead of the season, then he may resort to shortage gaming and rationing. Short gaming and rationing result in lower service levels at the retailer end. This may create a friction between the vendor and retailer, ultimately reflecting in a bad word-of-mouth due to stockouts among consumers during season sales. Retailers must, therefore, reflect on all these factors before making their decision on pre-season purchases.

Yield management strategies

One of the ways in which retailers can deal with the problem of seasonal sales is to adopt the technique otherwise commonly adopted by many service organisations like airlines; cine theatres etc., called yield management. Yield management techniques may be appropriate in any situation where:

- Capacity is relatively fixed.

- Demand can be segmented into clearly identified partitions.

- Inventory is perishable.

- The product or service is sold well in advance.

- Demand fluctuates substantially.

- Marginal sales costs and production costs are low, but capacity change costs are high.

In the retailing context, this would particularly be applicable for seasonal sales. The value of the merchandise may decline with the conclusion of a particular season associated with normal product usage (e.g. umbrellas during rainy season), or with the culmination of a well-defined shopping period (e.g., the "Christmas holiday" shopping period). Knowledge of customer price sensitivity as it pertains to a shopping period, coupled with the appropriate use of discount pricing, can maximise the revenue gained from sales of a seasonal product associated with a specific holiday.

Service providers most often ascertain shopper/non-shopper probabilities based on experience involving:

- Sales patterns

- Demand patterns by market segment

- Effects of price changes

All these require capturing of consumer behaviour on a constant basis. Effective Yield Management applications depend on excellent information systems to track critical aspects of the business. This means that response to offer of prior booking in the case of retail outlets selling 2/4-wheelers or other consumer durables, tracking of the inquiries on price ranges by different consumer segments that can be captured through shopping cards and the differential response to price changes need to be monitored to effect changes appropriately.

Shopping/season period

The length of the shopping period and consumers' reaction to prices make an interesting observation. Typically, the price sensitivity of the inventoried items decreases as the end of an "advance" (shopping) period nears. This means that the shopping period culminates with use of the product or service at a particular (scheduled) point in time. Most service industries would fall into this category. Examples include the theatre industry, sporting events, hotel rooms, transportation industries, and advertising space. This would mean that consumers would pay even a higher price towards the eve of a sporting event to buy a ticket. In the case of physical products, shopping periods culminate with product usage when the end of the shopping period coincides with a specific gift giving occasion (e.g. a birthday) or some special event (e.g. returning to school). In both of these instances, as the end of the shopping period approaches, the consumer may feel temporal pressure i.e., pressure of time to "find the right gift" or to "be ready for school," and as such may be willing to purchase an item at a higher price. In addition, temporal pressures may act to increase consumers' search costs, resulting in a decreased amount of shopping effort and an increase in the size of consideration sets. Again, the net effect is that the consumer is willing to accept a higher priced alternative.

In contrast those are situations where the price sensitivity of inventoried items increases as the end of the (shopping) period approaches. Most fashion or style goods retailers face such a situation, and would consider a pricing policy of marking down items (decreasing price) as the period ends. This is especially true of new fashions that are released across all products especially apparel during the Diwali season in India. The price sensitivity for fashion goods increases because the shopping period coincides with the product usage period. Therefore, the reason why price sensitivity increases (or decreases) has to do with the temporal relationship between:

- Shopping period
- Product usage period

In the case of physical goods, Yield Management techniques may be appropriate if the shopping period culminates in product use, but may not be appropriate if the shopping period coincides with product use. Increased temporal distance from a holiday results in an increased amount of search (i.e. a greater number of planned store visits).

Mark down management

The typical pricing procedure in most industries where shopping period coincides with usage period (e.g. the fashion industry) is to mark down specific items as the season progresses. In order to correct a mistake in pricing, when merchandise is slow moving, obsolete, near the end of its selling season, or priced higher than that of the competition, retailers adopt a mark down policy. Buyers would also decide to mark down merchandise in order to make room for new items, to generate cash flow, or to increase traffic flow of customers. In either case, store managers usually build markdowns into the initial price of an item.

The success of the markdown policy, then, depends on:

- Timing
- Size of price reduction(s)

An examination of the factors that one should consider in determining the timing and size of price reductions may provide insights regarding factors that one should consider in planning the timing and size of price increases associated with a yield management pricing policy. In terms of timing of price reductions, certain retail establishments such as Filene's Basement utilise an automatic markdown policy. For Filene's, this involves a 25% reduction after 12 selling days, a 50% reduction after 18 selling days, and a 75% reduction after 24 selling days. After 30 selling days, stores give away unsold items to charity. Obviously, the policy works because sale historically leaves after 30 days a small amount of inventory. Most retailers, however, face much less-certain demand conditions and will vary the timing of their markdown procedures.

Successful timing dictates that retailers maintain good records. This means keeping track of the types of merchandise that have required mark-downs in the past, as well as keeping track of what is not selling in the current season. Part of keeping good records is doing "sell-through" analyses. A sell-through analysis involves a comparison between actual and planned sales, to determine whether early markdowns are required or whether the store needs more merchandise to satisfy demand.

Assortment

Assortment perishability is a function of the speed at which a typical assortment loses value or becomes obsolete over time. Assortment heterogeneity on the other hand is the degree of between-store variability in product assortments among firms competing in the same retail sector. Heterogeneity of supply (i.e., product assortments) results in heterogeneity in demand as buyers learn of and respond to different product offerings. The different response patterns then lead to imbalances in supply and demand and to market dynamism as sellers shift their efforts to serve attractive segments. This type of market dynamism leads to price dynamism, as sellers of more/less-preferred products raise/lower prices in response to market shifts and imbalances. Thus, overall price promotion activity increases as assortment heterogeneity and market dynamism increase. This means that heterogeneity is one of the sure ways of dealing with competition in the case of season sales to avoid price wars.

Grocery & Season shopping

Grocery stores need to look at special requirements of groceries during season need as an interesting phenomenon. Grocery shopping behaviour has three unique characteristics that suggest a relationship between shopping behaviour and preference for different price formats:

- Consumers typically shop for *multiple* items on a given trip.

- For most of these items, they are usually unable to determine actual prices before visiting the store.

- Grocery shopping is repetitive—while individual trips may differ somewhat, most consumers settle into specific shopping patterns with respect to the average basket size per trip and frequency of shopping.

Together, these three factors suggest that store choices (if influenced at all by pricing) will be influenced by prices for a "basket" of multiple items; price expectations (rather than actual prices) will be the mechanism for this influence, it may be useful to segment consumers according to fundamental differences in shopping behaviour.

Small basket shoppers i.e., those who satisfy a relatively small proportion of their total demand for groceries on each shopping trip, have greater flexibility with respect to taking advantage of price variation over time. These are the households that, all other things remaining equal, will prefer to shop in a HILO store (a retailer who believes in variation of prices between high and low) because they can get a lower overall average price through opportunistic purchase behaviour. In case of these shoppers, the expected basket attractiveness will be higher in a store whose format offers greater variability in price, even at higher average prices. Conversely, the large basket shopper (who must purchase a relatively large proportion of their total grocery demand on each trip) will prefer to shop in an EDLP store (everyday low pricing strategy meaning low prices all through the year) where the overall expected price across a wide variety of categories is lower. It would be worthwhile to distinguish shoppers as the small and large basket shoppers and therefore use it effectively in the case of grocery retailing even during the season.

Guarantees

Guarantees on prices can also be a mechanism to woo consumers towards your store during a season. They could be of several types. A price-matching guarantee is defined as the retail offer to lower retail prices to meet or beat competitive prices within a specified period after the purchase. Some retailers use it as an aggressive competitive tactic and openly advertise. A low price guarantee refers to the retail offer to reimburse the price difference if outlet lowers the in-store retail price within a specified period after the purchase. Low price guarantee is a limited version of the price-matching guarantee, as it applies only to the store where the consumer made the purchase. Retailers use it to reduce the perceived financial risk of buying from the store now versus waiting until a big sale comes up, and it allows for price discrimination between consumers who are informed about price changes after the purchase and uninformed consumers. The ethicality of this aspect of implementation needs to be pondered over. Satisfaction guarantee is the retail offer to refund the whole price within a specified period after the purchase, if the customer is not satisfied with the purchase. Store managers can use it to reduce consumer perceptions of financial and performance risk, as the consumer can return the product for any reason if she/he is not satisfied with the purchase. Although conceptually different from price-matching guarantee, satisfaction guarantee also ensures the consumer s/he can get the lowest price, because the customer can return the product if s/he finds a lower price at a competitor.

All the types of guarantees mentioned above are in some form or the other, followed by many Indian retailers especially during the season sale. However, a unique guarantee like basket guarantee can be experimented. Shopping basket guarantee refers to the retail promise of the best price for the shopping basket of frequently purchased goods. Shopping basket guarantee is limited to a specific subset of products (e.g., 50 items) included in the shopping basket. The lowest price is guaranteed only for the whole set of products in the basket, not for individual items. If the consumer can find the same set of products anywhere else for less, the retailer promises to refund the price difference.

The game during season sale especially with prices is with respect to consumer price reference-points. There are three reference points that we can observe in consumers - looking back (at past prices), looking across (at comparison prices), and looking inward (to costs). If retailers can help win over consumers, by pricing products so that these reference points may not directly come into operation, the retailer can obtain success in pricing strategy for season sales.

CHAPTER FIVE

Trading Area and Site Analysis

SHOPPING TRIP AND PARKING

An automobile revolution preceded the Indian organised retail revolution. The range and variety of automobiles available for the Indian consumers have increased phenomenally since the mid 1990s. This development is crucial, as one of the key elements of retail development is mode of travel and travel time. Government of India in recent times has been laying increasing emphasis on infrastructure, especially developing better roads- even if it means the golden quadrilateral in a big way. Cheap consumer loans from several banks have facilitated affordability of automobiles. This has meant that the large middle class in the country has taken to automobile buying and usage in a big way. Other than for work, one major use of automobiles is for shopping. The vehicularisation of the Indian consumer is spawning a new generation of retail concepts that are themselves profoundly altering the country's retail landscape. In India in particular like in other developing nations, people are what they drive. In addition, more and more these days, they drive to shop.

Impact on consuming communities

Pre-liberalisation, communities developed around pedestrian-oriented, mixed-use town centres offer highly diversified activities to serve a relatively small trade area before automobile usage started. Many Indians lived, worked, shopped and played in small-town settings. Even large urban centres developed around boroughs or districts with town centre characteristics. The dynamics of such communities tended to support general, not specialised, retail opportunities. People ate lunch at the local diner and men took their dates to the local movie theatre. However, four wheels and somewhere to go have marked a defining characteristic of post liberalisation prosperity. With mobility came the slow but inevitable decline of the town centre as a naturally evolving community.

As development shifted away from a pedestrian orientation to meet the demands of a vehicular society, communities began to take on new characteristics. Today, communities are more dispersed than earlier years. A 25% building-to-land ratio is typical - with lower densities and an explosion of new retail concepts. Retail activity also is more isolated as distances between stores grow. Moreover, in some respects, location is less important as consumers begin to measure distance in minutes, not miles. The clock is ticking, as consumers are willing to travel farther to shop, retailers draw from a larger area. Faced with a trade area of 300,000 people instead of 3,000, they naturally begin to specialise.

Outcome on retail activity

Retail activity is divided into two main types: convenience and destination. Convenience retail - service stations, drug stores, fast-food restaurants, dry cleaners, banks, etc. - are essential "pit stops" that exist somewhere between home, place of work and other retail destinations. Transactions at these pit stops normally take 15 minutes or less. Successful convenience retailers require ample exposure to a high volume of customers and good vehicular access. The evolution of convenience activities along with consumer demand for a more vehicle-friendly world have given way to some surprising recent changes: the "co-branding" of service stations with fast-food restaurants; the flight of drug stores from neighbourhood centres to highly visible, freestanding locations at major intersections; and the strategic location of bank ATMs.

The summary of developments in the retail sector can read like this - prospective entrepreneurs will develop convenience retail wherever there is demand, high visibility, lots of traffic and easy vehicular access. Likewise, convenience goods and services will continue to grow around major destination locales. Destination retail centres, on the other hand, will increase in size, with greater focus on providing selection and service as well as enhancing the shopping experience. They aim for high consumer awareness, with the goal of becoming "the place to go" when a purchase decision is being made. Moreover, as specialty/entertainment centres continue to evolve, there may be a return to a modernised, vehicle-friendly version of the old town centre.

As consumers on the go become more health conscious, specialist retailers are serving blended fruit drinks often mixed with protein powder and other nutritional supplements which can be a new development. Consumers would drink these occasionally to cut fat from their diets and add essential nutrients. In the drugstore category, retailers experience tremendous levels of increased prescriptions. Price is not really the issue. It is the convenience and credibility of the pharmacy. In addition to freestanding stores, trends in the drugstore industry could include drive-through pharmacies, one-hour photo labs and 24-hour stores all combined into a one stop shop. Branded service retailing is also set to boom as in the case of hair care to obtain fast and standardised service.

Parking

The single most important factor that would have a significant impact on a travelling shopper in this vehicularised scenario would be parking space. The most desirable and least expensive way to provide the required parking is to build a surface lot. Yet, in some areas, land is hard to come by. If so, structured parking is a common alternative. However, there are drawbacks to building a parking structure. They can be extremely difficult to be made aesthetically pleasing and can absorb a significant amount of the construction budget.

Parking garage as another option can be a challenge for owners and visitors. No one wants to enter an environment where he or she feels unsafe. Historically, urban parking facilities have this reputation. The dark walls and ceilings are cold and claustrophobic. Poor lighting and endless spaces invite feelings of uncertainty and insecurity as patrons search for an elevator. Contrast this with on-grade parking. Visitors feel more comfortable walking in the open when they can simply walk directly to a well-marked mall entrance. This is particularly true if open areas are well lit and attractive. Landscaping makes the parking lot even more friendly and pleasing to the eye.

Location for parking

The location of the parking structure is also a major consideration. Building garages under retail buildings is the least desirable option. This route requires telegraphing a support system for the above building structure down through the parking deck. Builders must use beams to bring the building loads onto a column spacing that is compatible with the geometry of parking structure. In this scenario, the added support structures may hinder the optimum open feeling. A column-reducing strategy is to develop a long-span layout. Short-span parking structures usually require more support columns per space. Besides giving a feeling of openness, long-span systems make manoeuvering in the garage easier.

Traffic flow within a structure is yet another consideration with express ramps offering another opportunity to improve a parking garage. Mall owners build express ramps to direct the flow of traffic from one floor to the next. These ramps can skip floors for quick entrance and exit to upper levels. With no cars parked on the ramps, traffic does not have to yield to cars or pedestrians exiting or entering designated spaces. However, parked ramps yield more parking spaces. Owners need to weigh the option of more parking spaces versus better traffic circulation. Access options also affect traffic circulation. Free parking allows for the least amount of traffic resistance. Cars do not stop for tickets or pay parking fees. If the goal is to discourage non-shopping centre patrons from using the parking structure, outlet owners can employ various systems. Parking space owners can use inexpensive or reimbursable charges for the average stay of about two hours. For additional time, the rates get higher, helping to keep the parking facility available for the retailers' patrons.

Access options

A garage can benefit from multiple access options. More the entrances into a parking garage make traffic easier in the facility. This design provides ease of entry and exit to and from the parking facility. It also gives shoppers easy access directly to the desired level of retail. Elevators and stairwells also require careful planning. Once visitors park cars, they have to find their way out. These facilities should be centrally located and well marked. When possible, designers should create open stairwells and transparent elevators. The open feeling makes visitors feel comfortable. High visibility of the access areas prevents guests from feeling trapped or lost. Bright, creative, way-finding signage systems make shoppers' arrival more pleasant.

Way-finding signage systems make a parking facility inviting. They offer comfort, assistance and security. As parking structures become the choice of many popular centres, builders place more emphasis on attractiveness, safety and accessibility. Parking structures can be one of the first things a shopper sees when entering the premises, and they are often the last hurdle to cross after a harried day of shopping. Their potential effect on the shopping experience, therefore, can be as influencing and lasting as the mall itself. For that reason, builders of parking structures and centre managers need to recognise the importance of collaborating in parking areas' design and development.

Top design qualities

Convenience is the top design quality of a successful parking structure. Next come safety and appearance. Especially as the economy continues to thrive, high-end retailers will spend more on the appearance of parking structures. The economy can be a big factor in a decision to build a multilevel structure. The top design features are: architectural facades that complement and/or blend in with the surrounding buildings of the mall area; vehicle and pedestrian circulation; glass stairways and elevators; and facilitating a safe environment with natural and artificial light, wider column spacing and wide span beams for overall visual openness.

Security risks

The attraction of new and large retail formats adds a new dimension to be tackled i.e. security in the parking areas. In addition to bike patrols and truck/car patrols, there is a feature that tends to keep the youth groups from gathering in garages. This feature is adding a sound system in the garage that plays classical music at all times. This resulted in a major reduction in the youth groups loitering especially in the west. Future parking garages should have "high speed" entrances and exits, frequently seen at airports, to allow customers to get in and out quickly. The garage floors themselves then do not become ramps but instead become flat parking areas. As far as leasing goes, we should encourage more stores to construct entrances to their stores from the parking garage, since so many customers are using garages.

In any new parking structure, security is a paramount issue. However, in a multi-use structure, assuring a safe parking experience can be more challenging, since the structure may serve a number of types of parkers. For instance, if the facility's primary constituencies are comprised of retail and student parkers, security features must be able to accommodate both groups, each of which will have different parking habits. Shoppers, for example, are more likely to be short-term parkers. They will only be in the structure for a couple of hours, and the latest they are likely to leave the building is when the stores close. On the other hand, students are more likely to be long-term parkers, and may need to use the structure late into the night if they stay on-campus to study after their classes are over.

Partnership

Urban shopping centres are struggling to meet their parking needs. The solution to this problem may be to collaborate with local institutions that have their own parking needs, but face the same financial challenges in building new parking. By collaborating, developers and institutions alike can share the financial burden of constructing new parking. Local commercial businesses, government agencies, and institutions such as universities and museums can be potential partners. The make-up of the ideal partnership depends on local conditions and the individual requirements of each potential partner. For instance, a simple joint venture involving a single institution and a retail developer may make sense in one city, whereas a more complex relationship comprised of several different partners may work best somewhere else.

While the benefits of sharing development costs are easy to recognise, there are additional long-term financial advantages. For instance, such a partnership allows each member of the ownership team to share the responsibility for managing and maintaining the structure. This can significantly reduce the operational costs borne by each of the partners. There are non-financial benefits, as well. Most significantly, shopping centre owners can use the partnership to increase their customer base. For instance, teaming up with a college or university will assure a steady flow of student parkers into the building. These students become potential customers of the shopping centre when they park in the structure. These benefits are particularly strong in mixed-use parking structures in which parking and retail services are in the same building. Each time a patron parks or picks up their vehicle, they are in close proximity to the building's retail tenants. Parkers — particularly parking regulars — often grow to rely on those retail establishments because of the convenience their proximity provides.

Maintenance

As more and more shopping centres include entertainment areas, parking structures need to meet the increased traffic demand. This involves more developer focus on parking structure durability and the resulting design/builder warrantees that the parking decks remain in top condition for many years. Developers also should consider including more services within the parking structure itself. Valet parking will become more and more popular in urban areas where consumers are rushed for time.

The challenge for designers is to create a structure that would meet the parking needs of each of these constituencies, while seamlessly blending into this very exclusive neighbourhood.

Failure to maintain a pavement system on a routine basis can erode its lifecycle. Shopping centre owners expect their parking lots to last a long time, but most also realize that they have a role in making that happen. The lifecycle of a parking lot generally ranges from 20 to 30 years, according to some experts, who add that within that period, there most likely will be at least one complete resurfacing or overlay.

Some of the signs of structural damage include depressions in the lot, rutting and alligatoring otherwise known as fatigue cracking. Traffic is the primary culprit in these types of problems, which start under the surface and rise to the top. High-traffic areas such as truck loading and unloading areas and driving lanes require thicker asphalt than parking areas do. However, traffic load is not the only major cause of parking lot failure. Environment is an equal partner, causing a variety of surface problems. Block cracking, weak edges and water infiltration are all results of the combination of sunlight and water on a pavement.

Retail textbooks talk of several laws that relate shopping with time and travel distance. With the increased use of personal transportation by shoppers in India, retailers need to look at the attendant outcomes for their businesses. Retail formats that serve the needs of time starved, long travelled consumers are bound to develop. At the same time, retailers should turn their attention also to parking, as it can be a decisive factor in satisfying the customer.

AIRPORT RETAILING

Location is a key dimension of retailing. Non-traditional locations are now emerging as key areas to target for retailing. Airport retailing is a new phenomenon even in the west. However, with international travel becoming very common and affordable, utilising retailing opportunities in the airport are becoming important for retailers. Terms like concessions and concessionaires fill the arena of airport retailing in the global context. We need to understand these terminologies to go further into the depth of airport retailing. A concession represents a shop, restaurant, bar, or car rental counter located at an airport, on a ship, or at a hotel or attraction. Someone who holds or operates a concession is called a concessionaire. With crowds at airports growing annually, the trend in recent years has been to turn terminals into shopping mall-like facilities. Transforming waiting passengers into money-spending shoppers have become the goal of many major airport operators. Delays make keeping waiting and stranded passengers busy all the more important - and, perversely, increases airport retail areas' profit generating potential.

Analysts project world's airport retailing market to be around 1% of total retail sales. More remarkably, industry sources forecast airport sales to grow on an average at a much higher pace as compared to general retail. Although airport terminals may offer a plethora of opportunities to retailers, there are also significant challenges because of a terminal's unique nature, vis-à-vis retailing - the primary purpose for visiting an airport terminal is either to travel or to bid farewell/greet those who are travelling, and certainly not to shop. The presence of time pressures i.e. everything that happens in an airport terminal is driven around flight schedules and in particular the requirement to have departing aircraft leave on time, make shopping not an altogether interesting proposition. Heightened emotions i.e. many of the elements in the facilitation process, leading from arrival at the terminal to aircraft departure, include potentially emotionally charged experiences, therefore leading to very finicky service encounters.

Airport retail, which once was little more than newspapers, magazines, aspirin, bland food and burnt coffee, is now a billion dollar business. Today's airports are attracting familiar names; like Mont Blanc while also striving to offer tourists some local flavour. Builders are designing new airport retail operations to look like upscale suburban shopping centres. At a number of airports, governments do not permit merchants to charge more than they would at a traditional mall. Larger airports are increasingly forming partnerships with development companies that invest in the retail operation but have no stake in individual stores. Under this model, an airport has to pay the developer, but it also stands to gain more from the relationship with high-profile retailers that can generate higher sales. Retailers are always looking for locations where there are many people with disposable incomes. Airports satisfy those criteria, and people are captive and have lots of time to kill. Airports have also become even more attractive in recent times, since customers have to arrive for flights earlier to go through security, thus having more time to shop.

Types of airport retailers

Retailers of all types — convenience, shopping, and specialty goods retailers—have found airports attractive. Airports have always had convenience goods retailers, e.g., books, confectionery, fast food. Shopping for goods is becoming more popular since people have more time to shop. They can buy merchandise for themselves and gifts for others. Airport shops are a great way to rid oneself of the guilt of being away from kids and spouse. Finally, airports are excellent locations for specialty goods such as high-end wrist watches, jewelry, leather, and clothing. This has been true in European airports for years. Airport clientele typically has a higher than average income. Tourists and business travellers with time to kill are avid shoppers. In addition, these specialty shops are great places to display merchandise, even if the customer ends up buying when he/she gets home. The goods sold in airports can be categorised into the following groups: Luxury goods, such as chocolates, crystal and diamonds; Travel goods, which facilitate comfortable travel such as sunglasses, convenience foods, drugs, books and magazines;. Refreshment goods, such as might be available from bars, cafes, restaurants and other food outlets' and Traditional national or regional products, or souvenirs and gifts, including high quality confectionery. Portable and mostly small, with a relatively high value to their volume are characteristics of most goods on offer at airports. Stores must consider that their customers will likely already have carry-on luggage. Thus, large items and merchandise that is not easily transported or shippable will not do well at airport locations.

Marketing

Urban planners have remarked that airports are developing into not only the key urban gateways but also the central squares of the 21st century. Terminal builders are incorporating social roles in a new wave of terminal building that presents tremendous opportunity for specialised retailers. Every new private airport management project needs to develop a balanced assessment of the management of retail in airports, ranging from total volume that can be supported to retail mix and layout to pricing policy and capital investment.

While many airports in developed countries have developed mall-like concession areas, very few have executives with a background in marketing. Managing foot traffic and guiding people to shops and restaurants - skills that are second nature for shopping mall managers, do not come easily to airport managers. This is particularly since the authorities do not provide funding to many airports to advertise and market within terminals. Airportads.com, that educates airport executives on the basics of terminal advertising and managing foot traffic, allows airports to custom build their own advertising campaigns and order materials needed for that campaign on-line. Large illuminated advertisements standing on the floor are common. Most retail outlets have a standard shop banner over the entrance. Airport retailers use brand names extensively within stores to attract attention. In some stores, banners over the shelves display the product range display brands. Retailers promote international brands strongly among all brands. There is a sense in which international brands dominate the retail outlet and indeed the entire shopping experience. One of the attractions of international brands in this context is that they side step the issue of language. English is a significant language for promotional messages in many outlets.

Consumer behaviour

Travellers targeted as consumers by airport retailers are forcibly waiting. In particular, travellers in transit between two stages of a journey may be waiting between one to three hours, or even longer, and are looking for something to do to fill their time. They are experiencing enforced leisure in an environment in which they may have little to do. They will sit, walk around and browse and stores would see them as a captive audience for marketing messages. Other features of the customer profiles are: The customer group is very heterogeneous; it comprises members of many different cultures and many different native languages. The general concourse of the departure lounge sees a mix of all classes of travellers, including both business class and tourist class. This might raise issues of customer compatibility. Many people are likely to be under an expectation that they will take a gift back to their friends or family and if they have not already made an appropriate purchase are likely to feel under pressure to make such a purchase. Customers may be in family groups, but compared with other retail environments there is a high proportion of lone male shoppers. Shops have recognised lone male shoppers to have different purchasing habits from those in family groups. Travellers will be reluctant to carry too much in addition to their luggage and indeed may be constrained by weight limits and space on aircraft. They need to relax, especially if they are engaged in long distance travel. They are subject to a sense of disorientation in relation to time and place, because they are in transit. Travellers will have a variable frequency of experience of the departure lounge. Some will be seasoned travellers, whilst other will be new or relatively new to the experience. Retailers have to deal with these different types of customers differently. The new emphasis on shopping after having passed through security has posed a challenge for shopping centres that are largely in areas preceding the security checkpoints. It would be much more difficult to convince retailers to take pre-security space.

Airport retail purchases will be impulsive, and will be often triggered by browsing. This browsing may be in respect of a specific type of product, such as a bottle of perfume, or even a specific product such as a bottle of Chanel. In these instances, the purchaser has already decided what to buy and there is likely to be no other outlet offering the same product. Comparative shopping between retail outlets is not an option, although comparative shopping between brands might be. This one factor contributes to the relative insignificance of price in this retail environment. The two other factors that also reduce purchaser's price sensitivity are currency and brands. International customers pay in a range of different currencies and often use credit or debit cards. If they are paying in a currency with which they are not familiar, their perceptions of price will be less well honed. Since customers may be in countries in which local brands are unfamiliar, international brands take on a particular significance. Many airports have a unique identity that reflects the community they serve and the passengers who use them. Successful airport retailing depends on creating the right blend of international brands, local concepts, and tailor-made outlets that perfectly match the business objectives of the airport and demands of its passengers. Moreover, when it comes to providing food and beverage outlets, striking the right balance is essential. In most traditional retail establishments, the targeted consumer is female. However, some airports report that men are doing over 80% of all purchasing. This means that your message must be bold enough to breakthrough the clutter of the average male mind. Large graphics or photographs may also help the typical male to grasp a concept quickly and easily.

The international context

The Nuance Group, largest airport retailer in the world, is a fully-owned subsidiary of SAirRelations, the SAirGroup division. It specialises in travel retail, catering and hotel management. This retailer has developed several formats like The Beauty Zone that target primarily younger and more price-conscious customer. It has deliberately devised offers to provide a wide range of toiletries and beauty items that for the customer on the move. Five specialty shops offering a wide range of quality watches and jewelry, fun watches, toys, accessories and confectionery are other formats. Nuance has had an eventful history since the company was established in

1992. What started out as the amalgamation of the duty-free operations of Swissair and Crossair has grown to become the world's largest airport retailer and the global number one in duty-free sales. Nuance has achieved this phenomenal growth through acquisitions, particularly of Allders International Duty-Free in 1996. BAA plc is into airport retailing in many major airports in the United Kingdom and through World Duty Free, the Company's wholly-owned tax and duty-free business, which specializes in luxury brands, operates 64 stores across the United Kingdom airports. BAA provides over one million square meters of commercial accommodation for more than 900 organisations at its airports. It is also involved in airport-related property development.

The Indian scenario

By 2010, Indian airports were likely to handle 90-100 million passengers including 59 million domestic and 35 million international passengers. India is seeking to improve its airport infrastructure at an estimated cost of Rs. 400 billion over the next five years. It is one of the most dynamic markets in aviation today. There are currently 17 million passengers moving through its airports each year, a figure expected to grow by 25% in each of the coming years. The government is also trying to upgrade 30 smaller airports around the country. In the last three years, privately-owned airlines have proliferated, leading to congestion at many of India's airports. India's two main airports, which together handle almost half of the country's air traffic. Airport privatisation is in the offing though not in full measure immediately. These developments augur well for targeting airport retailing as one of the avenues for spreading retailing in India in the not so distant future.

Cochin International Airport is a unique experiment in airport management in India. Kochi airport is the only Indian airport owned and operated by a company set up with equity participation from the Kerala government — it has a 26% stake — while private investors, mostly Keralites from the UAE, own the remaining 74%. Alpha Kreol, a 50:50 joint venture between Sharjah-based Kreol Trading and Alpha Retail, will undertake the management and supply of goods to the duty free shops at the airport. The Alpha-Kreol joint venture is the first operation of its kind in the duty free industry in India, which so far has been the monopoly of the state-run India Tourism Development Corporation. The contract to operate the shops is for a period of 10 years. The joint venture partners have invested $2.2m for the project. The partners will split the duty free facility into two sections — the outlet one spread over an area of 6,432 sq ft at the arrival lounge and the shop at the departure lounge will cover 2,000 sq ft. An additional 270 sq ft shop will be located at the last checkout point at the terminal. This is one of the first organised private airport retailing efforts in India in a new airport management set up. Flemingo DFS Pvt. Ltd., one of another the country's duty-free player, has a range confined mainly to culinary stuff (spices, nuts and tea) at the Flemingo departure shops at the country's airports.

New initiatives

Logan's Airmall in the US or Amsterdam Airport Schiphol (AAS) managed Airport City reflect the new reality in air travel. Presentation, customer service, merchandise selection, and promotion are the key in their operations. Airport City, a teaming complex with shops, restaurants, multimedia facilities, banks, a casino and all the other things that make a city appealing and alive redefine experience of retailing at an airport. From the consumer end, airport retailers' facility in accepting return products by many outlets provides long-term comfort. More and more airports, viewing themselves as the front door to the city that they serve, are trying to capture the look and feel of the city in the terminal. This provides employment to locals and helps in highlighting the city. England's Manchester Airport greets travellers with an unusual facility that stands apart from the familiar duty-free shops and airport retail outlets that typically sell newspapers, novels, and souvenirs.

The Gene Shop, a joint venture between the Centre for Professional Ethics at the University of Central Lancashire, Preston, and the Royal Manchester Children's Hospital's (RMCH) department of clinical genetics, is intended to provide people with an opportunity to shop around for free information about genetics and how genes and genetic diseases can affect their everyday lives. The Gene Shop uses interactive touch-screen computer programmes and displays about inherited diseases to provide the travelling public an opportunity to learn more about genetics and genetic diseases. The main obstacle to airport shopping is that you expect somebody to rip you off — partly because souvenirs and even items like chewing gum cost more at the airport than outside. Many concession managers abroad now offer a money-back guarantee for travellers who spot identical items at lower prices at a regular mall in the city.

The massive growth in passenger traffic throughout India goes hand in hand with equally impressive investment in fleet by several airlines. The growth of low cost airlines, the impact of new generation aircraft, and the potential of the India represent a great future for airport retailing. The knowledge of airline schedules in advance help in airport retail planning and therefore it can be a very professionally managed activity in India. Let us wait for airport retailing to take off!

RETAIL LOCATION AS A STRATEGIC DECISION

"I have cornered the most vantage location and I am assured for the rest of my life that my outlet would succeed" - this used to be the thinking of many of the traditional retailers even in the most advanced part of the world just a decade ago. However as retailing is being saturated, location as it relates to opening and closing of stores has achieved greater sophistication. As organised retailing grows in India, professional retail entities and managers have several IT enabled techniques now in making a scientific decision regarding locating the retail outlet. Prospective retailers use the latest innovations and methodologies in the location research process to identify and quantify factors that affect store sales performance. In today's competitive retail environment, sales and market share preservation and growth are critical to survival. It is not surprising then that most successful retailers are constantly engaged in self-evaluation, of which an important component is ongoing assessment of a retailer's store deployment plans. Making better site location decisions for the retail sector is about staying ahead of the competition, entering a new market, or just familiarising themselves with the new advancements in methods and technology facing their industry today.

Location quotient

Economic and business geography are disciplines that are emerging to facilitate location decision-making. In each of these disciplines, it would be useful to discuss an oft-mentioned concept called location quotient. The location quotient is most frequently used in economic geography and locational analysis, but it has much wider applicability. The location quotient (LQ) is an index for comparing an area's share of a particular activity with the area's share of some basic or aggregate phenomenon. Is employment in manufacturing or services concentrated in some area (s), or evenly distributed across the map? Location quotients compare the distribution of an activity to some base or standard, in this case to total employment. One can re-express the question as follows: Is manufacturing or service employment more or less concentrated than total employment?

The location quotient for a given activity for area i is the ratio of the percentage of the total regional activity in area i to the percentage of the total base in area i. A location quotient is thus the ratio of two percentages and is, therefore, dimensionless. The location quotient for manufacturing in area A is $(5/100)/(150/1000) = 5/15 = 0.333$. That is, region A has 5% of the manufacturing employment of the region but 15% of the total employment in all sectors. Based on its share of total employment, we would expect region A to have 15% of the manufacturing employment. It has only 5%, or 0.333, as much as would be expected. We can interpret Location quotients by using the following conventions:

- If LQ>1, this indicates a relative concentration of the activity in the area compared to the region as a whole.

- If LQ =1, the area has a share of the activity in accordance with its share of the base.

- If LQ<1, the area has less of a share of the activity than is more generally, or regionally, found.

If we have a complete table of location quotients for two employment sectors as below, they can indicate which areas of the map fall into these categories:

Location Quotient

Area	Manufacturing	Services
A	0.333	0.667
B	1.400	1.100
C	0.750	0.750
D	0.677	1.333

For manufacturing, the location quotient reveals a concentration in area B and less than expected shares in each of the three other areas. For services, however, the distribution is much less concentrated, with relative concentrations in areas B and D and less than expected shares in A and C. Mapping these location quotients can reveal spatial patterns.

The selection of the base or standard distribution used in the denominator of location quotients is subject to choice. Usually, if the activities are part of some aggregate, then users use the aggregate as the base. In this example, it makes sense to compare the concentration of various industrial sectors to the total employment in all sectors. However, it is also possible to use area populations as the standard of comparison. In that case, we would be comparing distribution of sectoral employment to distribution of population. Alternatively, the base activity could also be defined as the actual land area in each of the areas of the region. Retail sector can apply the same concept to get an idea about the indirect estimate of the saturation of the retail outlets in an area as well as purchasing power. Density of the retail outlets in comparison with density for the region and a similar comparison with purchasing power provides an understanding of location quotient in the retailing milieu. This would help in deciding on opening or closing outlets in an area.

Other forms of locational analysis

We need to understand few other terms in locational analysis. Isostante is a term used to refer to the boundary between two market areas served by two market centres with varying prices and transport costs. The Isostante specifies the points with equal delivered prices from both centres. The delineation of this boundary helps us to theoretically use the price and transport cost in order to make a decision on the location of stores. Similarly the "range of a good" signifies the maximum distance customers are willing to travel or incur transport costs for in order to purchase a good at a given (f.o.b.) price. The range of a good refers mainly to the demand side and is defined by the maximum distance consumers are willing to travel (or pay transport costs for) for a good or service at a given f.o.b. price at the point of supply. This implies that each product category, product and brand has an attractiveness or power of influence on the consumer. This defines the trading area influence of the consumer. Thus, we can use this concept effectively in delineating the primary, secondary and tertiary trading areas.

Range and its dimensions

The "threshold range" is the minimum radius of a market area needed to generate sufficient demand to support the supply of a good. It refers to the minimum (potentially also the maximum) market area which a supplier needs (or can sell to) to make his undertaking viable. More specifically, "given the equilibrium f.o.b. market price, the threshold range represents the distance to the perimeter of an area enclosing the minimum level of aggregate demand (or a minimum population) which is sufficient to permit the commercial supply of the good. This specifies an area that permits only normal profits to be made."

The range of the good as well threshold range represents theoretical (equilibrium) concepts associated with market area analysis and central place theory: the range (of the good) has to be larger than the threshold range. The threshold is usually associated with the intersections between (or the point of tangency of) the spatial demand function and the downward- sloping average-cost curve (for the f.o.b. - case). The significance of these concepts relates to the equilibrium conditions for market areas i.e. what kinds of market areas we would expect under defined conditions. These concepts allow us to introduce the full gamut of supply-side (cost) and demand considerations and differentiation, related to the particular product and its production/ supply as well as differences in preferences and ability to pay among consumers as well as differences in transport costs and demand densities.

Location in metros - the areas of organised retail growth

The emergence of the industrial city, a product of capitalism, resulted in lower transportation and communication costs for entrepreneurs who needed to interact with one another; hence, most commercial and industrial enterprise is concentrated in and around the most accessible part of the city - the Central Business District (CBD). Retail firms especially are attracted to cities and thus aid in the city's growth because of two opposing forces. These forces are scale of economies and transportation costs. Two types of agglomeration economies account for city growth: Localisation economies refer to declining average costs for firms as the output of the industry of which they are a part of, increase. Urbanisation economies are referred to declining average costs for cities, as firms increase their levels of activity. These dimensions of growth in the Indian context are clearly visible in metros and therefore the growth of organised retailing in the metros has been growing accordingly.

Classical location theory states that activity is located in cities according to the outcome of the competitive bidding process. People willing and able to pay the highest price for a particular site win the competition. Competitive bidding processes change according to effective demand, public tastes and standards, and land use regulation. The maximum rent that a particular user pays for the site is called the ceiling rent. The growth in commercial property and intense competition in metros have in effect created a competitive bidding process for the property in metros. This has a clear influence on property available for retail outlet.

Accessibility to employment and services, and general supply and demand factors that impact bid prices, influence residential location decisions. Key demand factors in the housing market are population; inflation-adjusted or 'real' income per person or household; and home buyers' expectations of the future change in home prices. Important supply factors are the availability of items needed in building new housing units (land, labour, and construction equipment and materials) and construction standards or building codes. In India, in the last few years, availability of housing loans at a very competitive interest rate and the entry of banks in this field have made building homes a much easier process within the reach of the middle class. This has resulted in a boom in the housing market. This phenomenon has an implication for retailers, as there are chances of retail outlets springing up in new residential areas where the density of the population can sustain a retail outlet. The assumption that firms want to maximise profits is the basis for firms' locational decisions. If intra-urban accessibility is important to sales a firm should be willing to make higher bids that for locations that are central to all potential customers.

Nature of metro development

Because of automobile-based inter-urban dispersal, the city has evolved into a restructured form called multi-centered metropolis. Classical models cannot accommodate this new reality easily. The rapid spread of urban India owes much to the nature of the radial and circumferential road network, which results in near equal levels of convergence time across the metropolitan area, destroying the region wide advantage of the CBD. Low housing interest rates reinforced the trend towards single-family housing in the suburbs. Intercity neighbourhood redevelopment involves gentrification - property upgrading by high income settlers that frequently results in the displacement of low-income residents. Jobs are moving out with modern technology and development, and so are shopping centres and entertainment. The need for the city, as far as the middle class is concerned, has diminished. Affordable housing is a major problem in today's modern cities, and planned public housing projects have not solved big city problems. The inner city is home to the metropolitan disadvantaged and includes a few specialised services, where suburban and satellite cities house the affluent and support a range of services that were previously city-bound. Local and regional planners increasingly support the notion of increasing the supply of housing in job-rich areas, and the quantity of jobs in housing rich areas. The concept is jobs/housing balance. The suburbs create most new employment opportunities matched to the work skills of inner city residents. This is known as the spatial mismatch theory. Thus, the poor are faced with the problem of either finding work in a stagnating industrial area, the inner city, or commuting longer distances to keep up with the dispersing job market through reverse commuting. This also has an influence on the location of the retail outlets. The nature of the target segment of the retail outlet therefore determines the location of the outlet

Locational patterns of cities include: transportation cities aligned along transportation routes and at junctions of different types of transportation; specialised function centres that develop around a localised physical resource; uniform pattern of centres, referred to as central places that exchange goods and services with their hinterland. Central-place theory emphasises that cities perform extensive services for their hinterland. Business conducted totally within the hinterland is called settlement-forming trade. Activity that is directed to outside markets is called settlement-building trade. Business conducted with residents of the centre is called settlement-serving trade. It should be clear, what is the nature of the store that we have, in order to locate the store accordingly.

Development of central places

Central places serve large areas around the city. These areas are called hinterlands, tributary areas, trade or market areas, or urban fields. Areas of dominant influence (ADI) also called daily urban systems, is that area that describes the extent of the social, economic, and cultural ties between a city and its tributary region. Newspaper circulation and commuting are conceptually good indicators. People in the tributary area, look to the regional newspaper for information on sales and social events or to the city as an employment location. A good measure for locating outlets is to use this movement of people.

It is possible to order centres and create a hierarchy of central places. Highest order good offered by the centre determines the order of a centre. A central place hierarchy can be regarded as a multiple system of nested centres and market areas. Low order centres and their market areas nest under the area of higher order centres. As the hierarchical level increases, the number of trade centres decreases. The large centres are widely spaced while the hamlets are the most numerous. The determination of the size of the retail outlet in a location especially the city implies application of the same concept. As the size of the outlet, increases in the CBD of the city, its primary trading area increases and therefore the number of such outlets are less.

Hierarchy

Space preference structures measure the trade-off between a journey's distance to shop for goods and services, and the town size. The larger the town size, greater the positive mental stimulus, while the increased distance to the town centre is a negative mental stimulus. Rural residents receive a certain payoff to go a certain distance. Town size as a surrogate for the market basket of shopping possibilities that exist there measures the payoff. A central place hierarchy of goods and services also exists inside the city. This hierarchy is the retail hierarchy, and urban residents display a similar behaviour to rural residents. Shoppers obtain low order goods from the closest places and higher order goods from higher order centres.

Typically, location models identify as "best" that new location, which maximises some measures of overall financial performance for the organisation, often the total revenue. In doing so, the model usually allows new locations of the organisation (as long as total revenue is maximised) to cannibalise revenue from old locations. While this poses no problem to the corporate-owned chain, franchise systems are different. A current franchisee would be understandably upset if a new franchisee location cannibalises revenue at his/her, no matter that system-wide revenue increases. From the franchisee's perspective, the lost sales have been pirated away, just as surely as if by a competing system. Therefore, location also plays an important role in determining franchisee site-selection decision.

CHAPTER SIX

Store Atmospherics

RETAIL ATMOSPHERICS

Environmental psychology is an area that has a profound influence on retailing. The whole subject of retail atmospherics is a result of the application of environmental psychology in retailing. This has tremendous influence on shopping behaviour. The two major types of variables that affect shopping behaviour are external variables (e.g., window displays, entrances, etc.) and Interior variables (e.g., music, odour, lighting, etc.). While the external variables greatly affect store traffic and sales, research has found Interior variables to impact sales, time spent in the store and approach/avoidance behaviour. The layout and design of a store (e.g., traffic flow, allocation of floor space, layout of merchandise, traffic patterns etc.) has been found to influence unplanned purchases and perceptions of price value. Point-to-purchase communication and store decoration (e.g., product displays, signage, background features that affect human senses etc.) also influence sales. Research involving human variables (e.g., employee characteristics, crowding, etc.) reported that these variables generally influence consumer evaluations of the shopping experience. Store environments might influence shopping behaviour through mediating emotional states. The store environment contains various stimuli that the customer's senses perceive and each stimulus offers many options with regard to variability. For example, store music varies by volume, tempo, pitch and texture and by the specific songs played. In addition, a store manager can combine factors to create a unique atmosphere. To project an upscale image, a manager might choose classical music, subdued colours, elegant perfumes, cool temperatures, sparsely displayed merchandise, and low lighting.

Linking shopping behaviour to environmental factors and ambience, all retailers need to track factors through changes in emotional states, perceptions of shopping duration, and their merchandise evaluations. Music is one of the key environmental variables that can affect shoppers. In research done in the US, shoppers reported that (perception) shopping was a longer activity when exposed to familiar music. Shoppers related shorter times in the familiar music condition to time misperceptions. Environmental factors like music affect, thus, time spent in the store, propensity to make a purchase, and satisfaction with the experience.

Environmental Psychology in Retailing

Pleasure, Arousal, and Dominance in the minds of the consumers are the immediate effects of environmental cues given by the stores. The first is an effectual reaction, labelled Pleasure-Displeasure. This entails whether individuals perceive the environment as enjoyable or not enjoyable. For example, playing popular film or classical songs in Hindi should enhance shoppers' enjoyment in most stores in North India, whereas unpopular music might diminish it. The second dimension relates to Arousal. It assesses how much the environment stimulates the individual. Playing slow instrumental music may result in slower customer movement through a supermarket relative to no music or fast music. This result perhaps is due to a decrease in arousal. The third dimension is Dominance which concerns whether individuals feel dominant (in control) or submissive (under control) in the said environment. This shopper feeling could relate to environmental aspects like the height of the ceiling that makes one feel small/in control.

The dominant colour in the store also creates a response. Individuals associate the colour red with active, assertive, and rebellious moods whereas they associate blue with sedate tranquillity and suppression of feelings. The right choice of colour helps the retailer portray the nature of mood. This kind of decision is important in apparel retailing as well as furniture retailing as the choice of apparel as well as furniture greatly depends on the lifestyle of the target set of customers. A store could construct environments to encourage or discourage approach behaviours. For example, bright colours might encourage individuals to enter a fast food restaurant, whereas uncomfortable seating might discourage long stays.

While we discuss these factors in the context of brick and mortar retailing, the development of the Web as a retailing medium, needs us to understand the implications of web atmospherics.

E-tailing perspective

Analogous to brick and mortar retailing, in e-tailing, factors like Website organisation, server performance, product data, search option, and shopping carts all contribute to a positive web shopping experience. The easy navigability in the Website for a consumer who wishes to buy through the net is one of the first facilitating factors. Server performance directly affects the waiting time that is required for obtaining results of searches. The easy access to product data and a click and browser friendly search option, add to the convenience of the consumer.

Negative correlation between waiting time and evaluation of service satisfaction in brick-and-mortar retail stores needs to be examined too. Though store atmospheric variables can mitigate this, the association is strong. Similarly, system response time is inversely related to computer user satisfaction (i.e., the longer the wait, the greater the dissatisfaction). Demographic variables like the age, stage of the life cycle and gender may moderate perceptions of the convenience which the Web provides and the choice of the channel to make a purchase. This means that the younger unmarried segment of the population would have a better appreciation of the problems of Web purchasing and therefore may tolerate the disadvantages better than the older population. The degree of perceived irritation induced by displeasing aspects of the Web-shopping environment again would change based on the segment targeted. One of the better ways of segmenting customers would be to track the frequency of shopping over the Web that would determine the tolerance/intolerance levels of Web atmospherics.

In brick and mortar retailing, shopping is tending to move more towards "shoppertainment" i.e. a large dose of social activity and entertainment, especially in a country like India. In the case of the Web, shopping is absent. The lack of a clear social dimension is expected and especially given the fact that Web shopping is mostly a solitary activity. However, the shopper is interacting with the Internet Service Provider when faced with heavy Internet traffic and waiting time to load a web page. This organisational interaction, instead of the social interaction with other shoppers and sales associates (as one would find in a brick-and-mortar retail shopping experience) is a crucial dimension that a retailer requires to track to be a better Web-based marketer.

Inadequate instructions and complicated payment method are areas that might have a profound influence in the form of lost sales. A Website that is not easy to read may irritate older age groups, resulting in losing their way on the Website and showing a lack of confidence in the product service. This is because older consumers are more familiar with brick-and-mortar retailers where product service can be assessed prior to purchase. Frequent shoppers on the Web are more irritated by the waiting time to check this out. This makes sense since frequent shoppers are more experienced and may not tolerate delays. This is also true of the waiting time for a Web page to load.

The unpleasant visual surroundings in the location they shop on the Web may irritate older consumers less, whereas the change of visuals and attractiveness may be very crucial for young shoppers. However unpleasant visual surroundings would irritate the less frequent web shoppers more.

Time, music and shopping

Time is an important factor in retail shopping, partially because studies show a simple correlation between time spent shopping and shopping and amount purchased. In addition, retail experts argue that time is as much a constraint on consumption as money and those predictions that individuals would have more time at their discretion in the future than in the past have not proven to be true. For example, dual career families with children coping with transportation difficulties in dense metropolitan areas may feel intense time pressure when shopping. Consequently, it is reasonable to expect individuals to budget their time, including shopping times. People simply do not enjoy waiting too long or wasting time. Shoppers overestimate their waiting time less when they report a high level of shopping enjoyment, relative to other activities. Thus, retailers would be prudent to minimise perceived as well as actual time spent shopping for their patrons.

Music affects shopping time perception. The nature of music - foreground music or background music would have a differential effect based on the age of the shoppers. Music also affects actual shopping times. Individuals tend to stay longer when listening to the slow music compared to the fast music. How loud is the music and length of the song also makes a difference. There is conventional wisdom, which says that "time flies when you are having fun." Nevertheless, the type of music could mediate this. Therefore, retailers must make very conscious efforts to select music based on its listener responses and familiarity as well as its other qualities.

Environmental music varying in its perceived familiarity to the shoppers might affect individuals engaged in shopping activity. Individuals listening to familiar music will be more aroused and will spend more time shopping than individuals listening to unfamiliar music. This makes it imperative for the retailer to choose familiar music that is in tune with consumers from the primary trading area. This can also positively effect product evaluations. Individuals feel more comfortable in an environment featuring familiar atmospheric elements.

Implications for retail design

Retailing is a business that involves a lot of creativity. The store manager needs to create an excitement in the store always so that the regular consumer is in for a delightful surprise all the time. However, the catch is that a loyal consumer of a store expects some standard aspects of the retail outlet not to be changed. These generally pertain to the ambience of the store. Retailers in general and retail designers in particular need to make a fine balance between amount of change and the anticipated response to the same. The play with the elements of the atmospherics mix (if I may call it so!) must also relate to the geographical area that the retailer serves. On the other hand, the retailer would want to maintain standardisation across the stores for identity as well as cost benefits. The customer like the retailer is resistant to change and therefore would always be negative to change in atmospherics. Therefore, proactiveness, understanding of trend and competition as well as pioneering efforts through constant experimentation are the virtues that would help the retailer in making the best of the atmospherics.

STORE DESIGN

The development of a competitive situation in the Indian physical store retailing market place now places a heavy responsibility on brick and mortar retail marketers to position their entities uniquely compared to their competitors. In this situation, one of the tangible ways of looking at differentiation is to concentrate on the physical design components of the store. A dramatic and fun store design along with visual graphics could act as key drivers in design for differentiation. Customers want to visit stores with ambience, where shopping is an enjoyable experience rather than a simple visit to pick up a product. Some stores encourage interaction between customers and the product, but store design and style remain a powerful pull for customers and will keep them coming back. In order to turn these lookers (window shoppers!) into buyers an attractive and dramatic graphic design is one that can help.

The retailer needs to formulate graphics and designs that tie directly into the images and products sold. The process entails far more than a splash of colour here and a dab of colour there. It means starting with the product and exploring options that highlight the products or services to encourage sales. It is about marketing and not designs for design's sake. The Internet has been motivating retailers to find new and exciting ways to lure and invite customers. A dynamic retail environment, combined with physical product/ customer interaction, provides a competitive advantage to brick and mortar retailers compared to e-tailers. One of the lessons that a store can transfer from e-tailing to physical store design is the ambience in an e-mall offered through variety in graphics.

Design and store image

The retailer needs to be aware of design and its positive influence on store image. Many retailers become so used to their current design that they give little thought to possibilities. Retailers should try entering their store, as a customer would, for the first time. Empathising with the customer is the first step towards change in store ambience. The questions that need to be asked are—is there something to invite the customer into your store? Is something to promote curiosity. That first impression says a lot about who you are and what you have to sell. If the store looks drab and boring, that perception reflects your image and the quality of your products and services. The next step is to decide what you want the image to be and then design around it. For example, if the store's image is technology based, make sure there are elements within the store that support a technological message.

Traffic flow

The store must design traffic flow in consonance with its image. A discount store may have little space and therefore stimulates faster movement of customers and will be backed by faster delivery to manage a huge crowd on a regular basis. In the case of relatively premium stores, there is a need to give customers plenty of room to move around and allow for easy access to the cash register. Any visual or products that draw a lot of attention, should be easily accessible. One should be cautious about drawing customer's attention to off-limits areas. In services marketing, physical evidence (to rhyme with other 6Ps) as part of the 7Ps must be consistent to project a unique image. In that respect, design of the store plays a crucial role.

The foremost question to ask before putting on the thinking cap on store design is – what is the store's main objective - is it impulse purchases, lingering customers or education? Answering these questions will give the retailer a new perspective on how to make the store customer-friendly.

The play with colours

Once the retailer identifies a brand image and determines the feel, flow and objective, he should consider the element of colour. On the most basic physical level we all share similar responses to colour. Wavelengths of reflected light (colour) stimulate our nervous and endocrine systems, creating distinct biological responses. Our heart rate and blood pressure can increase while observing intensely saturated red and orange hues. We can become sleepy, anxious, or even get headaches while gazing upon large areas of bright whites or greys. Alternatively, we can achieve a sense of well-being when surrounded by a combination of cool and warm hues. However, for the most part, these responses happen beyond our awareness. How do all these instinctual responses relate to retail? By relating to a person's innate responses, colour can make the difference between whether a customer buys one item or 20. Colours that surround consumers influence them to some degree.

The key to using colours for specific purposes within a retail environment is to understand both the physiological and psychological influences. In a retail atmosphere, the main goal is to help the customer simultaneously identify with both the environment and the products, generating a healthy sale and a satisfied customer. Following are the questions to consider and some basic principles that a retail chain may use as guidelines, when choosing his/her retail colour palette:

- Define goals and culture of the business.

- Who are the customers?

- What should they experience?

- Are they teenagers, 30-something parents or seniors?

- Do you want to generate excitement or quiet interest?

- Do you want to create a space that is festive, trendy, utilitarian and funky, or elegant and sophisticated? Is the physical space large, small or intimate?

- Is there sufficient available natural light?

- Consider the psychological associations we have with various colours:

  Red: Assertive, exciting, passionate, warm

  Pink: Stimulates desire for sweets

Orange: Sociable, "folk-style," implies affordability; currently a trend colour

Blue: Relaxing, refreshing, cool; symbolises trust, integrity, and intuition

Green: Nurturing; has universal appeal; can be showy, dynamic

Brown and earth colours: Stable, secure, friendly, receptive; relates to instinct

Yellow: Cheerful, communicative, casual, youthful

Purple/Violet: Deep version is mysterious, serious; pastel shade is a favourite with young girls!

White: Unifies; brings life to other colours; culturally ambiguous; cold/impersonal, sterile

Black: Culturally ambiguous, formal

Grey: Implies ambiguity when mixed in hues; trendy metallic/pearl versions are more mysterious

Creating a successful palette is all about balance. Combinations of colour and lighting will influence any response. Therefore, the balance of hue, value, contrast and light reflectance is the key. Strong colour, high contrast, and more patterning will create a more stimulating environment. Close tones and lower light reflectance values will create a place where people will linger. Strong hues and mixed materials for visual interest can punctuate comfortable, sophisticated neutrals and more subtle textures.

Colour is a vast subject. New research is continually deepening our understanding of its power to evoke emotions. We could study it for a lifetime and one fact will remain tried and true — there really is more to colour than meets the eye. The challenge is creating a successful colour palette that allows its influence on customers to work for you.

Colours should be consistent with the corporate look. Retailers should carry colour schemes throughout the store and coordinate it with their fixtures. The dominant colour scheme acts as a reminder for the store when the consumer encounters colour in any other setting. It helps in aided recall of the store. When using bright splashes of colour, it needs to be ensured that let the customers' eyes do not get distracted. Surrounding areas of bright colour with areas of neutrality, give the eyes specific focal points with direction toward the product.

Graphics

Once the shop owner selects colours, he should consider incorporating graphic images that feature products, welcome and thank-you signs, or general artwork relating to the store's image. Other considerations for graphics are counter cards, tile printing, textured graphics, fabric banners and photomurals. Today's technology allows for photographic reproductions on almost any surface, from floors and walls, to many different fabrics and tiles. A designer can create a larger-than-life graphic by electrostatically printing an image onto an adhesive vinyl, and then applying the adhesive vinyl to the wall in multiple panels, in a similar fashion as a wallpaper. This material works well because maintenance workers can easily clean it. Using these tips, retailers can turn stores into dynamic retail environments. Remember, if the store's objective is fun; make it a fun place to shop. Educate customers about products, if that is the goal. Interact with customers by letting them know you want them to visit. Successful stores are becoming destinations that captivate, intrigue and make your customers smile. Try using colour graphics, and once the crowds flock to see that beautifully designed store, make sure the product is still great too!

Floor designs

Eye-catching floor designs have shoppers watching where they walk. Shopping centres are following the model of amusement parks in their efforts to create a fun, and themed atmosphere.

As a result, retail property owners are using every available space, from ceilings to floors, to make the shopping centre an interesting environment with the use of more colour, design, shape, depth and themes. The retail industry is using flooring as a new medium to introduce unique designs and intricate patterns into common areas and retail spaces. Water-jet technology enables engineers to cut floor products ranging from ceramic and stone into intricate shapes. The cut materials are then used to create distinctive patterns, such as mosaics or murals.

Floor designs are becoming more popular, particularly in malls with multiple levels or atriums that give shoppers a bird's-eye view of floor design. When you see it from above, it creates a far more dramatic effect. Oftentimes, shopping centres add designs that complement a property's name, theme or logo. Technology available now provides the means to cut intricate shapes in a variety of materials, such as tile, stone, metal and vinyl flooring. Recent innovations in water-jet technology have been instrumental in advancing the trend in intricate floor designs. For example, water-jet technology is now available to make cuts that are more sophisticated. The cost of the application has also dropped in recent years. Materials used to create floor designs include ceramic tile, terrazzo and stone. Ceramic has become one of the most popular choices for creating distinctive designs. This is because designers can cut it into any number of intricate shapes, and the tile comes in thousands of colours. Regardless of the chosen material or technique, the overall trend in the retail industry is to use flooring products to enhance the design scheme of a shopping centre or retail store. It is not always the merchandise. The decoration of the store attracts the buyer.

Another flooring trend has retailers moving their own floor designs farther out into common areas of malls to attract customers. Retailers can use flooring like signage to lead shoppers into a store. Retailers and shopping centre owners alike are using a variety of flooring products to capture shopper attention. Designers are searching for stone-flooring products that feature a variety of textures. The textured stone can provide greater slip-resistance compared with other products. The texture also can be used as an aesthetic feature to provide more variation to the polished flooring. For example, textured-stone pieces can be used in conjunction with polished stone to create decorative patterns or borders.

One of the most popular uses of ceramic tiles these days is to create a mosaic design within the floor pattern. Designs range from creating an image, such as a rosette, to duplicating a company logo in a tiled entryway. All aspects of retail, from the main floor of a shopping centre itself all the way into tenant stores, whether they are restaurant or retail use ceramic. Ceramic tile offers a very strong combination of great aesthetic and design capability, along with positive performance attributes such as durability, slip-resistance, scratch-resistance and good maintenance properties. Typically, ceramic tile is easier to clean than other flooring materials. Ceramic tile also holds a tremendous design potential in the variety of sizes, shapes and colours. Performance characteristics drive largely that choice. For example, the colour of a tile goes completely through the body of the product. Therefore, there are no worries about scratching or wearing-off of glazes. Another trend is the use of larger-sized tiles.

Wood/carpet for store decor

The light-coloured wood is used to complement store decor. It provides a nice backdrop for fixtures and products, and it adds certain warmth that you do not get from a tile, and a natural feel that you do not get from a carpet. One new trend among retailers selecting hardwood flooring is to use dark-hued wood. The richer wood colours are becoming more prevalent in bar and restaurant décor. Stores that favour carpets are opting for bolder colours and designs. Traditionally, retail stores have used inexpensive cut-pile carpeting in solid colours. A carpet's patterns can even help to disguise food and drink stains.

Matting

Making entrance decisions regarding flooring products for store and shopping centre entryways often depend more on practicalities than aesthetics. Not only are retail property owners concerned with using non-slip surfaces, but also the products need to prevent visitors from tracking dirt and mud throughout the shopping area. A common solution for retail centres is .to use floor mats in vestibules and entryways to prevent slipping and trap dirt and moisture. Now, rather than covering up expensive tile or stone, some shopping centres are choosing to install recessed matting as their flooring product.

Shopping centre owners are using matting as their sole flooring product instead of simply a fixture. Although shopping centres have moved toward floor products that feature greater slip-resistance, such as textured stone, those products are not very effective in trapping dirt or moisture. Since matting is a necessity, some shopping centres have decided to cut costs by installing recessed matting. The recessed vestibule matting allows for both function and aesthetics because the perimeter, or non-traffic areas, can still feature decorative tile or ceramic borders.

The eyes of retail shoppers, although sharp and exacting, are often encouraged to appreciate the forest for its trees. If the store design succeeds in its mission, then its smaller components - such as colour choice or fixture materials - lose their individual significance as they contribute to a refined, unified environment. To shoppers, the store makes its design and image impressions as a whole, while unselfishly giving the merchandise the store's top billing. However, for designers, a retail environment may truly succeed by what shoppers do not consciously absorb. The designer must harmoniously match, manipulate and enjoin each building block component of retail store design its materials, colours and textures to create a warm, inviting retail space. The retailer needs to appreciate the impact of the primary design elements in the creating an image for the store.

SPACE VALUATION IN A MALL

37 malls in Mumbai, 10 in Hyderabad, 15 in Bangalore, 220 malls in all of India by end 2007 this is the estimate of various agencies involved in assessing the future of commercial property development in India. The real estate sector is booming thanks to the low interest regime for home loans. One of the other factors that are providing a fillip to real estate is the boom in commercial property development especially retail property development. India has been witnessing tremendous investments in retail property development in anticipation of a greater shift towards organised retailing. Moreover, with the convergence of retailing, entertainment and the tourism sectors, the retail-property-development industry in India has taken to mega mall development, to suit the needs of all the three sectors in a single location. With this kind of development, it would be interesting to look at the economics of mall development and specifically the way in which mall developers manage space.

Before malls appeared on the retailing scene, the locus of retailing activity in major Indian cities was the central business district, populated by well-known department stores. A department store resembles a collection of smaller stores offering a variety of goods and services but under single ownership. In addition, department stores in central business districts were multi-floor structures, so the shopping cost of going from one store to another was higher than the cost of cross-store shopping in a typical mall. In a few cities, specialised developers did purchase large blocks of central city land and then offered leases to department stores and other stores at differential rents. Increased automobile ownership, an enhanced urban road network, and growing suburban markets have clearly hastened the displacement of the central business district in major Indian cities by the suburban mall. If additional benefits offered by the anchor were not priced in central business districts but were in the new malls located outside the central business districts in cities and in the suburbs, then major department stores would be more eager to leave the central business district for malls located elsewhere in the city or in the suburbs. Therefore, there is a need to understand how pricing must be done better to take care of benefits offered.

Mall represents a set of co-located retail outlets in a large area with lot of amenities. In the retail sector, mall development must be a planned development of the property to attract the right mix of tenants. There is need to plan the location of the mall in anticipation of increased footfalls. For the mall developer as well as potential tenants, understanding of the retail environment becomes crucial while investing in malls.

Benefits of a mall

Consumers reduce search costs by shopping at malls. However, the agglomeration of stores inevitably creates issues for various stores because the success of a mall store depends, in part, on the presence of other stores within the mall, especially on the presence of the mall's anchor stores. A common claim is that consumers are attracted to malls because of the presence of well-known anchor stores—invariably department stores with recognised names. By generating mall traffic, anchors create benefits by indirectly increasing sales and/or reducing promotion and other costs of a host of smaller mall stores. Lesser-known stores can exploit the reputation of anchors. This would mean, mall developers would provide rent subsidies to anchors and would charge higher rents to other mall tenants. A mall store benefits from store agglomeration because more consumers are attracted to the mall. The disadvantage is that each mall store faces competition from stores within the mall. In general, larger stores have more established reputations and are more likely to create benefits, no matter what type of mall.

Types of tenants

Each tenant in a mall can be classified into one of three types based on the reputation or brand name of the store: member of a national chain member of local chain; or independent store. A national chain could be a retail business that operates in at least four metropolitan areas that are located in three or more states. An independent store could be a business operating in two or fewer outlets in only one metropolitan area. A local chain could be a business that does not fall in the other two categories. This classification makes sense in terms of the propensity to pay for the mall space. Moreover, this could also make a difference with respect to owning or not owning the store.

The anchor

In the USA that anchors' rent per square foot is at least 72% lower than what a developer would normally charge a hypothetical store with a similar level of sales in a mall. One of the options available to a mall developer is to fill the mall with specialty stores that generate more sales per square foot and pay more rent per square foot, than traditional department stores. However, mall developers offer huge discounts to department stores because these anchors create traffic and increase the sales of other stores, which in turn is responsible for the higher rents developers charge other mall tenants. In the Indian context, such information is not available for researching. We may find a similar approach in mall developers marketing space.

First mover

A developer's first step in creating a new mall is the signing of the mall anchors to long-term contracts typically with duration of 25 or more years. Developers benefit in two ways from signing anchors first. They obtain lower-cost financing and second, they can charge other mall tenants higher rents if the mall tenants know that well known anchors will be in the mall. The other mall tenants know that their sales per square foot depend on the drawing power of the anchors. Because anchors do most of the advertising done by all stores in a mall, a mall store also knows that its promotional budget will be lower if it locates within rather than outside a mall. In India, especially developers develop even residential apartments in this manner.

Contracts

Mall lease contracts in the US have two components, a base (fixed) monthly rent and an average component that equals a sharing fraction times the difference between actual store sales and a pre-specified threshold value for sales. In the Indian context, sales of individual stores in the mall including the anchor are not transparent information available to the mall developer. In view of this, there is hardly a possibility of a change in the lease terms between anchors and other mall tenants. Financial and operational size and presence of the prospective anchor or tenant could make a difference in terms of the rents charged by the mall developer.

On an average, anchor stores occupy over 58% of total leasable space in US malls and yet pay only 10% of the total rent collected by the developer. The anchor stores' tremendous draw/footfalls can only explain the sheer size of this subsidy. In the Indian scenario, there is need to carefully value the presence of an anchor store and therefore price the space offered to them accordingly. This is more so in a situation where mall developers develop malls even without a clear anchor/anchor characteristics in mind.

The mall developer depends on each store owner to exert effort not only to maximise their own store's profit, and consequently their willingness to pay more rent, but also to generate more traffic to other stores as well. At the same time, success of the entire mall depends on how the developer maintains the mall over time—keeping it clean, remodelling it every few years, attracting the best stores, updating the mix of stores, keeping the mall competitive with other malls in the area, etc. As these actions from both parties are difficult to contract over, developers cannot use fixed rental contracts to align incentives. Therefore, in India soon, fixed rental contracts would give way to variable rate rental contracts that vary based on the sales of the tenants.

Anchors with well-established local market reputations are often in a commanding bargaining situation so that developers pay for some or all of the construction costs and agree to pay for remodelling costs even though the anchor technically owns the structure. One of the ways of tackling this situation is to make anchors own the retail space. If many anchors own their buildings and sign long-term contracts, mall owners can avoid shirking by anchors.

The mall developer is in an unenviable position while holding the supply of commercial retail property in any developing city. However, the crucial test of his decision-making skills depends primarily on how he deals with the valuation of space and manages selling place. Price discrimination is the key to dealing with this situation. Price discrimination can be across several dimensions as listed above. The better mall developer understands it operationally but the better would be space management in a mall.

ENTERTAINMENT AND RETAIL

Multiplex in a mall is the *mantra* for managing convergence of retailing and entertainment in India. The merging of entertainment and retail is one of the biggest trends facing stores, malls today. Shopping centres and business districts are using entertainment to set themselves apart from competition. Many innovative examples of how developers combine entertainment and retail exist in our country's urban areas. The idea of providing shoppers with a pleasurable experience offers an opportunity to increase sales. Organised retail outlets are attempting to attract large footfalls by setting up malls, which cater to every consumer group. In recent times, theatre chains in the form of multiplexes are being set up all over the country. Multiplexes, which provide high quality viewing experience, are fast emerging as one of the key drivers of footfalls in a number of organised retail outlets resulting in a renewed interest in investment and growth of movie exhibition business in India. The major players in the development of multiplexes are PVR cinemas, Adlabs Films, E-City Entertainment, Shringar Cinemas, Wave Cinemas and Inox Leisure. Multiplexes provide a steady stream of returning visitors to the mall, and have become a powerful anchor that increase patronage and attract new restaurants. But as the movie industry is moving towards multiplexes in part to combat the growing entertainment options at home, entertainment has also been used in the restaurant industry as casual dining establishments provided a sit-down atmosphere, table service, good prices, and televisions. Retailers view entertainment environments as luring shoppers who might otherwise choose home shopping by mail, television, and computer as the several new distribution channels are getting acceptable, especially due to paucity of time.

Stages in shopping centre development

It would be worthwhile to look at the development of shopping centres in the USA to see how entertainment has influenced it. The shopping centre is largely an American concept and the growth of the shopping centre industry has been documented well by their retail industry. It is thus appropriate to use the American context as a basis for identifying the five stages of shopping centre developments. The first stage and therefore the type of shopping centres that started in the USA such as Raleigh in 1949, while essentially reflecting a traditional retail strip format, was centrally managed with a uniformly themed appearance. A further innovation was that it focused on separating the pedestrian from the car. The second stage centres, which began to develop in 1958, took this concept further and separated the pedestrian from the outdoors by making the centres fully enclosed. In these climate-controlled consumer spaces, builders incorporated a further element -the leisure/entertainment dimension. Examples of these features included cinemas, cafes, children's amusements and the provision of entertainment such as live performances and fashion parades. The third stage saw developers more explicitly badge, market and manage leisure and entertainment in shopping centres as part of the shopping centre concept. Such a change began to occur in the US in the 1980's, as the traditional shopping centre anchors, the department stores, went into a period of decline. Shopping centre managers sought different approaches, such as themed restaurants, theme parks, much larger cinema complexes and a greater focus on food. Specialisation, with centres focusing upon one particular retail area, such as fashion, bulky goods, furniture, home and garden, food or convenience, often in a large retail format characterised the fourth stage.

There was no longer an assumption that centres will provide a one-stop shopping service, but rather, they catered to a segmented and highly mobile consumer population. These kind of centres were the most popular shopping centres in the 1990's. The fifth stage of shopping centres is still emerging. Key characteristics, however, are an increase in mixed-use developments, such as factory outlets, cinema, food, office, residential and convenience goods. This gives us an idea as to how entertainment that started in the second stage of development of shopping centres have remained almost a permanent fixture in organised retail, even in the USA.

Role of entertainment in retail

Many mall developers and managers have focused on making the shopping experience more entertaining or amusing, by adding movie theatres or live performances that consumers passively view. Perceptions about the entertainment value of a mall are key determinants of mall evaluation. The entertainment portion of the shopping mall does not need to be necessarily outside of the shopping experience—finding unusual or special stores is often entertaining. Entertainment, if looked at as an absorptive and passive experience, would mean that a shopper would describe shopping as both an activity as well as a passive (just looking) experience. Entertainment, in general, is important to tourists (including teens) visiting malls and makes a difference in mall choice. Teens, however, may be just as interested in escapist or play experiences that allow them to actively immerse themselves in consumption (either physically or virtually), e.g., theme park, virtual reality games or skateboard parks. Tourists (including teens) are looking for exciting and recreational activities. Mall owners are looking to entertainment retail to create a customer draw to other retailers in a centre. Regional malls are adding cinemas (often with 10 or more screens), restaurants, and other forms of entertainment to enhance the customer drawing power of a mall and extend that drawing power into the evening hours. Mall operators argue that making the mall an interesting entertainment venue has enhanced mall brand image not only with adults, but with teens and young adults as well.

Entertainment is also important in many downtown and regional development initiatives. Downtown areas are great places to bring together retail and entertainment. In many malls, communities, museums, sports centres and food and beverage facilities already exist. Developers can package these to create a pleasurable and more interesting shopping experience. Unfortunately, new retail/entertainment developments require a critical mass of residents and tourists. Further, entertainment facilities are very expensive to build and may only be feasible in larger market areas. Nevertheless, various opportunities might make sense in smaller communities. The creation of entertainment opportunities is especially important to our small communities. Not only do special events, festivals, parades, and businesses such as theatres provide much needed entertainment for their residents, they also have a positive impact on the surrounding business community. While the mall owner does not always design special events to ring cash registers, they do bring people and provide valuable exposure to businesses, architecture, exciting window displays, revitalisation progress, public spaces, and other assets that can help shape the interesting atmosphere of the area. If we can create a good experience for them, they will come back and support our business community.

Emphasis of entertainment in the US

By offering low prices, broad selection and expertise in given areas, category killers took a huge chunk of the retail market. Their annual sales made up about one-third of overall U.S. retail revenues in the 1990s. Malls, specialty stores, grocery stores, restaurants, and other retailers, knowing they could not compete with category killers' prices, decided to stress the quality of the shopping *experience* they offered, rather than just the products they sold. The Mall of America in Bloomington, Minnesota, completed in 1992, is America's premier entertainment mall. It boasts an indoor amusement park, Camp Snoopy, and the Underwater World Aquarium with walkthrough tunnels. The 43 million visitors per year enable the mall to rake in sales of $540 per square foot, on an average. In the restaurant business, Planet Hollywood, the Rainforest Café, and EatZi's restaurants sparked a parallel development in the late 1980s that came to be called "foodtainment." In November 1999, Vans Inc. of Los Angeles opened a 60,000-square-foot, $4 million, skating park and off-road bike track at the Ontario Mills Mall— offering its customers both entertainment and a place to try out products. It has also opened up a completely new revenue stream for the mall: customers who come just for the entertainment. In the first two weeks, one customer logged half dozen visits at $14 each!

In the toy industry, Wizards of the Coast, a 16-store Hasbro chain, got into the act against the toy-store category killers. Wizards offers its patrons fantasy games, collectible game cards, and Pokémon tournaments. A third of typical stores consist of game rooms with tables for trading cards and playing tournaments, plus banks of networked computers on which the young customers can play video games together. Wizards learned the same thing Van's did in the sportswear game: the entertainment is often worth more than the products. Card trading is free, but networked computer time is $7 per hour—and customers are lining up to pay it!

Entertainment Anchors in the US

Many regional malls are adding entertainment centres to appeal to the after-6 pm crowd and create a new downtown for the community. The Mall of America and Mills outlet malls are examples of how mall developers can combine retail and entertainment on a large scale. Entertainment anchors found in regional malls may include:

Theme Restaurants: Americans now view eating as the number one way to unwind and relax according to a recent Salomon Brothers report on the restaurant industry. Hard Rock Café, Planet Hollywood and the Rainforest Café combine dining with entertainment. They aim to transport patrons to an exotic and entertaining atmosphere, then offer merchandise that guests can take home as souvenirs.

Family Entertainment Centres: Indoor centres typically have more than 20,000 square feet with features that appeal to families with young children. They include climbing and play equipment, small-scale rides, video arcades, games, redemption games, food, beverage, and merchandise.

Theatres: Large mega-theatre complexes are drawing huge crowds in various areas around the country. In other areas, selected shopping centres offer high-impact film technology such as IMAX and Omnimax. They are giving new life to tired malls and are boosting sales of neighbouring businesses, especially those that sell software, videos and CDs.

High-Tech Entertainment Centres: These centres range from 10,000 to 40,000 square feet. They elevate the traditional video arcade to the next level by introducing sophisticated games, simulators and virtual reality in a themed environment.

In-store entertainment

Retailers can create innovative ways to provide shoppers with pleasurable experiences. They attempt to get people into the store, stimulate their emotions, keep them there and encourage them to buy. The following are examples of in-store entertainment:

Merchandise Demonstration Areas: Many sporting goods stores allow customers to try out sporting goods in the store before they pay.

Life Enhancement Activities: Specialty kitchen stores offer cooking lessons. Specialty stores dealing with building products offer "how-to" classes for its customers on a variety of home maintenance topics.

Children's Entertainment: Several children's stores offer children cartoons on an oversized screen in the store or provide child play areas in the store. Some of them also attract parents along with them by providing parenting lessons/other entertainment.

Relaxation: Many stores offered live soothing music and other forms of relaxation for shoppers as a form of entertainment.

Indian scenario

There are several examples of entertainment getting prominence in retailing in India. Multiplexes are becoming the anchor tenants of many of the upcoming malls and multiplexes themselves are wooing customers in different ways. A multiplex at Nariman Point has an art gallery, especially to encourage upcoming talent in the field. An interesting space for art curators, the gallery has around 11 artists appointed in their fold. Every month, the gallery displays works of one of the eleven with the price list and their contacts. These artists dabble in all kinds of art - abstract, portraits, along with paintings in different mediums. The gallery replaces the paintings as soon as it sells them. The art gallery came into being because of a rule, which requires every multiplex to have an art gallery. This multiplex is also conducting many activities surrounding the gallery. Portrait artists for the guests on the first anniversary, on Valentine's Day, a caricature artist sitting at the gallery are some such activities. The multiplex also conducts different activities such as Art Appreciation and Kids' workshops.

A look at potential malls will give an idea of the importance given to entertainment by retail developers –

A mall in Delhi - an area of 90,000 sq ft, the complex will have parking facilities for nearly 2,000 cars. A crèche, for around 30 children, and a special kids zone are also being set up. The Cineplex, with a total seating capacity of 900, will have seats with attached computer panels for ordering F&B items from one's seat in the hall. Also a part of the mall will be a Club. The company is looking at roping in 500 members for the club. The facilities on offer include a swimming pool, gym, beauty salon, bar and restaurants.

A multiplex in Vizag - the complex will comprise a mega shopping mall, a family entertainment centre, four theatres with 70mm screens, food courts and a restaurant. The complex will have parking space for 900 vehicles. A cellar and sub-cellar will accommodate these cars. The complex will also have banking facilities, coffee shops, fast-food outlets, multi-cuisine restaurants, pubs and gaming zone.

The state government, too, has been encouraging development of multiplexes especially where the old theatres are under renovation. For example, the Chandigarh administration has decided to increase the Floor Area Ratio (FAR) of the plots on which builders would be building multiplexes. The government would be increase the FAR from the existing 2 to 3 for up to one-acre plots. The FAR of plots measuring over one acre, which presently is 1.75, has been increased to 2.625. Other relaxations promised by the administration include an end to redtapism. Under the policy, the administration has allowed maximum FAR of up to 50 per cent of the minimum FAR within the same height after payment of conversion charges. The administration took the decision to make optimum utilization of available plots and to rationalize the FAR of cinema halls opting for conversion.

Entertainment to retail

Many theatre chains in the US have moved to include other forms of entertainment under their roofs, like roller rinks and miniature golf, to capitalize on the time people spend there. Carmike Cinemas, based in Columbus, Ga., the industry leader, recently opened its second joint venture with Wal-Mart, a concept called Hollywood Connection, in Goshen, Ind. The idea was that if people are going to be spending time at the movies, you try to capture more of that. It becomes a four-hour experience, instead of a two-hour experience. At another theatre chain, the attractions include coin-operated video games and General Motors cars on display (part of a marketing deal General Motors Corp. made with the theatre). It was not until the movie theatre industry shifted to multiplexes that chains realised the full potential of entertainment. In London, the Hard Rock Café successfully merged the concept of dining with pop culture. Customers experienced dining among images, memorabilia, and the music of musicians and actors. The concept proved to be popular and the Hard Rock Café soon became a tourist destination in its own right. Thus, entertainment and retailing are coexisting effectively even if the shift is from entertainment to retailing.

Entertainment centres

Entertainment venues seemed to have the flexibility to be located nearly anywhere, and generated trips and revenue. Developers saw entertainment venues as destinations in terms of their economic and revitalization potential. Race, income, and culture segregate as urban authorities develop suburbs. They lack urban space. Thus, merely building an entertainment venue would not guarantee success. Arcades and movie theatres would find they would not survive on entertainment alone, or in an area viewed as unsafe. Hence, the demand for the right location would become increasingly competitive. In the future, CBD locations would answer many marketing issues in entertainment centre development. We can view CBDs as cultural entertainment destinations in the not so distant future as they offer a central location, parking, financial incentives, connections, and people, all of which are vital to the success of these centres.

The goal of the entertainment centres for the city or developer is to create tax revenue, or to sell food, or merchandise, but for the visitor the overriding concept was to have fun. Entertainment is the draw and a large part of what creates the unique experience of the centre. The trick is to create a centre with the right balance of retail and entertainment. Too much retail in a shopping centre would make the visitor; view it as an ordinary shopping mall. Conversely, too many entertainment options would make shoppers forget to make purchases.

Thus, to create the balance of retail, entertainment, and, in essence, the level of fun, developers, and cities followed some basic rules of the trade. A good concept was not enough. Simply having a brilliant idea would not make a successful venture. For example in the USA in 1992, the Edison brothers had an idea to recreate the Star Trek experience for everyone. They hoped to put this experience in local shopping malls, but the concept failed largely because the owners had not realized the full potential of the medium. A few years after they debuted, they sold out to Paramount Inc. Paramount expanded the concept and incorporated it into their project. The entertainment centre had to be unique in architecture and design, so the tenants. They needed to offer the visitor something different from what he could find in the local shopping malls. This was a demanding task. High rents often prevented the establishment of local small businesses. Bigger malls copied their success too easily. What is today's truly special and unique experience is tomorrow's national chain. Another dimension was technology. Technology assisted in offering exciting and new experiences, but the centre itself could not be too high-tech. Behind the scenes there could be as many bells and whistles as it took to create the experience, such as laser shows on the food court ceilings, but merely having high-tech wizardry would not help market an entertainment centre. In addition, such high-tech products were expensive to produce and quickly became boring to the repeat visitor. The greatest design, performers, or products usually grew stale eventually. To be successful, the entertainment centres kept its offerings new and exciting. While they relied heavily on the tourist trade, they made the realization that local business was just as important, as locals could more easily repeat their business and could balance the fluctuations in the tourist industry. As with technology, entertainment centres endeavoured to keep the centre fresh. This created a balance in the types of retailers and balance of the costs of goods and services provided in the centre.

The key for retailers is to avoid getting so caught up in providing experiences that they forget their primary focus, which is selling goods and services. Consumer spending on entertainment has increased significantly in recent years. Real incomes are rising and households headed by 30- to 50-years old – a group that spends heavily on entertainment are increasing. As consumers reach their peak earning years, their propensity to dine out and seek entertainment will increase. Consumers want to use their time better by combining shopping and leisure. In recent years, shopping has become a chore with people spending less time in malls. Entertainment has emerged as a strategy that can influence where people shop and how long they spend shopping.

CHAPTER SEVEN

Retail Strategy and Challenges

INDEPENDENT VS. CHAIN STORES

You've Got Mail - a 1998 release movie starring Meg Ryan (owns an independent children's bookstore) and Tom Hanks runs (runs a chain of mega bookstores). The story is about Tom Hanks, opening one mega bookstore. It is just around the corner from Meg Ryan's, threatening to run her out of business. This is a romantic comedy centering on the whole chain store/ independent store clash. The making of the movie on the story woven around a conflict between two types of stores symbolises the level of intense competition and the feelings that revolve around these two types of stores. While the United States, where the retailing scenario has reached saturation, is facing such a problem, it may not be too far in the distant future that we in India would see such issues cropping up. Organised retailing making rapid strides would be a threatening development for many of the independent retailers in the country. In this context, therefore it is apt to look at the various dimensions of this potential conflict.

One of the biggest criticisms against the supermarkets or big chain stores is that as they expand, they destroy small-town charm, a wonderful, rare community and a rare and special place. However, in the U.S., the chain stores have overcome this by initiating neighbourhood meetings. Chain stores design new stores by working with the community to get inputs on the development of the site. Moreover, the neighbourhood receives a notice of the public hearing. These efforts try to assuage the feelings of the community and at the same time also results in the attachment to the developments in the store. The combined experience of an Old World store employee does not match with the trained chain store employee. The knowledge about the consumer for a long time employee at an independent store is much higher due to his long association with the consumer. These results in a much natural-friendly service compared to the chain store. This also stretches on to after sales service. Let us take the case of a musical instruments store, a case of repair of the guitar would probably be handled for free in an independent store by an experienced service person whereas the same may not be true of a chain store that would operate on a policy of charging for repairs.

Criticism against chain stores

There are other reasons where independent stores score over chain stores. Industry watchers have found chain stores guilty of such anti-competitive practices as colluding with suppliers to get wholesale rates lower than the industry standard that other stores have to settle for. However, this kind of collusion is also not yielding much result, as there have been successful attempts even in India of independent grocery retailers coming together for buying. Another emotional point that local small and independent retailers use against the chain stores is that buying local keeps your money circulating locally. This helps your local economy by boosting sales taxes and property values. Reportedly, in the U.S., chain stores persecute employees for attempting to unionise. The situation may not be far off to visualise in India. This is especially true due to the pressures of unemployment in India and the retail sector possessing the potential to employ large numbers. The contrast in the independent store scene in the Indian context is that family members employed in retail business never take into account the opportunity cost of their presence. This means that one can never estimate the right value of the cost of labour. One of the strongest criticisms against chain stores is that - every chain store is pretty much the same. The kind of standardisation that takes place in a chain store in order to obtain economies of scale as well as to present a consistent positioning, gets rid of its uniqueness in a local context. The extent of adaptation to the local situation can at best be minimal or else the character of a chain store may be lost.

The Australian government not so long back constituted a commission that looked into the concentration of the retailing business. During the course of the commission's term, it provided opportunity to all the sections of the retail sector to depose before the commission. The verbatim reproduction of the discussions in the commission's hearing make interesting reading. One of the interesting insights that one gets out of the commission's report is the extent to which the deep pockets of major chains result in merger and acquisition of regional chains in to the major chain. The commission sees an oligopolistic situation, which results in lesser variety as an anti-competitive measure. Experts see encouragement to specialty independent stores as one of the ways of maintaining the competition and the heterogeneity of the products available.

Advantages of independent stores

One of the advantages of an independent store in the present Internet age is the web presence of a local specialty store. This will let you buy from your local store with all the convenience offered by online competitors. Moreover, in the case of U.S. book stores, it has been observed that local independent stores are more likely to have the courage and freedom to stock controversial titles whereas national chains more likely to cave in to regional pressure groups and pull titles from shelves nationwide. In addition, every independent store has its own unique character. They provide variety in the midst of a monotony of standardised products available from chain stores.

The superstore and chain stores have become the industry standard in only a few short years. These superstores carry tens of thousands of stock keeping units of various products in well-lighted, wood-panelled layouts. In the case of bookstores, these stores resemble more like comfortable library reading rooms than traditional, cramped bookstores. Customers get huge discounts on books from best-seller lists and may spend hours browsing through a dizzying array of categories. Shoppers can relax in reading chairs to peruse books before deciding to buy. Top-name authors stop by for autograph parties, and poetry and literary groups schedule meetings and readings for regular customers who sip espressos from the coffee bar.

Disadvantages of independent stores

Some of the disadvantages of independent stores are that most of them are tiny, under-stocked, and poorly staffed. Customers now would tend to visit such stores only if a store specialises in a unique niche or offers a unique atmosphere or service. Owners typically operated the traditional neighbourhood store during hours of convenience to them. That is, they were likely to be closed at night and on Sundays and holidays-prime leisure hours for consumers who want to shop. Small floor plans and small budgets meant that there was no depth of selection from which to choose. In some cases, small staff and poor employee training meant customers' questions went unanswered. There was little money with which to advertise. There was rarely enough volume to attract special events. Special orders and other unique customer needs were often unfulfilled. Profit levels were small, so discount prices were not possible.

Today's most successful, individually owned stores tend to be unique specialty shops catering to a clearly defined segment of the market. For example, popular are crafts stores that appeal only to consumers who want to make ceramic items such as pottery, paint these items in the store and fire them in the store's kiln. These true niche operations have limited growth potential. Mom-and-pop stores that succeed today must do so on the strength of personal service and individual relationships with their customers. For example, independently owned flower shops still thrive by operating personal charge accounts for their customers and by remembering their customers' favourite flowers, gift recipients, birthdays and anniversaries. Likewise, most major cities have at least one large, independent hardware store that stays on top by having extremely knowledgeable and patient floor personnel who have known their customers for years. In the absence of personal relationships with the employees in an independent store, many shoppers opt for the apparent stability and reliability (and frequently discounted prices) of a chain store. Shoppers, who decide to buy from a major chain, rather than a mom-and-pop store, know that a chain store is more likely to be around in the future if the customer has a problem. If the customer moves, it is likely that the chain store will have a location in the next town or neighbourhood. Chains are also more likely to have a defined and enforced money-back guarantee policy.

Chain store management

Some of the accusations against the chain store are that the products available in these stores are generally inferior to an independent store. This is because chain stores need to achieve consistency and it is a lot easier to do this at a lower quality threshold. Moreover, it is simpler to train staff and narrow product range results in lesser product fails and better quality control. There is less choice. If the next nearest store stocks the same product at the same price, there is no incentive to go further afield. It is fewer hassles keeping a limited number of product lines. Chains spare store managers the task of making choices about what to stock. However, in spite of all these disadvantages, the independents lost the battle in the developed world because of financial reasons. When a new chain store is set up, the company has reserves of cash and profits from its other stores to fund heavy cost cutting at the new stores. The big chains can afford the large initial investment to purchase a store in a prime site, not something that an ordinary independent store could do very easily. This prime location makes it easier to get more noticeable and in the retailing business, location does play a very important role.

Independent store response

There seems to be some light at the end of the tunnel for independent stores. According to recent reports, big chain supermarkets in the U.K. are unable to satisfy demand for organic products. This implies that people are prepared to dig a little deeper in their pockets for tastier food. Moreover, there seems to be contempt for just going for the bland tasting but nicely polished and consistent products that consumers otherwise have to endure in food chain stores. One of the reasons attributed to specialty spicy food taking off in the U.K. in recent years is the boredom with standardisation of the traditional British fare. Supermarkets are the biggest impact chain stores. They achieved this because they could offer cheaper food, the convenience of the one stop shop which initially offered a higher quality product than many complacent grocers. As the retailing wheel gains momentum, the independent specialty outlets gain importance, leading to a change in the strategies of the chain stores.

It may sound strange, but it is true that many times the range of the brands/products offered in a superstore might be smaller than in an independent store for specific categories. Considering this, we can say that the existence of independent stores help in keeping the broad variety and the vast number of existing product categories, since the scope of choice that they make possible to the consumer, is much larger. A consumer should consider the different qualities of service offered in an independent store and in a chain/superstore. If one goes into an independent shop, it is more likely that the salesperson is able to give him/her all the information necessary on a brand/product. In a chain store or in a superstore "the shop floor staff may be regarded by some as minimum-wage shelf-stockers with little knowledge of the brands/products". In other words, consumers may more directly link independent bookshops with quality while volume of sales and the mass market would relate to the chains. In order to reach big volume of sales, superstores usually practice high margin of discounts on several of their brands/products. Consumers might see this practice as a depreciation of the value of brands. If one enters into a superstore she/he will see discount signs and promotional displays all around it, and the discounted brands will be much easier to access than the other ones because of the large number of promotions usually found within the supermarkets.

Defending superstores

Some of the most critical aspects consumers need to consider in this analysis are the deals involving superstores and suppliers, through which retailers sell displays and the best places on the shelves. The superstore chains may have a cooperative marketing scheme that involves suppliers paying to promote brands by buying placement in the stores and advertising in newspapers and magazines under the chains' names. Add to this that superstores chains can decisively influence sales when get behind a brand. One of the dangers that we can visualise with this kind of an approach is that when the independent stores disappear, there is the risk that quality of the brands supplied and displayed do not matter anymore, as long as they can generate large volumes of sales.

There is another current view that defends the superstores as being an element of culture democratisation. It argues that the superstores are always very well located, and also offer a huge variety of brands/products at different quality and prices, making products much more accessible to a larger number of people. Superstores are attracting people who earlier did not enter a small shop before because there was no shop nearby. One of the main roles of the superstores so far has been popularising the habit of shopping, in the sense that the boom of the chains, and the appearance of the superstores, the market for products has been growing. Thus, superstore chains can claim credit for enlarging the market for various products. Concerning discounts, if on the one hand high margin of discounts offered might decrease the value of brands/products, on the other hand the same high margin of discount might be providing the retail industry's growth, and more than this–its survival. Suppliers need to make a profit to continue investing in new brands/product categories, and nowadays there are many more products competing for the consumer's shopping expenditure. From this point of view, discounts not only appreciate brands/ product categories, but also make superstores fundamental for the retail industry's wealthy future.

Chain superstores have been playing an important role in changing the concept of shops. Shops have changed from places that only sell products into places with a nice and warm atmosphere, where people can relax, have coffee, browse the shelves, and buy products. Due to this new atmosphere, people spend more time within the shop and look at a larger number of brands/ product categories. Even if they do not buy anything, the superstores still work as a tool of culture dissemination, because they allow people to know and absorb more.

Last, but not the least, the main argument against the cooperative scheme is that although superstores sell their displays and best space on their shelves to suppliers, they will only display brands with good sales potential. If a brand has no potential, the chain would not be displayed visibly on it, not even for good money, because the amount of money that the shop would lose compared to the revenue generated by displaying a "better" brand would be bigger. However, no one is obliged to buy the brands that are specially displayed - it is a democratic system. If people buy them, it is because they consider those brands/product categories to be good ones or at least, to be good value for their money. Why should anyone judge whether brands that people want to buy are good or bad, and what would be the criteria for judging? Also why should this judgment be considered more important than people's opinion? The concept of "good' or "quality" is extremely difficult to be bound. People have the right to buy whatever they consider more convenient for them, and the superstores might work just as a facilitator in this process: They are merely showing more visibility to the brands that might attract more people's interest.

The debate of Independent versus Chain store is decades old. It started ever since the concept of chain stores flooded the U.S.. The concept has also picked up in other developed countries. In this context, it would be worthwhile to look at some of the recommendations of the independent retailers association of Australia. These included:

- Capping retail grocery market share of major chains by 80%.

- Introducing legislation providing stiff penalties for abuse of market and divestiture powers.

- Making mandatory economic and social impact statements for all new shopping centres and significant retail developments.

- Establishing new national watchdog to monitor market share of major chains with mandatory bi-annual public reports on retail grocery prices and anti-competitive behaviour.

- Requiring disclosure to manufacturers' trading terms and conditions on a confidential basis to ensure transparent and fair pricing policies (with six-month reviews).

These are the kinds of issues that may crop up with the introduction of FDI in the retailing sector and the development of the superstore retail chains. While the Indian retailing scenario is different and provides scope for enough competition, the pros and cons of both forms of stores discussed may be weighed before formulating policies for the retail sector.

HR CHALLENGES IN RETAILING

The development of organised retailing in India poses a challenge of human resource development to serve the needs of this sector. There has been development in the form of several business schools embarking on retail management specialisations to suit the future needs of this sector. The big organised retailers have transformed their existing training establishment into institutes of retail management. However, it would be worthwhile to understand the needs of the sector, given the trends that experts have observed in the west.

The Wal-Mart model is looked at as the best model to emulate all around the world and especially in the developing countries especially when it comes to offering products at prices that are competitive. An extremely efficient production process characterises this model. The operations that make up the heart of retailing – buying products, distributing them to stores, and selling them to customers – are streamlined and linked in one continuous "just-in-time" chain. Wal-Mart pioneered the concept of using technology to manage inventory, and in recent years has invested several million dollars in its information system. In contrast to this taut efficiency, retailers pay little attention to the human resource side of the equation. The retail transformation model as epitomised by Wal-Mart is a restructuring model based on technology and process, not on developing human resources. Low-wage strategies, unskilled jobs, imposition of two-tiered wage systems and substitution of contingent for full-time workers are some methodologies adopted by Wal-Mart in achieving 'cost leadership'. The stereotype of retail jobs – part-time, high turnover, low wages, and no benefits – holds considerable truth.

In this context, therefore it would be useful to see the typical dimensions of work atmosphere in retailing. This sector is heavily weighted towards front-line workers, more than any other sector in the economy. Women are in fact quite concentrated in industries such as apparel stores. The nature of jobs as well as the composition of the workforce presents a special picture that needs to be tackled. New issues like timing of stores and gender related inconveniences might also crop up.

Nature of retailing

The retailer in New Delhi does not compete with firms in Thailand, but rather with others in the same region. This is not to say that service industries have been immune to globalisation. In fact, retail chains outsource specific operations such as data processing. However, the core of service delivery remains face-to-face interaction. To a significant degree, then, the forces that govern competition, product markets, and workplace strategies remain firmly rooted in the domestic sector. Therefore, in retailing one needs to contend with a situation where the retailer creates jobs exciting enough for youngsters to join. Employee retention through job enlargement in retail plays a crucial role as job markets perform better for skilled personnel. In the Indian context, the labour market situation would be complex. While literacy and skill enhancements are happening at the potential employee level, retailers are creating jobs at the same pace. On the other hand, new retail jobs may benefit from unskilled labourers. In both the cases, the retail company has a task to handle in terms of human resource development from entirely different perspectives.

Taylorisation

In much of the retail industry, the task content of front-line jobs has historically been low, segmented, and "Taylorised", requiring little skill or training. There have already been large investments in the machinery and processes surrounding these low-skill jobs. Supplier network firms in developed retail markets like the U.S. are mostly tied to these jobs. In this scenario, the potential gains from focusing on improving the productivity of operations far outweigh those that chains may reap from instituting a wholesale change in how they deploy human resources, – in that the risks and costs are lower. Interactive service work is not as amenable to Taylorisation or the engineering approach to work design typical of manufacturing. However, this in fact is what low cost standardised retailing strategises to achieve. A cycle of low wages, little training, low morale, and high turnover, leads to customer dissatisfaction and therefore loss of sales. If this vicious cycle needs to be broken, then the only way is to concentrate on specific service requirements of consumers and empowering front line employees.

Retailing in the typical service marketing mould emphasises on people, processes and physical presentation. While process and physical presentation are greatly controllable, people part of the service marketing is a difficult dimension to handle. It involves satisfaction of employees through internal marketing and therefore creating better interaction marketing and external marketing. The prescription for satisfactory internal marketing would involve a focus on increased worker discretion in meeting customer needs, the empowerment of front-line workers to carry out their customer contact roles, integration of employees into a winning team and concentration on service quality.

Types of service differentiation

One of the crucial differentiating factors in retailing could be the nature of service delivered by the store. This differentiating factor has great implications in terms of human resource development. If we discuss the two extreme forms of differentiation based on service, we would get an idea of its impact on retail employees. The first form of retailing differentiation by a store could be stressing personalised and in-depth service. A classic example is Nordstrom's famed sales workers, who are essentially personal consultants who build long-term relationships with their upper class clientele, informing them of sales and new products, setting aside items and even making purchases for the customer over the phone. This practice is called Clientelling.

Clientelling

Clientelling has spread in the retail industry, especially in America. In some American stores, sales associates can access a client database and submit structured queries about a customer's buying habits, in order to tailor their service. This form of customer relationship building would result in the requirement of many employees, particularly skillful in communication and analytical in understanding buying patterns on a continuous as well as customised basis, to succeed in retail marketing. This scenario is analogous to the personalised financial services offered to high net worth individuals by the banking sector in the country. In India, this segment is small and not the one who would take to organised retail efforts in this direction in a big way. In markets for high-income customers or products requiring expert advice, multi-skilled and better-trained workers are required – they need to have the technical background to give advice, soft skills to build relationships with customers, and ability and knowledge to make decisions on their own. In these niches, jobs are often above average for the industry.

The (consumer) market scenario, which is emerging in India, is what we can describe as below. There is a growing labour force participation of women and an increase in working hours. There is need for double incomes to sustain a relatively better quality of living. Here the market that is developing is one that is not in need of a high quality service. The market being tapped here is consumers who are pressed for time, who shop for value, who know what they want and get annoyed at invasive sales staff. What is, therefore, expected is a standardised quick service.

Service segmentation

The two definitions of quality service – depth versus speed – are based on a segmentation of the market. They can be the basis for segmentation of job quality. In the retail market as it develops in India, some firms may choose to compete for larger shares of standardised products produced by low wage workers carrying out relatively simple tasks. Other firms may choose to tailor production to a high value-added, high quality product at the upper end of the same market. Both strategies may prove successful in generating profits, but with quite different consequences for workers' wages. In the first instance, job satisfaction as well as wages is much better than the second situation where repetitive standardised work makes interaction marketing lose its sheen over a period time. Man-Man interaction unlike man–machine interaction in a production shop floor in quality, dips by even perception!

Trends in Indian retailing

Hypermarkets in each metropolitan city in India targeting price conscious consumers, providing mind boggling assortment of products is the trend of the future as is mall retailing. Each of these forms of retailing involves extensive use of labour for various activities. Increase in labour force and variability in demand and human resource requirements also pose difficulties in scheduling. Computers can have a major impact on staff scheduling which now is a time-consuming and inefficient process. Scheduling software can help find the most efficient and least costly allocation of labour, taking into account, worker availability, payroll budget, individual skills, and productivities. This can greatly reduce retailer's payroll costs. The task of affixing price labels to every item in the store was once time-consuming, especially when prices changed or during sales, but is now becoming obsolete with the advent of barcodes. The counting of products in stock, once done manually by a slew of workers at night, is now increasingly done either automatically (i.e., when cash registers record that a product has been sold), or by fewer workers who use hand-held scanning computers. The growing practice of having outside vendors stock their own pre-packaged and pre-priced products (and sometimes even sell them) also reduces the amount of in-store labour.

The retailer sees this type of effect at the back end of retailing, the warehouse, where increased computerisation and scanning has actually reduced the need for skilled labour, or labour altogether. It has generally not brought an upskilling of core front-line jobs. The retail sector (and other low-wage service industries like it) simply serves as a temporary way station for most workers. The image is of teenagers earning extra spending money, mothers wanting to get out of the house for a few hours a week, retirees looking for something to occupy their time especially in the U.S. A typical Wal-Mart store has one store manager, four assistant managers, and 235 non-salaried workers, who are paid by the hour. The question is whether replication of the model in India would be helpful for the employment situation facing India. One of the key issues facing the retail industry as it develops, is the management of skilled as well as unskilled employees and their potential career plans. In the case of the unskilled employee who would start as a front line salesperson or as an in-store employee in any department, would need constant training to keep him updated at the same time job rotation. However, the upward career ladder has limited opportunities because of decreased hierarchy levels and increased use of information technology. At the managerial level as the operation gets detailed, managing on a regular basis might tend to become monotonous unless the retail entity has an urge for creativity. In other words it must always look for new ways of developing retailing. The use of games and contests in store for employees becomes a routine after a period. If, therefore, the retailer has to sustain employee interest for a longer career in retailing, he has to tackle these issues. There must be a strong statement of commitment to better development of human resources on a continuous basis. The concurrent development of multiple formats of retailing would provide required impetus and interest in retail as a career. A sustained effort in partnership with educational institutions is also required to remove the stigma of retailing jobs.

E-RETAILING AND NET MALL STRATEGY

The Indian retailing scene has not been as encouraging with respect to e-retailing as a concept. This has been mainly because of the reach and quality of access as well as the medium used in transaction. However, these aspects in the immediate future may not be a limiting feature for the spread of Internet retailing. Tremendous efforts are on to spread IT to rural areas and increased rural connectivity is being experimented through cheap wireless connectivity, indigenously developed. We have also been successful in developing applications in several local languages to suit the requirements of different states in India. In view of these positive developments, E-retailing is set to stage a major comeback in India. Add to this, the effect of a favourable monsoon, the spread of computers in rural areas etc. In the short term (5-10 years), retail stores will have nothing to fear from the Internet. The size of the Internet population will stay relatively small and at least half the population will lack the equipment, skill or inclination to use computers for home shopping. Security issues will also have to be resolved in this period before people learn to trust the medium.

Even in 20 years time, when some 60%-70% of the population will have regular access to the Internet, several forms of retail establishments will still be required. The largest category will be those that deal in inspection goods: car yards, fashion houses, jewellers, restaurants, cinemas etc. Products that have high transport costs, such as groceries and home hardware, will most likely operate in a slightly different fashion. Consumers will purchase goods on-line and retailers then would deliver to homes or pick them up from local warehouse outlets. Established firms will find it costly to maintain both retail outlets and local warehouses. Initially, major retail chains will resist online ordering because of their investment in retail premises. Over time, online ordering will gain in popularity as consumers take advantage of the lower prices and greater convenience offered by warehouse outlets.

Firms dealing with information goods are at greatest risk. Banking, education, investment services, insurance, software retailers and travel agents are examples of information-based products that have low delivery costs from a virtual shop front. If Internet traders develop a reputation for passing on large cost savings - savings that result from not owning a network of retail outlets - then traditional businesses could be faced with large reductions in demand within a 10-year framework.

Problems with on-line retail experience

Some of the existing issues in developed countries where online retailing is very popular relate to consumer use experience. About two-thirds of online stores have ineffective search engines, leaving customers frustrated and apt to do business with a competitor. While analysts rate a few top e-retailers, like LandsEnd, Petco and L.L. Bean, highly for their sites' search capabilities, the majority of on-line stores treat search engines like an afterthought. That means millions of shoppers are left groping through online stores, doing repetitive searches, thinking up more and more descriptive words, browsing aimlessly through page after page — until they leave to shop at another Web site or even a brick-and-mortar store.

A majority of the online retailers cannot properly match misspelled search terms with the correct product. In addition, there is an absence of any offer to help shoppers sort their search results, such as allowing them to pick out a certain brand, price range or availability. Moreover, most of them fail to allow customers to describe the item they are searching for in their own terms, instead of demanding a specific name or title. E-retailers themselves were unhappy about online fundamentals such as site navigation and setting up online accounts. However, industry experts rate better aspects like the online ordering process, site functionality, and content.

Online marketing and segmentation

Online retailers rather miss out basics of marketing in e tailing. With the advent of technology and therefore the facility available to track the customer though clicks, one of the easiest forms of segmentation that most online retailers adopted was segmentation based on transaction data. However with increase in competition many online retailers realise attitudinal data is more effective than transactional data for segmenting customers, though even in develoued countries many retailers do not perform any segmentation. Among those performing segmentation, only a miniscule minority use attitudinal information to segment customers. In addition, these are the dangers of untargeted sales promotions and untargeted newsletters. These leave even potential consumers unhappy at the idea of on-line shopping. While most online retailers recognise the importance of knowing customer behaviour and preferences, few have the skills or resources to acquire such information.

It may be worthwhile to note in the Indian context, that despite escalating number of retailers selling online abroad, revenues are still concentrated in a few mature sites. In addition, multi-channel retailers such as Dell Computer, Charles Schwab, Eddie Bauer, and Lands End experience greater revenue, better conversion rates and more customer loyalty. Moreover, research has found that online retailers also invest heavily to expand their reach and customer base. Online retailers reinvest 6% of their revenue in marketing and advertising, compared with 4 % for most traditional stores. Moreover, online retailer marketing and advertising costs per order generated is $26 as compared with $2.50 for traditional stores.

Consumer effects

The best thing a company can do for a consumer is to make sure that the site is easy to navigate; make consumer service telephone numbers easy to find; make sure search engines are top-of-the-line; and help people answer basic questions. From the standpoint of an individual buyer, the Internet offers a convenient, hassle-free medium to shop at, one that offers both privacy and is not limited by stringent time schedules or constraints of a store-level inventory. Additionally, the web provides a number of buyer-empowering sites that permit an easy comparison of prices and features of products that are available from different e-tailers. This comparison contributes to more informed decision-making. Comprehensive evaluation was not possible earlier in the traditional shopping context. Buyers earlier often faced an array of choices and had to bear onerous search costs if they wished to evaluate their alternatives in greater depth. However, the ease and convenience of comparison shopping that is possible today on the Internet tends to cause many prospective buyers becoming deal-prone as they are better able to sift through value propositions of their offered choices. This new-found facility represents a negative development for online retailers because it stands to hasten a phenomenon known as cost transparency which dilutes brand loyalty and makes consumers reluctant to paying any "unreasonable" price premiums.

Retailer effects

A key threat that the Internet poses to retailers is the seamless access to information of product attributes that consumers are able to secure at no or very little cost. Information has a way of making buyers more sensitive to prices and therefore more averse to paying an excessive premium. For the first time in the history of economic exchange, the seller presents the buyer with a wealth of information about competitive offerings, their attributes and characteristics, as well as objective (third party) evaluations of their quality. Moreover, the Internet equips the buyer with sophisticated software tools that process the complex information and determine the value that each represents on a host of buyer-specified yardsticks. Not surprisingly, marketers are, therefore, compelled to compete on price and ultimately end up engaging in a self-sacrificing price war.

Viewed from the perspective of suppliers, the Internet represents a new and inexpensive distribution channel that provides direct and instant access to prospective buyers on a global level. Additionally, it facilitates implementation of hitherto difficult marketing objectives of personalised (or relationship) marketing and securing consumer involvement at various stages of new product development. The Net may allow suppliers to co-opt customer competencies and leverage *their* knowledge for such expensive and risky tasks as product design and testing, in ways never possible before. An oft-cited instance is how Microsoft Windows 2000 software was beta-tested by more than 200,000 unpaid consumer volunteers who pointed out bugs and made invaluable suggestions that significantly decreased the time-to-market the product.

Benefits to consumers/retailers

Some of the benefits of e-retailing are that Web convenience makes the job of shopping for the consumer easy and the marketer to fulfil the order. Potential for Impulse Purchase is quite high given that a click of the mouse helps you buy anything that a retailer shows. The tremendous scope for customisation and versioning capability makes the product/service to the online retailer to sell to every customer in a unique manner, thus achieving the idea of mass customisation. Therefore, the estimation of the market potential also becomes much more reliable. The utility of on-line search capabilities makes the job of comparison-shopping for shopping goods easier. Retailers themselves incorporate Comprehensive Information Provision on the site in some cases and make the job for the buyer that much easier.

The benefits for the retailer are in terms of technological facility to provide better visualisation. In addition, Exploitation of Network Effects helps in spreading word of mouth (mail) communication better. Technology helps in on-going communication with the consumer as well as a greater and in-depth understanding of the consumer through customer information. Advanced visualisation techniques like graphics technology (animation, sound/image effects) gives many opportunities to present a product in a way that the consumer will be impressed and motivated to buy it. Online retailing allows on-click purchasing (for registered customers or members) which leaves virtually no time for second thoughts or reasoning about the purchase of the product. This helps in expediting the purchase.

Visitor centricity

The point that the e-retailer, however, has to bear in mind is that the interface provided must be visitor centric. This means that the web pages in the website must be fast loading and transaction enabling. The website of the online retailer should utilise productivity software that does not burden the shopper. For example: Auto-responder, send information to the visitor immediately upon request at the site; Shopping cart software - simplifies the shopping process; Statistics analyser - analysed site traffic to help improve the site and email package, automate list management and correspondence to improve communication.

Internet mall

Internet malls are subsidiaries of major Internet portals, which attract millions of visitors through news, games, and many other forms of entertainment. Yahoo! Shopping, eShop at msn.com, or Shop@AOL at aol.com are some of the leaders. Rediff shopping in the Indian context is one of the pioneers in this space. Similar to conventional malls, Internet malls have numerous affiliated stores, thrive on their ability to attract consumers, and derive their revenue streams by collecting fees from their member stores. However, Internet malls differ from conventional malls in at least two major ways. First, Internet malls have an open structure, i.e., even when an online store is affiliated with an Internet mall, consumers can still access that store directly. For example, the popular electronic store JandR is a member of Yahoo! Shopping. A consumer who wants to shop at JandR can find it at the Electronics section of Yahoo! Shopping. Alternatively, this consumer can simply go to www.jandr.com. If a brick and mortar store is located in a conventional mall, then consumers have to go to the mall to shop at that store. By contrast, online stores have virtual locations and consumers can access them directly. This is regardless of whether they are affiliated with an Internet mall or not.

E-mall vs. Conventional Mall

Internet malls distinguish themselves by the presence of search engines and featured stores. The search engine allows a customer to compare prices for a product across stores more easily than in a conventional mall, where a consumer needs to have a sharp memory and endure several shopping trips in order to comparison shop. A featured store has its logo embedded in a large icon that is placed in a prominent spot on the Internet mall's web page. With a single click, the internet mall directs a consumer to the featured store. Note that when using the search engine, consumers take the initiative in determining where to shop, whereas the Internet mall guides them to the featured store. The presence of search-engine and featured-stores lead to consumer shopping behaviour that is significantly different from that in conventional malls. Growth in one-stop shopping and consumer's economising on shopping time has led to the proliferation of product assortments in grocery stores and supermarkets. In the presence of general-purpose search engines, online stores compete with each other regardless of whether they are in or outside of Internet malls. Since consumers differ in their ability and willingness to search, the search engine facilitates price comparisons for those who are price sensitive, while featured stores provide one-stop shopping to those who are price insensitive.

An Internet mall reduces price competition among online stores by leveraging two notable features: the search engine and the featured store. The search engine facilitates price comparisons but requires consumers to spend time going through pages of search results. In contrast, consumers are directed to the featured store with a single click. Consumers trade off price reductions with reductions in search time, leading to higher prices in the featured stores and a consequent softening of price competition. Search costs are the product of a category specific search time and unit time cost. To choose between search engine driven comparison-shopping and featured store shopping, consumers form price expectations that help them compare the reduction in price obtained by searching with the cost of the search itself. As search costs increase, the price differential between the featured stores and non-featured stores becomes larger, as is also the case when more shoppers purchase through the mall. A mall should feature stores free when more shoppers purchase through it and when consumer search costs are substantial. Conversely, it should charge fees to feature stores when fewer people purchase there and search costs are low. Finally, while a large mall should charge percentage fees to participating stores, a small Internet mall may optimally offer free participation to online stores.

The various decisions in the Internet mall relate to the fee structure, nature of featuring of the individual store, nature of price setting and nature of searching and buying in an Internet mall. Internet malls can be expected featured store shoppers to pay a higher price, but the price differential should be no greater than the savings in search costs they would incur if they used the search engine. By contrast, E-mall comparison shoppers purchase from either the low price store, which can be the non-featured store (more frequently) or the featured store (less frequently). These decisions referred above differ significantly from the conventional brick and mortar mall.

The developments in online retailing mimic the developments in brick and mortar retailing. However, the nature of interface with the consumer makes E-tailing more amenable to digital goods marketing, compared to goods that need a feel and touch. In that respect, there lies a fundamental product level segmentation. In terms of the consumer as the competition hots up in the online retailing arena, new ways of tracking customers would be required in order to be efficient marketers.

RETAIL ENTERTAINMENT CONVERGENCE

Convergence is happening in the retail industry. The entire industry abroad and slowly in India too is readying itself to the fact that entertainment and retail are converging. Projects like Fun Republic, E city, Forum Mall, Millennium Plaza, Hakone are proof to this development. Retail analysts expect the Family Entertainment Centre sector in India as a concept to grow at a rapid pace. They expect the number of centres to double in the coming three years with investment increasing from Rs. 3,000 million to Rs 20,000 million. In this context, it would be worthwhile to reflect on the aspects that are important as elements of entertainment retail.

Shopping centre owners and managers are always looking for ways to boost traffic and increase sales. In addition, entertainment operators continually seek new venues that will help increase their bottomlines. Both have similar strategies for reaching their goals. Entertainment venues thrive on traffic and bring in traffic. Serving as a traffic generator is the best thing a family entertainment centre has to offer to the promoter. While the benefits of mixing entertainment with retail are easy to see, shopping centre owners and managers, as well as entertainment operators, realise that they need to overcome obstacles. One of the disadvantages of putting an entertainment centre inside a mall involves the hours of operation. A mall's operating hours are generally not the same as those of the entertainment centre. Late hours kept by the entertainment centre also create a security issue, both for the mall itself and for the visitors to the centre. In addition, parking may not be as convenient. An entertainment provider must first determine if it can afford a shopping centre's base rent. Entertainment venues do not make the best retail tenants because rents and overrides from other retail-type tenants are generally much better. The cost of doing business in a retail setting has turned some entertainment operators away from malls in the U.S.A.

Types of entertainment

Entertainment is becoming more of an area, which can be, will be and should be combined with shopping and movie theatres. Knowing when a retail/entertainment mix will work, is the first step on the road to success. There needs to be a clear picture of what entertainment is and should be for a particular setting. While entertainment can range from games and rides to movie theatres and skating rinks to restaurants and food courts, there are few operators in the industry that have combined all of these components successfully even in the U.S.A. While there are exceptions, most people who are successful in the food business have not done a very good job in the entertainment business, and vice versa. Historically, operators of one have not understood operators of the other. When considering entertainment, mall owners and managers have traditionally worked with movie theatres. In addition, while they are increasingly learning more about other entertainment options, their experience with operating them is limited.

Consumer end

The neo-rich consumers in India have started to invest in leisure differently, spending more on activities rich in amusement or diversion value but requiring little time to enjoy. Instead of the former 7 to 14-day long trips, overnight trips, long weekends at nearby hotels and resorts, and three-day cruises, all have become popular as disposable income and time became scarcer. These changes in leisure spending, driven by concerns over job security and the time constraints imposed by an increasing number of two-income families make traditional avenues of entertainment more difficult to schedule.

A value-packed shopping experience includes the anticipation felt as the customer thinks of visiting the entertainment-spiked retail centre. It also includes the customer's heightened experience as he moves happily around a shopping world laced with visual, auditory, and other sensory and emotional delights. Finally, the customer remembers the shopping experience and expands that memory into anticipation of the next visit. Exploitation of entertainment promises to redefine how the consumer perceives value. As a result, retailing is going through massive format changes that will alter the shopping experience, perhaps permanently.

A typical retail + entertainment combination

The most frequently encountered version of the "pure" entertainment centre consists of a multi-screen cinema; two or three high-atmosphere, "brand-name" restaurants; perhaps a nightclub or two; and an eclectic mix of tenants. Tenants are of local, regional and/or national repute and offer unique goods and services, or they present ordinary goods in a unique and entertaining way. The mall builder spares virtually no expense to create an architecturally compelling street scene for the entertainment centre. Ambiance through imaginative architecture, sensitive site planning, and a liberal use of street performers, carts and kiosks complete a "value-added" environment.

It is relatively easy to find entertainment for the mall. Dozens of entertainment providers are packaging affordable, exciting experiences. Attractions are not a problem. The trick is to create an entertainment mix and integrate it into the mall in a way that increases traffic and lengthens the average shopper's stay. The right combination of attractions can measurably increase the mall's trading area. Although entertainment can boost traffic at a mall, can it increase the sales volume of existing tenants? Undoubtedly, entertainment brings new people to the mall. Theoretically, once these potential shoppers experience the ambiance, they will return repeatedly and will soon start buying things other than entertainment. The Mall of America, which was built from scratch as entertainment retail, has certainly shown that entertainment on a grand scale brings shoppers by the millions.

Restaurants offering good food in a high atmosphere are going to prosper. Nightclubs and dinner theatres will proliferate. Participation retail, such as bookstores with reading and socialising centres, will become the order of the day. Urban entertainment districts have attracted hundreds of municipal and state government followers. Cities seem especially anxious to support these projects, as they see entertainment as the saviour of their most neglected commercial areas. When builders build such projects, they are often on a massive scale involving many city blocks and huge acreage. The hope is that shoppers and businesses will be drawn back to what had been a struggling, decaying area. Revitalisation efforts incorporate movies, special purpose live-entertainment theatres, interesting restaurants, game arcades and mini theme parks. Given the state of many of our cities, the future of this type of development seems assured.

Entertainment centres with strong initial impact have some common features. They have two or three strong, exciting anchor tenants that generate repeat visits. The location is well known. There is a large daytime population in the market area. The primary market area has 3 to 4 million people. The project has strong marketing and experienced, focused management. The project is different, unique, and has an exciting atmosphere. A multiplex theatre may be part of it, but that is not enough to sustain long-term success. Uniqueness has a way of fading quickly. The mall developer keeps the project focused on entertainment. The restaurants and entertainment components are kept fresh. A desirable experience is provided and maintained. Sheer size will not overwhelm the market over time.

The following are some of the developmental and operational elements that are essential to a successful centre: Sites must be accessible. High crime areas should be avoided. Local government must be committed to maintaining the uniqueness of the area. Zoning and other necessary legislative changes must be forthcoming. Sufficient police protection must be available. Owners should be in constant touch with local governments and document the contribution which the project is making to the betterment of the community. Owners should avoid creating any teen hangouts. The centre must provide enough parking. Shared parking means night time availability only. Customers should not be required to walk long distances from parking to the project. Centre owners should have needed agreements with, and cooperation from, neighbourhood property owners. Adequate public transportation should provide access to the site. The merchant's association should be active and on good terms with neighbouring local merchants.

The cine screen as the entertainer

The number of movie screens nationwide has increased, but the number of locations has stayed pretty much the same. The large-format business is dramatically different from the motion picture exhibition business. Consumers are willing to drive 30 kilometers, past 25 one- or two-screen theatres to get to a complex that offered a different experience. You did not have to call around and find out exactly what time a movie was playing. You could just go, and it would be playing on several screens 15 minutes apart. When you add to that a number of restaurants, you find that you can park your car once, see a movie in an acceptable period, have dinner and then go home. There is no hunting and searching to find that experience. That is the crux of an entertainment centre today. Technology and high design give today's megaplexes a traffic draw of palatial proportions. These megaplexes (not mere multiplexes anymore) are often found as anchors of sprawling entertainment centres — they are a major generator of traffic, but they also attract shoppers who might only have come to the complex to shop.

Experts estimate that about 10% of audience members' time is spent outside the motion picture viewing area, in the theatre lobby and other areas. Thus, megaplexes have transformed the lobbies and entrances to theatres into experiential environments full of visual and visceral appeal. In addition, the transformation of theatres from the small "miniplex" to grand "megaplex" is recognition of the growing importance of urban entertainment venues that use theatres as anchor tenants. The competition for the consumers' time has also created greater competition for moviegoer dollars. These megaplexes are rich in amenities and visual imagery and they also offer a compact form of entertainment for the time-challenged consumer.

Components of a retail + entertainment centre

The primary purpose of a customer's visit is what makes a centre into an entertainment centre. If customers come to a centre to obtain entertainment, then it is an entertainment centre. If customers come to shop, then it is a shopping centre. Three components make up entertainment centres: architecture, people generators, and programming or marketing. An entertainment centre has distinctive architecture that aims to make people feel good. Original malls with enclosed corridors and stores on both sides are shopping destinations. An entertainment destination has a more comfortable and human side to its design. People generators; include theatres, museums, concert halls, restaurants and nightclubs. However, none of these by themselves can create an entertainment centre. People generators will attract people, not necessarily to see a movie but to do something — anything fun — where other people are. A centre must use programming and marketing to add spark to a development with new and exciting events. In terms of physical characteristics, height is important. Taller buildings provide flexibility for the accommodation of various types of entertainment. Another challenge is how to make buildings timeless. Everyone wants to be avant-garde, but avant-garde suggests a time, and what is avant-garde today may be trendy and old in 10 years.

Retail entertainment-centre promoter issues

As retail entertainment continues to evolve and become a greater factor in the shopping centre industry, promoters will need to be prepared for some of the positive and negative impacts that a retail entertainment tenant will have on shopping centre operations. Because most shopping centre lease forms have been prepared for use with traditional retail tenants, promoters should consider whether their existing lease forms would be adequate for use with retail entertainment tenants. Promoters should be prepared to negotiate everything from rent to design and to the use clause.

Rent/Tenant Improvement Costs: Promoters often are willing to accept lower base rent from retail entertainment tenants in exchange for the increased customer traffic they generate and the resulting increase in the percentage rents generated by other tenants. However, lower base rent may be met with equally lower percentage rent if the definition of gross receipts is not specifically adapted for entertainment tenants. For example, the definition of gross receipts for a movie theatre complex in a property-owner lease-form might provide for the averaging of weekly gross admissions receipts to avoid disproportionately high receipts for short periods. It may include gross receipts generated by "4-wall" deals and exclude gross receipts from video games and the sale of refreshments and merchandise.

The definition of gross receipts for a themed restaurant might provide for the inclusion of gross receipts generated by private parties and events and the exclusion of gross receipts from video games and the sale of licensed merchandise. In addition, because entertainment tenants have unique space requirements, promoters may face higher tenant improvement costs at both lease commencement and lease expiration.

Hours of operation/security/parking: Retail entertainment tenants usually have extended hours of operation and generate the greatest traffic at night or on weekends. As a result, during these times, customers of traditional retail tenants often have problems finding parking. Certain types of retail entertainment tenants attract more teenagers and children, which can significantly increase security and insurance costs.

In addition, retail entertainment tenants often will seek the right to host their own premiers, promotions and events within their tenant spaces. Promoters should ensure that retail entertainment leases require the tenant to provide adequate security and parking for such events, at the tenant's sole cost and expense; prohibit the use of the common area without the property owner's consent; and limit the frequency of such events.

Use/Exclusives: A retail entertainment lease should specifically define the types of uses that the retail entertainment tenant will be permitted to operate within its space. Because of constantly changing technology and the nature of the entertainment business, a retail entertainment tenant will want maximum flexibility with respect to its tenant space and may seek the right to operate any use that is a "technological evolution" of the current use. However, an imprecisely worded or overly broad use clause could result in a loss of the property owner's flexibility in maintaining an appropriate tenant mix or result in the violation of another tenant's exclusive.

Signage: Signage, location and visibility are especially important to retail entertainment tenants. For example, many retail entertainment tenants will only agree to use their standard signs and logos, and they will want such signs and logos to be as visible as possible. Promoters should examine their existing lease language, sign criteria and local laws well in advance of seeking a retail entertainment tenant to ensure that the property owner will be able to grant the signage rights that will be required by such tenant.

Merchants association/promotional fund: Retail entertainment tenants often will balk at making a contribution to a merchants association or a promotional fund because these tenants generate traffic for other tenants of the shopping centre and spend a great deal of money on marketing and promotion.

Years ago, developers wrestled with these same questions, minus the word "entertainment." Indeed, malls remain the original form of retail entertainment: clusters of shops, boutiques and department stores aiming to provide all things exciting, thrilling and wonderful in any product category a consumer could possibly want. Coming of age at their birth, malls startled big retailers with a new and successful format, collecting numerous shops under one roof. Over the years, however, the concept has lost its freshness. Today, entertainment retail has startled traditional mall developers and retailers with a fresh format, one that aims, in various guises, at a single, fundamental goal to revive the sense of place and community.

RETAILING BANKING CONVERGENCE

Imagine the biggest retailing entities in the country – many find it difficult to think of public distribution system outlets, *khadi bhandars* or post offices. The reach of these entities is quite powerful compared to any of the other 'organised' popular retail entities in the country. We are all aware of banks using their premises to sell other financial products/services. Awaiting the bancassurance bill, insurance products are also being sold through specifically brick and mortar bank branches. Many observers of retailing as well as banking sectors are not aware that post offices in an otherwise emerging economy in India represent convergence of retailing and banking/financial services. The postal department in addition to postal services is into banking through the post office savings account. It offers insurance through postal life insurance and helps in transferring money through its network. Now in select post offices, several products like greeting cards are being sold and plans are afoot to convert prime post office locations into typical retail stores. It is all happening in India! Nothing represents greater potential for convergence than the post offices in India in its 150th year as an example of convergence of retailing and banking. Elsewhere in Europe and Japan, retailer banks are replacing retail banking.

Retail firms got unexpected help from established retail banks, which in their eagerness to cut costs and increase revenue from service fees on card payments seem to have paved the way for new entrants. These banks stimulated retail firms to enter into the card business by imposing payment fees. Their large investments in new cost efficient electronic-based banking formats and widespread launching of the concept of in-store-banking on the premises of retail firms widened customers' comprehension of what characterises a retail bank.

In this shift of economic power, from producers of goods to distributors of goods, the service economy is sparking much of the action. The service functions include advertising, marketing, information, transportation, inventory management, sales, service and billing. This distributive work can be organised into networks, coordinated by computers and communications technologies and used to build empires once considered too complicated or unwieldy to be managed effectively on a big scale or over huge distances. Over time, strong distribution channels can move more easily into neighbouring territories than in the past. Free of the need to invest heavily in manufacturing facilities, many service companies can use their existing contacts and powerful, flexible technology to sell new products. Thus, giant accounting firms have moved into consulting, Wal-Mart into the turf of supermarkets and pharmacies, and telecommunications giants into publishing. Just what may happen when companies with powerful distribution networks invade one another's territory is hard to say. In the media/communications field, for example, nobody knows which digital entertainment products will succeed in the emerging era, and it is difficult to predict how marketers would deliver digital entertainment to households. It could be through telephone lines, cable television or, as some predict, satellite broadcast. Depending on the outcome, different types of companies could predominate.

This very uncertainty over the type of technology and the type of competitors is pushing companies to seek distribution channels through outright control of them rather than through fuzzy alliances with independent entities.

The Swedish Story

Ikanobanken originates from the Ikano finance group, which is a financial subsidiary to IKEA established in 1988. The idea of starting a retailer bank was stimulated in the early 1990s by the banking crises after which the group applied for a bank charter that the government approved in 1994. The objective of the bank was and still is to be a complementary bank alternative to customers by becoming the most attractive player within the area of financial and supportive services, on targeted markets. Bank customers are, thus, encouraged to keep their current bank for ordinary payment services and to use Ikanobanken for their long-term savings. The ICA Bank sprung from the ICA store card business. However, the group considered banking as an interesting business opportunity already in 1995, when two of the largest Swedish banks imposed a new service fee on card payments. This fee drew a lot of public attention as many retailers responded by passing it on to customers paying with a card. In case they were using the selective store card of the retailer, however, the bank exempted consumers from this charge. This act of discrimination was very successful and led to massive applications for retailer-issued store cards. Grocery retailers like ICA and COOP have never experienced such a great customer interest for their store cards. Beside the deregulation of financial markets, the far-reaching innovations and advancements within the field of information technology have paved the way for the development and launching new banking formats. There are prospects for retailer banks to benefit from economies of scope by utilising the existing network of retailer stores. The efforts of grocery retail banks to use the store card business as a platform for the provision of financial products and services worked well.

In many cases, the retailer accomplishes the provision of financial services by co-operating with an established bank in the form of a strategic alliance. For retailers the provision of financial services may also be a way to increase customer loyalty. From a relationship perspective retail customers are, for instance, likely to be attracted by the opportunity to withdraw or deposit money when shopping. However, the picture looks different and less attractive for established retail banks. For them the entrance of retailers into financial services may be rather distressing. In case the retailer chooses to open a bank of its own, a new cost efficient competitor is born, but even in the case the retailer desires to cooperate with the bank, the risk of losing customers due to 'cannibalism' is imminent. Hence, even though established banks still have a dominating role in the retail banking market, the new entrants are definitely challenging their dominance.

Japanese Story

The story of the Japanese convenience stores shows how the path to banking retailing convergence took place. A key strategy for the leading Japanese convenience stores was to add continually services to attract traffic, even if these services do not contribute directly to profits. Thus, many have long offered copiers, fax services, and video games. Later they became payment points for electricity, gas, and water bills. One of the prominent convenience stores in Japan is Seven Eleven (SEJ). SEJ was the first and reports having 3% of the total Japanese payments market in 2000, which includes payments made through banks and the postal system. In February 1989, SEJ also became a payment-point for Daiichi Seimei (life insurance). As deregulation allowed, convenience stores added sales of money orders and postage stamps. The government allowed sale of rice in 1996. Foreign exchange services started in April 1998. Package shipping was started in the mid-1990s. SEJ works primarily with Yamato Unyu (Black Cat), by far Japan's largest package-delivery firm. During the year 2001, SEJ handled over 13.5 million packages. In November 1999, SEJ began accepting payment for purchases made over the Internet. Reservation services for travel packages became available beginning in late 2000. Many customers wanted the convenience of paying for their e-commerce purchases at the convenience stores in cash. Most convenience stores have combined their multimedia e-commerce strategy with 24-hour ATMs in addition to the multimedia kiosks. However, as under Japanese law, only banks can have ATMs, the convenience stores other than SEJ have invited one or more banks to locate ATMs in their stores. That means the bank controls the ATM. As IY and SEJ wanted to control the services available through the ATMs in their stores, they decided to organise their own bank to serve their 10 million customers per day, plus their 200,000 employees. This is despite the greater capital and systems reporting required.

Sony has affiliates that offer life and auto insurance, while it is also planning an e-bank. The participating banks expect to be able to close branches without sacrificing customer service since depending on store locations; ATMs accept different affiliated bank cards besides IY's. By the end of December 2001, there were about 2,200 of these ATMs installed, all in metropolitan Tokyo and adjacent areas. By the spring of 2002, over 3,600 stores will be served and over 7,100 throughout Japan by the spring of 2006. Services offered will eventually include bank accounts, remittances, and money transfers, debit card within the IY group, credit cards, purchase point cards, loans, Internet banking, and settlement services with member firms such as 7dream.com or Seven-Meal Service. There will also be services such as brokerage, insurance and credit cards offered through affiliated firms.

ATMs and IT as enablers of convergence

Installation costs have been about ¥2.5 million per ATM, and because an ATM is a bank branch under Japanese banking rules, Consumers can open the accounts only at a bank branch (or by mail). Therefore, SEJ can open accounts only in the stores with ATMs. In the first two months of operation (June and July 2001), about 10,000 accounts were opened. Not surprisingly, ATM use has been primarily on weekends and after 8 pm. Besides the Seven-Eleven convenience stores, ATMs ultimately will be placed in IY's other operations such as Denny's restaurants and IY's general merchandise stores. Because IY and SEJ control the bank, they control the services offered and the ATMs' functions. Therefore, they can target services important to their clients and can leverage advances in technology, since banks first introduced ATMs. Thus, these convenience stores ATMs are electronically sophisticated and can be programmed to handle a variety of functions over time as services evolve while also being very compact, which is important for storeowners. However, so far SEJ has not trained store personnel in these functions. Therefore, from a store's perspective they use ATMs to generate traffic, with the bank partners handling the actual service.

IY and SEJ's e-commerce support system is an extension of its already very sophisticated IT system that is largely independent of the Internet. It was in place when the potential of the Internet was widely recognised. Nevertheless, the company feels the advantages of a proprietary network are such that it would not have made the system Internet–based even if that had been an option. In addition, they were monitoring its use by others since Lawson and Mitsubishi Corp, as of the summer of 2001, 2000 of all Japanese convenience stores had ATMs using regional banks that were members of e-net and of these 70% were in FM shops. (The banks working with FM include Tokyo- Mitsubishi, Chiba Bank, Dai-ichi Kangyo, Mitsui Sumitomo, Mitsubishi Trust, Nagoya Bank, Michinoku Bank, Suruga Bank, 105th Bank, and Sumitomo Trust.) This is thus about the same number as they have installed multimedia kiosks in their stores, about 1500.

Payment mechanism – link to conversion

Banks come into the picture with respect to retailing entities due to the payment mechanism. There are three primary reasons associated with the increased importance of the payment system. First, customers wish to minimise transaction cost of paying for their purchases. For example, fuel companies have boosted fuel sales per station by installing pump-based card readers to speed up transactions, which reduces transaction cost in terms of customer's time. Second, payment devices can be and are being used to build brand loyalty (repeat purchases). Bank card issuers have found that rebates are particularly effective at encouraging repeated card usage across a wide variety of retail outlets. The power of rebate programmes has not been lost on retailers: many have agreed to issue jointly a "co-branded" Visa or MasterCard. Third, technological advances have greatly increased the value of information captured about customer preferences when consumers use credit cards instead of cash or checks. Purchase patterns are key ingredients in target marketing efforts to generate incremental sales. The card issuer captures the information, elevating the importance of which card he uses when a customer chooses to pay with plastic.

Merchants with proprietary card programmes lose such valuable information if their cardholders increasingly switch to bank cards. Consumers who frequently utilise a bank card in either retail or a gasoline outlet, do so to obtain rebates and shop with fewer cards. Consumers, who frequently utilise their retail cards, do so to simplify merchandise returns, obtain sales notices, and expect retailers to recognise them as loyal customers. Consumers who frequently utilise their fuel cards do so to maintain separate records of their fuel purchases and keep other credit lines open. For store cardholders, a co-branded rebate card is likely to appeal to three distinct groups: namely those with a desire to consolidate cards carried; those who are attracted by rebates and those who want to be identified as loyal customers (affinity buyers). That is, the co-branded store card appeal cuts across the set of reasons that characterise the behaviour of both substituters and non-substituters in the retail store environment. However, if the bank and retail entity belong to the same group, then the idea of a co-branded card vanishes and it is a single card.

Micro payments and banks – status of retailers

Banking is all about trust, and customers are resistant to switching financial services firms from a long-trusted one to an upstart merely because of a new-fangled feature or minor conflict. Therefore, keeping a standard in payment systems tends to be easy. Visa is a master of such incremental standard propagation. When they design a new feature, it is first "sold" internally to member-banks. Then, the banks agree to a common standard to support, say, a common method for activating new credit cards via 1-800 numbers to reduce postal fraud. Then, the multiple sources of payments clearing software systems must update their software to screen out a new class of payments attempted with "valid" but "inactive" cards that have not been initialised. Visa established the standard by defining it and then getting the banks - which buy the payments management software to agree to support it in advance. The captive software vendors must follow. They are not in as good a position to develop new features of their own and propose them as standards because they deal in a fractured, multi-party market. Only Visa has relationships with the whole consortium and is best positioned to maintain control by developing payment standards for banks. Standards in micro payments face all of these issues and more.

One obstacle to micro payment adoption for banks is the potential loss of revenue from micro payment technologies that remove validation from third party sources, such as banks. With some micro payment technologies, merchants have direct access to customer accounts and no bank authorisation of funds is required. Consequently, the bank loses transaction-processing fees. Intertrust has developed a solution. The Intertrust Commerce Architecture enables banks to become processors for micro payments on the internet. Banks would guarantee that they would receive payment in much the same manner that banks process checks. The bank would pay parties after a 15-day float and collect a fee for its services; which is similar to the fees charged when a consumer uses an ATM machine that does not belong to its bank. Thus, banks can move from being authorisation sources to being payment processors, and thrive with micro payment technology. However, this could happen if retailer banks do not develop efficient mechanisms of payment processing.

The international retail industry is undergoing paradigm shifts that are changing the way in which we can look forward to retailing developments in India. One of the views of service marketing considers products and services which are a part of a continuum. There are products with services and there are services that provide products. Retailing as a sector is seeing this convergence. Retailing started as a brick and mortar entity centuries back. The introduction and differentiation of retailing by the type of additional service provided to the consumer brought it closer to the services sector. The physical distribution of retail outlets brought the services close to the consumer. The use of information technology helped provide standardised services. The web gave an avenue for further distribution and convenience to the consumers. The financial service sector that facilitated development of retail industry provided an opportunity to retailers to use their consumer interaction by offering their services through the retail outlets.

This has resulted in steps further to integrate banking/financial services and retailing. One of the key elements of this convergence is the distribution strength of the retail outlets. Information technology has played a strong facilitating role. Thus, it has not been a convergence of retailing and banking but also information technology to ease transactions in day-to-day life for a variety of products and services.

BPO IN RETAILING

The concept of outsourcing is spreading fast in different types of organisations. Specifically, business process outsourcing is gaining ground. One of the pioneering sectors that took on this concept quite early is the retailing sector. Retailing as a concept can be looked at from various dimensions. One of the perspectives is viewing retailing activity as services marketing/management. In making, an effective/efficient job of retailing as services also requires the help of other services. The retail entity can either provide these services internally or procure it from specialised service providers. Thus, the typical make or buy situation in simplistic terms that triggers outsourcing thinking is quite typical of retailing too. A retail chain would involve three types of interactions – one with suppliers, second with consumers and the third with other formats/stores within the retail organisation. The various business processes involved in these interactions represent decision-making points for outsourcing. A retail ERP tries to bring in all the processes within the domain of the retail organisation and therefore assumes that the organisation has the capability to handle all processes effectively. However, if each of the business processes involved in these interactions is subject to the test of outsourcing feasibility/viability, there are several possibilities that emerge. Outsourcing is a viable business strategy because turning non-core functions over to external suppliers enables companies to leverage their resources, spread risks, and concentrate on issues that are critical to survival and future growth.

BPO

An article entitled "The Muddles over Outsourcing" written by Professors Jagdish Bhagwati, Arvind Panagariya and T N Srinivasan deal with the concept of business process outsourcing very well. In this article, the authors clearly state that outsourcing as a concept is related to trade in services and that it can be classified into four types. In this classification, they have looked at outsourcing as almost similar to classification of services marketing, where types of services are classified, considering service provider and receiver as major components. The authors have split services in the context of outsourcing into four types - Mode 1 - trade in services involving arms-length supply of services, with the supplier and buyer remaining in their respective locations. Mode 2 services are those provided by moving the service recipient to the location of the service provider. Example of Mode 2 services is education, medical assistance as well as tourism. In Mode 3, the service provider establishes a commercial presence in another country, requiring an element of direct foreign investment. The most prominent examples of Mode 3 services are banking and insurance. In Mode 4, the service seller moves to the location of the service buyer. Construction and consulting services are often provided through this mode. Also included in this category are medical and educational services provided by moving doctors and teachers to the location of the recipient. This clarity of thought on outsourcing is important for understanding outsourcing in retailing.

Retail context

The retail product is the store outlet, which comprises store location, layout, assortment and looks, as well as marketing functions like product presentation, pricing strategies and retail services. The store as a whole is the offering to the consumers. In a retail store, modules that can be outsourced are the categories. An excellent basis for identifying core categories is formed by ECR (efficient consumer response) work in companies, since ECR has sharpened the role and management of product categories especially in the grocery retailing business. Outsourcing has moved markedly from performing single functions more efficiently to reconfiguring whole processes in new ways. Rather than asking what our company could do, the question is why not outsourcing. The company should do only those activities where they can develop best-in-world capabilities. When we think about the outsourcing arguments from a retail industry viewpoint, the first consideration is whether a global manufacturer can form them more efficiently. Even though there is a globalisation trend in retailing, it is still a relatively local business. However, suppliers to retailers are in many product categories globally operating companies and the competition is global. The retailers could better utilise capabilities and big resources of global vendors. So far, retailers have mostly compared products and prices that they offer. When the outsourcing approach is applied, we should widen the viewpoint to include business processes and service concepts.

Outsourcing - Category Management

One of the forms of outsourcing that is gaining ground in the developed world is an outsourcing of two major processes in retailing - category management and stock replenishment. This is being termed as vendor managed category management. However, outsourcing category management is not a solution for all categories. The supplier taking care of one category must be able to offer all products in the category, or be able to purchase some products outside, maybe from a competitor. This however may be difficult in product categories where there are several competing strong brands. In these situations, a supplier may not be willing to give the management of the category to a competitor, retailer must retain category management in its own hands. The rule in outsourcing is that the buyer should outsource non-core functions from a best-in-world source, but his own capabilities should be developed and maintained in core functions and operations. In many categories, the retailer is best placed to provide category management process. The role of a category captain from the supplier side with several products in the category has increased as categories expand and the concept of category management becomes employee intensive.

DSD as outsourcing

Direct store delivery is in effect an often forgotten business process outsourcing in retailing for several years. To develop an efficient outsourcing strategy, retailers and retail chains should consider their attitude towards suppliers with direct deliveries. Retailers should systematically agree upon the division of the responsibility of functions between vendors and retailers. Outsourcing is not a systematically chosen strategy in grocery retailing. It has developed by evolution. Nevertheless, suppliers have been carrying out a part of retail operations for a long time. On the one hand, retailers consider DSD suppliers as harmful. They see suppliers delivering directly to the retail store causing traffic jams at the store backdoor, creating paperwork, increasing the materials handling work, and store management fear loss of control over the DSD categories. In addition, benefits of cross docking and consolidation are lost for the distributor or wholesaler upstream in the supply chain. The DSD suppliers generate higher productivity to the store by offering good service and fewer out-of-stocks, carrying out the category management process and adopting sophisticated replenishment methods, like continuous replenishment. The results indicate that DSD is a powerful weapon in increasing profits in the maturing retail industry Furthermore, the retail personnel have usually nothing against a supplier taking care of a part of their job such as shelving or ordering.

Logistics

Many firms have turned to logistics outsourcing as a way to restructure their distribution networks and to gain competitive advantages. Logistics outsourcing, the use of a third party logistics (3PL) provider for all or part of an organisation's logistics operations, has grown dramatically over the last several years. Logistics outsourcing has increasingly become an effective way to reduce costs and spread risks for traditional, and vertically integrated firms. More than 50% of Fortune 500 firms report having at least one contract with a third party logistics provider. The potential economic advantages of logistics outsourcing include elimination of infrastructure investments; access to world-class processes, products, services or technology; improved ability to react quickly to changes in business environments; risk sharing; better cash-flow; reducing operating costs; exchanging fixed costs with variable costs; access to resources not available in own organisation.

The contract logistics market has grown and providers of these services have increased in status and professionalism. However, the market is volatile. Retailers use many of the reasons cited for contracting out such as cost, customer service and management expertise to justify retention of the logistical service 'in house'. There is an impression that companies enter some form of partnership but in many cases, they pay lip service to the idea. Retail management is much more positive about the factors for retaining 'in house' distribution. There is little variance across business sectors and the very highly significant factors are those of maintaining control over the warehouse operation and being able to give their internal retail store division high levels of customer service. The retailer would contract out transport than the warehousing function, where cost effectiveness and utilisation of 'in house' company expertise are also significant factors for retaining own account warehousing.

Logistics – retail chain

In multi-site networks, where outsourcing is an acceptable strategic objective, it is likely that retail chains would use a mix of contractors. The management can use the introduction of innovative practices and the monitoring of standards, to improve not only efficiency, but to benchmark performance between contractors and between contractors and the 'in house' retail logistics operation. A grocery retailer abroad had an annual prize instituted for the best depot to act as an incentive to improve performance. In cases where a retailer has between one and three depots, the 'in house' logistics department often entirely contracts out or operates the network. The companies with newer retail formats have benefited from contractors' management expertise in establishing centralised distribution whereas companies with 'in house' logistics assets have a degree of inertia, which may militate against change and contracting out. Here the skills and core competencies have high asset specificity and are 'sunk costs' within the organisation. In the context of the historical evolution of retailers' distribution networks, companies, which centralised early, tended to develop an 'in house' operation. As these businesses evolved and moved into new geographic markets, retail chains outsourced complementary skills of medium asset specificity through a range of contractual relationships.

IT revolution in BPO

The advent of technology has changed the idea of business process outsourcing to a plane where information and knowledge management has become the key. This has resulted in small firms with good understanding of IT and its prowess, providing several services like vendor evaluation, real estate tracking, and site location and trading area analysis using GIS applications etc. These are pure play service organisations that add value to service delivery and success of the retail organisation. Malls outsource In-store services and space-management in addition to facility management. Call centres of large retail chains are outsourced and marketing analytic firms are involved in market research outsourcing. IT has spurred a range of business process outsourcing possibilities in retailing. Many IT companies in India started with retail clients as outsourcing partners for developing their IT backbone. Therefore, it may not be an exaggeration to say that retailing is the mother of the outsourcing business. Probably other sectors can learn many lessons from understanding success in BPO in the retail context.

RETAILING BANKING SERVICES

One of the key differences between India and the developed countries is the direction of convergence in case we envisage the same. While convenience stores like Seven Eleven have transformed into financial services retailer and into a bank, in the case of India, this cannot be the case. We do not have a chain of stores that has a national presence in the grocery segment or any other segment that commands the kind of distribution network that would help expand to financial services. The physical distribution of brick and mortar outlets provides the physical space for interactions in financial services, whereas in the case of pure-play financial services, physical retail space is minimal. Does that mean that extremely successful financial service retailers should not get into goods retailing? Is the convergence going forward from goods retailing to service retailing only and not the other way around?

One of the reasons professed by Oriental Bank of Commerce (OBC) when it took over Global Trust Bank (GTB) was to expand the presence of OBC in the south. GTB had a good presence in the southern states due to its retail branch network. Therefore, it would complement the relatively strong presence of OBC in the northern states. In the run up to the impending merger of public sector banks, one serious criteria looked at by many banks is the complementarity of the branch network that would help in increasing the retail distribution network of banks that are merging. In addition, the commonality of the IT infrastructure in terms of software and hardware that enables the effective functioning of the network matters. While this is the case of financial services or particularly banking services, manufacturing and marketing companies look at efficiency and effectiveness of the existing distribution channel of the merging entities in order to serve consumers better post merger in addition to the complementarity of the products.

The three state owned entities that have potential in converting their distribution network for retailing are the post office, LIC and the State Bank of India. This is in addition to the public distribution system that has a greater network.

The Indian postal department as a monopoly has more than 1.5 lakh post offices in the country. It has more than 5.5 lakh letter boxes. The postal life insurance is as old as 1884. In addition, it deals with about five basic policies that serve the large set of first time buyers of insurance and therefore has a huge scope in the fast developing life insurance market that has opened up recently. The post office as a bank helps us open a savings bank account and utilise services just as in the case of a bank. In addition there are about nine small savings schemes operated through the bank that greatly compete with other banking products for personal savings. Since the Indian postal department is an arm of the government, its decisions and speed of implementation, especially with respect to interest rates on the schemes and other benefits have an impact on how the public tends to save. Any small incentive is good enough in shifting consumers from banks to post offices. The post office monthly income scheme is a good example of what happened in recent years due to a drop in interest rates. One of the common ways of savings for a middle-income household had been to open a POMIS account, an SB account as well as an RD account together at the post office and provide for standard instructions for transfer of interest proceeds of the POMIS account through the SB a/c to the RD a/c. This means that investors divert a huge amount of savings to post offices and one of the reasons for the same is easy accessibility.

While the post office is a banking and financial service provider as described above, one of the major tasks that it performs is to convey communication through letters and transport goods from one place to another. In this task, the Indian postal services have developed an excellent reputation for themselves without the use of a concept of dead letter office! The transit mail service and RMS system, in addition to new forms of conveying information through e-mail, facing courier competition with better terms and conditions and a good branding, have equated their efforts with the best retailing entities in the world. They carry about 750 million letters a year. The entire logistics functions so very smoothly that the backbone of a typical retailing entity (in this case post office) that is retailing operations management runs very effectively. This is in addition to selling of postal material and transfer of money through money orders. These activities of the postal department make it actively suitable for the government to get it converted into a retail entity.

With the availability of prime real estate across the country in easy accessible locations even in rural areas, the potential of the post office is tremendous as a retailer. Already plans are afoot in building huge multistory structures in big cities to use real estate effectively for providing almost a one stop shop for not only buying postal items and posting letters in post offices but a place for buying other products like even groceries, greeting cards etc and do financial transaction in the post office premises. The use of the capacity of postal vans on road and rail can be more effective if it uses the same for transporting other products that the post office merchandises.

State Bank of India, which was born out of the Imperial Bank of India that existed before independence, is the bank that is the ubiquitous name for banking across the country. Its spread of around 10000 countrywide branches straddles across the urban and rural areas. With its over 20,000 crore deposits, 20 mutual fund schemes, 8 lakh credit cardholders and 250 crore worth of consumer finance, SBI represents a financial powerhouse. SBI has joint ventures for other related businesses like credit and debit cards, life insurance, merchant banking, securities trading etc. SBI by virtue of its physical spread across the country and being on merger with its associate banks would represent one of the largest brick and mortar financial services retailers in the country. Here again its possession of prime real estate that is a fit case for using the same efficiently for a joint venture to promote a physical goods retail entity that has a 'bank financing' relationship with SBI . Thus, SBI represents the power of a potentially serious contender for an entity that would be involved in banking and retailing as they converge.

LIC was the only life insurance company in the country until very recently when the Government opened up the life insurance segment. With more than two crore policyholders, 85,000 crore annual cash flows, and several schemes, LIC again represents a financial super power. Its housing finance subsidiary was almost the only place where customers would go for housing finance, before the government allowed banks in this business. With a huge customer base and strong presence in rural areas, the physical presence of LIC across the country is phenomenal. LIC is one of the major landmarks in Chennai. With the advent of competition and effective use of investment, the strategic stake of LIC in corporation bank is a forerunner for LIC representing the combination of an insurance company in banking post bank assurance. LIC boasts of a separate department, which deals with the enormous area of property that it owns across the country. An effective use of this would make it again a potential contender for a good brick and mortar retail entity.

India has been following the trend in western nations in several fields. However, in the context of convergence of banking and retailing, there does not seem to be a case due to the nature of development of retailing. We could probably see an innovation in financial service providers entering the physical brick and mortar retailing arena as its gets opened up and more organised. India would probably be a pioneer in this field and a trendsetter in this area. If this premonition comes true, the post office, LIC and SBI would be big entities that would challenge strongly, any player who would want to straddle across otherwise two sectors namely banking and financial services and retailing.

ENTRY STRATEGIES OF GLOBAL RETAILERS

One of the latest reports available on global retailers shows that the five top ranked global retailers have different national origin, different number of stores and sales and earnings not comparable from the dollar figures quoted. A survey on the penetration of global retailers in even developed economies shows that there has not been a great penetration of global retailers. If this is the case, is the fear of global retailers gobbling up local retailers an exaggerated version of what in reality could happen in emerging economies with the increased trend of globalisation in the retailing sector? This also poses a question as to whether globalisation in retailing is a new phenomenon. Woolworth's entry into Canada in 1907 and later into Europe; Sears Roebuck's expansion into Cuba in 1942; Marks and Spencer's entry into Canada in the early 70's; C&A's entry into several European countries in late 1960's etc. also dispel the myth that international retailing is a new phenomenon. There were some important overseas retail/ manufacturing networks established by manufacturers such as Bata Shoe Corporation of Canada and Singer Company of U.S.A, having set up hundreds of company owned or franchised outlets across the world in the 50's, 60's and 70's. We in India have been used to Bata stores for generations! Then why is it that there seems to be greater interest in investing in retailing, especially in developing/emerging economies.

While overall world demographic trends are slow to change, there remain important shifts that global retailers are monitoring. For example, comparisons across countries show varying growth rates in different age-specific groups. India's population is very young; nearly 44% of its inhabitants currently are below 20 years of age. In contrast, only 19% of Italy's consumers are under 20 years old, while 18% are above 65 years of age. This latter percentage is one of the highest in the world. These two countries highlight the growth differences between many low-income and high-income countries. By 2020, an estimated 35% of the population in the less developed countries will not have experienced their 20th birthday. In the more developed countries, the under-20 age groups will comprise only 22% of the total. This would mean an active population in a stage of their lifecycle that would be interested in shopping. If this means a big market and entry of global retailers is a matter of time, then one need to understand the mode of entry of these multinationals. Currently, the 250 world's largest retailers sell in 5.5 countries, on an average. Only five years ago, the average was 4.5 countries. The trend is even more noticeable in the U.S. Five years ago, only one-third of U.S. retailers sold outside of their home borders. Presently, 56% have stores in other countries and as home markets continue to become saturated, retailers will continue to look elsewhere for growth opportunities.

International/global retailing

The neglect of international retailing as an area of study has in some cases been because historically, it was a domestic market based industry, with core activities seen as primarily downstream in marketing, sales and service. Experts have viewed Industry sectors characterised by predominantly downstream value chain activities as very difficult to globalise, since they require a high proportion of local activities. For example, experts regard the retail sector as highly labour intensive, whereas it has become more capital intensive partly because of increasing use of information technology e.g. EPOS systems and the cost of large, well-situated sites. Further, potential change arises from political and economic restructuring that is taking place across the world. The formation of trading blocs and decreasing barriers to trade, have been instrumental in undermining the traditional cost structure of the retail industry, partly in terms of the ability to source worldwide and utilise trans-regional distribution systems. Because of these factors, upstream retail activities, such as purchasing, sourcing, logistics, distribution and warehousing functions have become increasingly important and large scale. It is here that international players can command greater power as compared to other local/domestic players.

Factors affecting global retailing

Hollander's book "Multinational Retailing", is widely regarded as the seminal work on retail internationalisation. The value-added service delivered to customers, through the performance of functions or activities represent the major source of competitive advantage for retailers. This value-add must be firmly based upon customer needs and values, and may comprise both tangible or functional and intangible or symbolic elements. Researchers recognise the importance of fully understanding the source of competitive advantage (and in particular, the role of intangible benefit) in the domestic market, before moving into foreign environments. The PLIN model for global expansion of specialty retailing suggests that retailers need to understand fully the role of Product, Lifestyle, Image and Niche in creating a differential advantage in the domestic market, before attempting to move overseas. The ability to offer the host market consumers a source of differentiation in the delivery of benefit is a key factor in international success. The international activities of European grocery retailers appeared to be more successful if the internationalisation process involved the importation of a new concept - such as the hypermarket or limited line discount store - to the host market. Once the source of this competitive and differential advantage is recognised, a key issue then becomes whether to replicate or modify the operation on entering a foreign market. This relates to the standard standardisation vs. adaptation debate in international marketing literature. In many sectors for international marketers to thrive, adaptation is necessary and this would be true of those who are planning entry through Greenfield ventures in retailing in India.

One of the most important things that has been learnt by international retailers is that formats, merchandising, store design and store location often have to be customised to local conditions to achieve success. Nevertheless, one should note that such 'tweaking' of the core concept or merchandising mix, while representing modification, is not a denial of global or regional operating benefits. Benetton may sell different colour and range combinations in its Asia-Pacific stores to its European ones, but this does not detract from the scale benefits the company gains in manufacturing, marketing, distribution and branding. Pizza Hut protects the core elements of its brand by copyrighting its individual product brand names, e.g. Perfect Pizza. It also ensures standardisation across markets by operating a strict specification of product ingredients. However, the concept is adapted to suit local needs; for example, some elements of the menu (such as desserts) will vary, as will store design, and even the way in which the retailer provides products to the customer. Co-operative agreements such as franchising and joint ventures and investment provide further alternatives to overseas market entry.

Business distance

One of the key factors that impact upon an entry strategy for global retailers is business distance. Business distance represents the gap between host and home environments in four areas: consumer behaviour, outlet or store format, networks and environment. Any retail format has a grounded history, built up over years of operation in the home environment, and thus one needs to understand fully the "fit" within the host environment. Without this understanding, "the decision to export a retail format to another cultural environment may drastically modify its initial competitive advantage". Many a time's retailers choose initial markets because of their geographical or cultural proximity to the domestic market. Clearly, companies try to minimise business risk through gaining experience of like markets by organic growth or acquisition (2 types of entry strategies) rather than higher risk markets which may be targeted by franchising or joint ventures (other entry strategies). This would be deemed "culturally proximate" expansion. Historically, well established U.S. retailers have tended to operate in the early stages of internationalisation in Canada, Mexico and even Cuba - "geographically proximate" markets. Push factors for entry include limited opportunities in the home market due to saturation, regulation or adverse trading conditions, while pull factors relate to seeking opportunities in new markets conducive for growth in retailing. Food retailing continues to be the dominant format among these large global retailers. Nine of the 10 largest global retailers sell food, and more than half of top 200 global retailers operate food related formats such as supermarkets, cash-and-carry or convenience stores. Specialty stores, however, continue to be the most popular format among global retailers. This shows that in terms of formats with which global retailers could enter India, food retail and specialty retail could be the dominant ones.

Types of global expansion/entry

For all retailing organisations with ambitions to operate in overseas markets, the methods of entry can vary from acquisition to franchising and licensing. Acquisition of a controlling interest in a foreign company provides immediate market share, sites, location, concept and distribution. It may also encompass a diversification of retailing activities. During 1988, the U.S. retailing sector saw the acquisition of Federated Department Stores by Campeau Corporation (Canada), the purchase of Brooks Brothers by Marks and Spencer (U.K.), and the diversion into the hotel and leisure sector by Seibu Saison (Japan), in its acquisition of the Intercontinental Hotel Corporation. Within Europe the Belgium retailer Delhaize le Lion has acquired a number of overseas stores in the U.S., (e.g. Giant Foods in 1985), and Portugal, (e.g. 40% stake acquired in Pingo Dote in 1986). The U.K. jewelry chain retailers has recently bought the U.S. firm, Sterling and Westhall, making it the largest jewelry chain in the world. A further example of such activity is that of European Home Products (U.K.), which has grown internationally, mainly by acquisition of a number of diverse consumer goods companies such as Singer (sewing and electrical products), buying the Spanish Ivarte electrical chain, in addition to the Scholl pedicare and footwear company in 1987. Although the parent company EHP is U.K. based, the focus of activities is firmly placed upon the whole of Europe, rather than on any individual country.

Franchising has been the route taken by retailing companies such as Body Shop (U.K.), Benetton (Italy), Stefanel (Italy), McDonalds (U.S.), PreMaman (France), and Yves Rocher (France). Joint ventures have been particularly favoured in countries such as Japan and India, which until recently retailers have found difficulty in penetration. In Japan, there have been a number of agreements between Seibu Saison and U.K. and U.S. companies such as McDonalds (U.S.), Mulberry (U.K.), and Paul Smith (U.K.). Organic growth is a strategy for developing overseas operations, which leading U.K. retailers, such as Laura Ashley, Sock Shop and Habitat (Storehouse), have taken in order to spread trading activities across a number of geographical locations. It is also the one pursued by the oil companies, global petrol retailing chains such as EXXON. The parent company retains ensures financial and management control over when organic growth happens through overseas operations.

We can look at International expansion of retailers in four ways

1. *Autochthonic* - Saturation in the domestic market is unimportant but the retailer's operation has limited global potential.

2. *Reactive* - Saturation in the domestic market is important and the retailer's operation has limited global potential.

3. *Expansive* - Saturation in the domestic market is important and the retailer's operation has considerable global potential.

4. *Proactive* - Saturation in the domestic market is unimportant but the retailer's operation has considerable global potential.

These four types of expansion modes reflect different compulsions/advantages of retailers. In order to understand entry strategies, we need to study the nature of forces that affect expansion by the retailer seeking entry in to the emerging market.

Retailers such as Benetton, Body Shop and McDonald's have such a large international operating chain that the consumer views them as global brands, and their original home base is not discernible to the public. Their ability to create and sustain a successful brand image - and the goodwill attached to it - is a key competitive advantage and not one previously thought available to service businesses such as retailing. In fact, the branding of services is a relatively recent and underutilised asset. This advantage of branding eases the transfer of the retail concept to different geographical locations across the world. Whereas previously, international branding was something considered only for products, the same factors, added to the commonality of tastes and preferences, now make possible the international success of certain types of retail concepts such as Laura Ashley. Therefore, international brands in retailing have the ability to survive on their own, regardless of the mode of entry. However, in emerging economies this would mean limited potential, as the formats are not price related.

A new type of cooperative agreement is emerging in Europe with buying associations and consortia. The Argyll / Casino / Ahold / Rinascente / Dansk / ICA and Migros Consortia involve retail chains from seven European countries. Retail consortia are not just joining to buy products. More sophisticated procurement benefit in the joint purchase of vehicles, computers, software and even the eventual international transfer of trading formats. With such potential synergies from collaboration, it is believed that differing degrees of joint venture as a mode of entry into international markets will start to gather pace. Indeed, whilst the cost of entry and risk element associated with acquisition and organic growth remains high, it may well quickly become the preferred route into international retail markets.

Factors related to entry strategies

Different entry strategies have specific characteristics. An entry strategy that affords a high degree of control is normally associated with high cost, such as acquisition, dominant shareholding or wholly owned green field investments. A second strategy involves medium cost and control, which is typically connected with 50:50 joint ventures. A low cost strategy implies a reduction in control, such as minority equity interests, franchise arrangements and in-store concessions. Several internal determinants of business by the organisation involved in international retailing like the degree of centralisation of decision-making, organisational culture, international experience, and size of the firm have an influential role in internationalisation. Research has shown that a more entrepreneurial culture, such as adhocracy, is likely to take more substantial business risks and enter markets through high cost/high control strategies, whereas a hierarchy or clan culture may be more likely to adopt a low cost/low control strategy. Larger retailers, with greater financial resources, are more likely to use acquisition as a mode of entry, whereas small retailers will evaluate the relative benefits of franchising, concessions, distributors and agents. Flag planting (establishing a cursory and very modest store presence) in a new country market, invariably, has been an expensive failure. Increasingly, global retailers are focusing on building local scale in high potential markets, rather than developing as wide an international coverage as possible.

Defences against global retailer entry

Global retailers could use local cultural capital to compete not only in local markets but also in the global arena. Ethnic retailers can perhaps make a brand of them and enter even a global retailing market, not with the financial capital and power of large size, but with an idea for a niche based on their unique cultural capital. International retailers have not been successful in transferring retailing formats from less developed countries to developed ones or from small countries to larger ones or from peripheral places to central core economies such as North America, Europe and Japan.

Success in global retailing is not pre-ordained – the relationships that consumers and shoppers have with their food, cooking, meal occasions, and eating differ substantially from one country to the next. For example, in the European region, food and culinary culture in

Italy is quite different from that in the U.K. Successful retailing in any country is contingent upon having a profound understanding of the wants of domestic shoppers. Taking a retail concept that works well in the middle of the U.S.A. and dropping it down in, say, India is a recipe for disaster! National/regional markets for food still differ and this limits buying scale opportunities for major players. Planning and labour union rules and regulations differ from market to market even within a country like India. Defensive mergers of local companies reduce acquisition targets. In view of these possibilities, the pessimistic view of global retailers sweeping the country away looks unconvincing.

The spectre of Wal-Mart arriving in a new market continues to concern retailers around the world. Many retailers are developing strategies focused on defending their territories against the Wal-Mart threat. Loblaw's in Canada is a case in point with a pre-emptive programme to for example expand its range of non-food items, increase private label products, and reduce food prices across the board. The discount German retailers Aldi and Lidl are inexorably expanding their networks across the globe – with a limited product range, and relatively unknown brands and/or private label products. These companies find ready markets in both mature Northern European countries (where they continue to expand their market share in all countries apart from Ireland), and in countries where household incomes are constrained and the overall spend on groceries is a significant proportion of total family income. Across the globe, national and regional retailers are expanding their fresh food offer to defend, even attack, the incursions of global retailers. Traditional wholesale markets must change categorically if they are to have a long-term future. It is instructive to look to the Paris Rungis wholesale market – for fruit and vegetables, meat, dairy and bakery products - which have redefined itself as a "one stop market" for safe, quality food. The survival and prospering of modern wholesale markets have both economic and social importance in emerging markets. Smaller-scale producers who will never have the size to link with large supermarket supply chains need access to a modern wholesale market network that can keep them in touch with entrepreneurial, forward-looking "mom and pop" retailers and food service businesses that will continue to compete even in a supermarket-dominated world.

A study of the entry strategies of global retailers in different markets shows several factors that force or facilitate global expansion. The entry itself is greatly restricted now with the importance given (by host country governments) to the impact of entry on the domestic players. This would mean utilisation of windows of opportunities whenever available (as in the case of Dairy Farm International in India) and in whatever form (cash and carry wholesale like Metro in India) and obtaining the first mover advantage. The links in sourcing (the likes of what Wal-Mart and other global retailers have with several companies in India) also act as an efficient facilitating mechanism for entry. However, entry is only the start of a great set of realities that global retailers would face when they start operating in emerging markets. A successful/sustainable global retailer needs to understand the peculiarities of operating in these markets.

CHAPTER EIGHT

Specialty Retailing

TOY RETAILING

The toy retailing industry in India is poised for growth in leaps and bounds due to the demographics of the country. In addition, the increase in purchasing power and greater propensity to spend would lead to much greater growth in the industry. However, as is seen in developed markets, toy retailing has not developed as a speciality retail format in spite of the development of the merchandise category. In the list of the top ten toy retailers in the U.S. until very recently, Toys R Us and KB toys were the major speciality toy retailers, whereas other store formats like hypermarkets were the largest sellers of toys.

Industry analysts estimate the growth rate of the Indian toy market at around 15%. This figure seems set to rocket upwards with the entry of speciality retailers who are targeting children. At the forefront of this retail wave is Toys Kemp, an offshoot of Ravi Melwani's Kemp Fort group. Melwani is out to create India's answer to Toys "R Us, and is targeting a network of 500 stores in the next two years. He has adopted the franchise route for this process, and has already set up over 15 stores across several cities including Chennai, New Delhi, Bangalore, Mumbai, Indore and Nasik. Moreover, on the drawing board are stores in Hyderabad, Bhubaneswar, Visakhapatnam, Pune and Ahmedabad, in addition to a 15,000 sq ft Toys Kemp store in New Delhi. Toys are first tested at the 50,000 sq ft toy store at Kemp Fort in Bangalore. The retailer tests around 100 toys each week and only around five make it through. Kemp Fort further distributes it to the franchisee stores. Chennai-based Jus! Kidding, a unit of Kids Mart India (Pvt) Ltd., which in turn is owned by real estate developer Mangal Thirth Estate is not an exclusive toy store, toys are one of its major product lines.

Factors affecting retailing

Parents consider several factors when buying toys including its safety, durability and design. The ability to combine all of these factors and keeping costs low ensures that top selling toys are possible. Many factors influence the success of a given toy or product line, including play value, perceived worth, eye-catching design, innovative line extensions, creative marketing, proper in-store exposure and reasonable availability. However, it is most likely a combination of factors, plus positive word of mouth (e.g., child-to-child, child influencing parents, etc.), that make a particular toy or category a bestseller. The ability to incorporate the features above would help toy retailers in becoming successful. A dedicated play area for experiencing play value, understanding child behaviour in buying toys and converting it into eye-catching design and visual merchandising are strong influencers for toy buying. The storeowner has to initiate positive word of mouth for the toys in the store as well as the store through an innovative marketing programme. These could involve loyalty points or referral points as well as schemes that persuade parents to come along with children for toy buying.

Video games and its impact

Video games have largely attracted both the young and old alike and have eroded the base of traditional toys. As advanced technology began to offer increasingly sophisticated game play, in late 1993 a progressive and forward-thinking coalition of U.S. manufacturers of video game (including CD-ROM) hardware, which became known as the Interactive Digital Software Association (IDSA), met to discuss a voluntary rating system for game software. They created the Entertainment Software Rating Board (ESRB) to review independently entertainment software. After extensive research and consultation with consumers, leading psychologists and child advocates, the ESRB developed a standardised system for rating computer and video games. The voluntary system developed by the Rating Board is similar to that used by the movie industry. It rates games by age category: EC (early childhood), for ages 3 and up; E (everyone), for ages 6 and up; T (teen), for ages 13 and up; M (mature), for ages 17 and up; and AO (adults only), for ages 18; and over and RP (rating pending). The rating system went into effect for games arriving on the market after November 1, 1994. The ESRB has rated more than 7,200 titles submitted by over 300 publishers and developers. There is a need for such a system in India, before foreign video games swamped the market and reached wrong hands. This can help retailers to be vigilant about what they sell and can help professional as well as ethical retailers to categorise their offering and inform the appropriateness of the offering.

Types of toys

Toys can be classified into different categories like infant/pre-school, dolls, plush, action figure toys, vehicles, ride-ons, games/puzzles and activity toys. Each can constitute a department in a speciality toy store. In addition, if any of these have enough merchandise to be managed as a separate store, there is a possibility of a store-in-store concept to be made operational or a super speciality store that concentrates on any one of these categories. In the Indian context, however with toy retailing in its nascent stage, traditional toy products like stuffed animals, games, action figures, dolls or crayons will always spark interest in the years to come.

One of the key developments world-over in the toy industry and the retailing part in particular is the use of licensed characters. Because licensed products depend heavily on the movie, show or character they are affiliated with, the product can either boom or bust often in response to the success of the actual license. Moreover, because retailers usually have to order toys eight months in advance, picking a winning product can prove to be tricky. In an effort to avoid surplus stock, several retailers tend to restrict the number of actual licensed products to a minimum. There is further trouble in the Indian context. In the open economy, there is greater exposure to the international developments and there are interesting new developments in India. Which character, Indian or foreign –given the media exposure would interest the toy buyers, is a difficult development to predict.

Expanding market base

Today's children are growing up faster than any generation before. With advances in technology, combined with their access to all levels of information through media and peers, this trend makes sense. This development, known as age compression, continues to challenge toy manufacturers to create new, innovative toys that capture the interest of children. While many have reported that the average age range of children buying toys is 0-8 years of age, there seems to be a glimmer of hope for toy companies worldwide. A small but critical shift is taking place among the so-called tweens, due to the introduction of high-tech toys that require a higher level of creative input and play that is more intelligent. One of the advantages, therefore, for toy retailers in India is a broadening of the market for toy buying and therefore greater sales.

Given the trend in developed countries, Independent-speciality-toy-retailers would continue to create an expanding niche in the marketplace. Smaller toy stores cannot access hot best selling toys; if they can, they are priced substantially higher than chain stores. Therefore, small store survival depends on product uniqueness and customer service. These are unique selling points in toy marketing. Speciality stores attract an increasing number of customers wanting toys not available elsewhere and toys that enhance child development. Examples of speciality products include nostalgia and retro toys, do-it-yourself toys, and exotic toys. These help in developing niches that are hard to penetrate.

Online toy retailing

Online retailing or e-retailing of toys is a development that we can correlate with the development of software-based toys. While online shopping of traditional toys means a way of reaching (distribution) of traditional toys, some of the sophisticated game consoles that run based on software could be supported by new software that could be downloaded through the web site. In addition on line games for children and adults of different ages may change the buying behaviour of toy buyers. Although eToys.com pioneered U.S. online toy retailing, other toy retailers rapidly addressed the e-commerce challenge. In one U.S. holiday season, competition in online sales hit eToys. Attacking from the street as well as from cyberspace are the classic bricks-and-mortar retailers like Toys R Us and KB Toys (after spinning off their Web sites as separate companies). Other toy retailers and manufacturers such as Noodle-Kiddoodle, Fisher-Price, Hasbro, FAO Schwartz, Zany-Brainy, and Mattel promptly followed their lead by launching their own online stores. Big box retailers (Wal-Mart, Costco, Sears, Kmart, JC Penny, and Target) are poised to carve slices of the online toy market. Cutthroat competition in online toy retailing has inspired creation of speciality online stores (SmartKids.com, HardToFindToys.com) and special features (e.g., online animated, systematic instructions for assembling toys provided by Netoy.com). Nevertheless, the biggest challenge from the competition against eToys.com came in summer 1999 when Amazon.com, the Internet guru of the book world, began selling toys through its toy section. The next battleground for toy retailing seems to be the web. If we extend geographical area to cover almost the entire world, then we in India would really have to face the onslaught. One way of trying to face this situation is to look for Indian characters, traditional Indian toys and increased promotion of ethnic toys that would help face the onslaught.

The toy industry is a highly seasonal industry. A relatively small number of products accounts for the bulk of industry toy sales. In addition, the identity of the top selling toys in the industry changes substantially from year-to-year and is hard to predict. The strong seasonality in toy sales and the hit-driven nature of demand contribute to frequent divergences between anticipated and realised demand. The supply of toys, however, generally does not respond rapidly to unanticipated demand due to the relatively long delivery cycles resulting from overseas production and water borne international shipments. In view of this situation, at the retailing end, the importance of supply chain management becomes important. Specifically, logistics – a combination of inventory management and transportation becomes crucial. Management of this aspect of marketing ensures that the service levels are high for the store. Merchandise management also depends on the same. Stringent product control measures would have an impact on the positive development of branded toys. This would help retailers, if in the future there were a greater sensitiveness to issues of safety of toys.

SPORTS GOODS RETAILING

A significant segment of the Indian population has turned to fitness and exercise as part of an evolving lifestyle. Whether that entails a trip to a health club, jog through the neighbourhood or simply yoga in the living room, these people have a renewed vigour towards keeping fit. There are programmes on health and fitness in almost all television channels. This has resulted in the increase in awareness about health and fitness goods/equipment as well as different sports. The increased awareness of fitness along with the influence of the western media has resulted in personal fitness equipment that has grown quite popular in India. The large number of equipment that manufacturers sell through the television shopping networks also substantiates this. In addition, new sports as they develop in the west also have an immediate impact on youngsters, as they are highly impressionable by the international media available in their living room. The development of indoor games like pool is an example. This augurs well for the diversified development of sports and games unlike the still typically cricket crazy India.

Indian sports goods industry

The Indian sports goods industry, which is now more than 100 years old, has matured into a very capable supplier of sports goods to almost every part of the world. The skilled labour force, which had mastered the art of manufacturing the traditional item of sports goods, is now also venturing into fabrication of more high tech equipment for new trendy sports in response to the demands of the global market. Today, all sectors of sports goods including sports equipment, sports apparel, sports footwear and sports accessories are flourishing sectors of production and export in India. Buyers of Indian goods include top international brands like Adidas, Asics, Dunlop, Decathlon, Fila, Gap, Kookabura, Maxfli, Mitre, Nike, Puma, Rawlings, Reebok, Spalding, Canterbury of New Zealand, Rip-Curl etc. However, due to the skewed nature of interest in only one major game in India, namely cricket, retailing in India for sports goods has so far mainly concentrated on selling cricket related accessories rather than several types of sports. However, off late there is an emerging interest in several types of games/sports. In view of this development as well as the catching up of retail as a phenomenon in India, there is great scope for development of sports goods retailing.

Sporting goods retail development

The availability of a strong manufacturing base for sports goods that meet international standards and at the same time a nascent market for sports goods provides a great combination for retailing to flourish in this sector. One of the examples of the new entrants could be sports wear manufacturer and retailer Sportiff India. It has entered the sports goods retail segment by opening its first store "Sports Locker" in Chennai. Sports enthusiasts can now pick up cricket, tennis, badminton and other sports' gear from this outlet spread over 3,000 sq.ft. "Sports Locker" stocks sporting equipments for games like cricket, tennis, badminton among others. According to the company, Sportiff India plans to open 15 such stores in Hyderabad, Bangalore, Mumbai, Delhi, Mysore, Chandigarh, Pune and Noida. As of now a large number of small sports goods store exist in cities. Top Indian and multinational footwear stores like Action, Nike etc dabble into sports goods through their footwear stores. However, we are yet to see the development of a national level sports goods chain.

The American model and the possibilities in India

An understanding of the American context can give an idea of the nature of the development of sports good retailing. The three major merchandise categories in the sporting goods U.S. retail scene are equipment, footwear, and clothing. Equipment can be accredited to bringing in the largest amount of sales. Footwear was the second largest source of revenue, followed by clothing. We could divide the universe of sports participation into several sectors like Fitness, Team, Racquet, Skating, Indoor Games, Personal Contact Sports, Extreme Sports, Recreational Exercise, Bicycling, Helmet Sports, Board Sports, Outdoors Activities, Shooting Sports, Fishing, Snow and Water Sports. According to Sporting Goods Manufacturing Association International's Recreation Market Report, manufacturers' sales of sporting goods equipment, sports apparel, athletic footwear, and recreational transport items in the U.S. totalled $68.6 billion in 2003 - a 0.5% increase over 2002. The six largest specific categories of sports goods sold in the U.S. were exercise equipment machines; golf; firearms/hunting; camping; team/institutional; and fishing. In the exercise equipment category, treadmill sales account for 26.4% of that category. Consumer spending for exercise equipment accounts for 81.3% of the entire exercise equipment category. In the absence of figures in the Indian retail context, there is a possibility that the same trend as in the West is also reflected in domestic sales. In team sports, the three largest categories were baseball/softball, basketball and soccer. Sports apparel is still the largest segment of the sports and recreation industry.

The top two sporting goods retailers constitute only 3% of the total revenue of the industry. The Sports Authority (TSA), Dick's Sporting Goods, Gart Sports, Foot Locker Champs and East Bay are the prominent sports goods retailers in the U.S. in terms of sales revenue. Men are the major target segment. This is a major surprise and therefore for a long time to come, retailers may not target women in India, given the level of retail development in shopping goods. The major formats of sports goods in the U.S. are Traditional sports goods retailers e.g., Champs. Speciality sporting goods like Athlete's Foot, large format like TSA and mass merchandisers like Wal-Mart. Incidentally, Wal-Mart was the largest seller of sporting goods in the U.S. last year. We may expect a different kind of development on the sports goods front, if the development of hyper marts in India is going to exceed speciality stores.

Facilities and services

Sporting goods stores need to be service/facility intensive compared to other product based retail formats. Consumers use these goods very regularly. Therefore, they are bound to have requirements in terms of servicing on a regular basis. Facilities at the U.S. retail outlets range from facility to test golf clubs in an indoor driving range to an archery range, providing hunting/fishing license, custom boot fitting, and equipment rental. Two of the biggest sections of a retail store are the apparel section and the footwear section. Both sections carry a variety of products in many different brands. The apparel section includes a wide range of clothing from gym shorts to rain jackets. The footwear section carries many different styles of shoes for every type of sport.

Consumers make a distinction between indoor and outdoor sports. In India, we see that some outdoor sports are getting a special thrust due to corporate attention on training employees for physical endurance too. Such activities are part of outbound programmes done by specialised agencies, at present. Soon, regular activities that require private ownership of related accessories and equipment may start. One of the big sections in the U.S. sporting goods stores is the different areas of outdoor sports, such as water sports and winter sports. Sporting goods stores have a wide variety of equipment, apparel, and sometimes instruction available in these sections of the store. The outdoor section is also a major attraction for consumers. This section usually has many displays such as tents, cooking utensils and sometimes even a rock wall for climbing practice. Consumers identify the fitness and exercise section through its gym set up, displaying barbells, treadmills, stair steppers, and all kinds of weight lifting machines. Finally, most sporting goods stores will include a game room section which will house goods for ping-pong, darts, billiard, air hockey, and fuse-ball.

U.S. sporting goods retailers are known throughout the retail industry as being very good at customer service both during the consumer's purchase and after the purchase. In each store, there is always an employee in each section of the store. They do this for two reasons; the first reason is so that the customer does not have to go searching the entire store looking for an employee to help them. Secondly, each section has an employee who specialises in that particular section, for example, if a customer needs assistance in the golf section, he can be sure that the employee working in that section is familiar with the latest technology in the golf world.

The stores in U.S. are also respected for their customer service, after the sale. Most stores offer a phone number for the customer to call for assistance with the more complicated products or the assembling processes of certain products. They provide repair services for most of their products, especially the big ones like basketball goal and exercise equipment. In addition, they generally have good return policies for their equipment, allowing customers to test out products and return them after a short trial if they do not like them. Shipping and handling is another convenience of sporting goods retailers because they offer to distribute many of their bigger products so the customer does not have to rent a truck to transport them home.

The retailers in India with a background in durable retailing would have no problem in handling these facilities. Almost all retailers in durable retailing are currently undertaking services as these. However, the major bottleneck would be the knowledge of different sports among the employees and therefore the appreciation of the finer details as required by customers. On the other hand, there would also be a requirement for a through education of the consumer on the attributes of the product as well as the game to promote buying.

Online sports goods retailing

The world's biggest online retailer Amazon is trying to transform itself into a shopping mall. In the last week of September 2003, Amazon opened a sporting-goods department where retailers such as Golfsmith International Inc. can sell golf clubs, baseball bats and other athletic gear. Teaming up with other merchants eliminated inventory risk for Amazon and reduced the amount of expertise it needed to forecast accurately hot products in unfamiliar categories. It was a more practical strategy for Amazon following the bursting of the dot-com bubble, as the flow of funding for more expansion was shut off. The arrangement also suited retailers, who realised they were better off focusing on their main bricks-and-mortar businesses. Amazon is applying the same thinking to sporting goods. Rather than reconfigure its warehouses to handle hundreds of thousands of different types of products — a number that would have multiplied to millions of goods when different sizes, colours and other variations were added — Amazon has gone looking for experts in the business.

It found several takers, including Golfsmith, a chain of golf superstores, who were eager to sell their goods to Amazon's 35 million users. It also ran into a problem: Some golf-equipment makers do not want to see their goods in the Amazon shopping mall. Golfsmith, for one, was told by the makers of Titleist, Callaway and Ping goods not to sell their clubs and other gear through Amazon, even though Golfsmith is authorised to sell those same brands through its own Web site. Ping has allowed four speciality golf retailers to sell Ping equipment through their Web sites. Callaway Golf Co. asked retailers not to sell new Callaway equipment through Amazon. However, it gave permission to proceed to Callaway Golf Pre-Owned, a separate company owned by Trade Up Commerce Inc., to sell used Callaway clubs there. Other big brands are fighting the sale of their goods through Amazon include Nike. In any event, Nike's efforts have not been very successful: Many Nike products are still widely available through Amazon, listed by Foot Locker Inc., Nordstrom Inc. and others. Amazon executives say there is still a huge selection of sporting goods on its site, even without the support of those brands, and that it will win over detractors. The company says it has partnerships with "hundreds" of retailers overall and more than 50 retailers in its new sporting goods store alone.

Fogdog sports – sporting goods e-retailer

Fogdog Sports is considered a "pure-play" Internet retailer and the leading online retailer of sporting goods. They offer an extensive product selection, detailed product information and competitive prices. They claim to have the largest selection of sporting goods online, with up to 60,000 distinct stock keeping units representing more than 600 brands in all major sports categories. This includes sporting equipment and apparel for competitive athletes, team sports and sports enthusiasts.

Fogdog utilises traditional and online advertising, direct marketing, and strategic relationships to build brand awareness and acquire customers. They advertise on Web portals, such as AOL, and target radio, print and outdoor media. The company also sponsors sporting activities such as the Let it Fly flag football tournament, mountain bike races, and the homerun hitting contest during All-Star weekend of Major League Baseball. Fogdog targets people with active lifestyles and want to position their website as the online sports store built for people who "live to play sports".

Ideal etailing site requirements — consumer perspective

The home page needs to be linked to about 20 major sporting areas. Each of these areas will start with a basic page from which links will send customers to other pages from which specific items may be selected and purchases made. The same will also be true with respect to sporting goods by type (*e.g.*, footwear, clothes), and to sporting goods by brand.

Each of the sub-home pages needs to contain:

- Columns listing and linking to 20 or so categories of items within the sub-home page area (*e.g.*, for baseball, the links would be to bats in general, aluminium bats, wood bats.

- Columns listing and linking to 10 or so special sales items.

- Links to informational articles on such topics as

    (i)   Rules of the game or sport,

    (ii)   What to look for in a piece of equipment to select intelligently the item best suited to your needs,

    (iii) Care of equipment.

- Drop down window to enable one to search and go to any product available on the site.

- Illustrate special sales promotional items.

Each web page needs to have graphical illustrations of the product or products that are available (*e.g.*, jerseys, pants, shoes, bats, balls, golf clubs, hats, caps), as well as the following:

- Links for descriptions of the item or items

- Links to any available product reviews

- Links to the records and stats of the stars in case of personalised items

- Links to other items that are peculiarly related to the particular item (a web page for a Baichung Bhutia signature jersey might link to another web page featuring his signature football).

- Drop down windows for (i) item selected [in the event of a multiple product web page]; (ii) colour/size of item selected; and (iii) any other distinguishing characteristic; and (iv) functional link to shopping cart web page.

The three major forces that will compete for the fitness of Indians with high personal disposable income are "magic pills", weight loss programmes and physical exercise. Younger children with parents in this category are now more comfortable with video and computer games. In the past, kids would play outside after school, but now kids are more interested in the latest Play Station 2 games rather than playing sports. These developments are affecting the U.S. market too. The Sports Authority one of the biggest sports goods retailers in the U.S. has started two programmes to encourage kids to get involved in outside activities. The first, "Get

Out and Play" works with the Boys and Girls Clubs of America to promote the benefits of playing outside to kids in the age group four through fourteen. "Be a Sports Authority" is the second similar programme aimed at getting children outside instead of inside in front of the TV or computer. In the Indian scenario, manufacturers as well as retailers of sports goods need to both educate consumers as well as promote retailing of sports goods.

PHARMA RETAILING

Imagine ordering prescribed medicines through the net, getting automatic refills on regular prescribed drugs, a loyalty programme and door delivery. These are some of the immediate possibilities in drug retailing in the country.

The drug store industry is a large and growing industry, especially after the mid 1990s. An important factor in driving industry growth is the increased life expectancy of the population brought about by the discovery and widespread usage of new life-saving drugs. Life expectancy has increased among both males and females in India. Longer life expectancy is slowly increasing the population of older people. In this emerging scenario, it is worthwhile to note that senior citizens (60 years and older) typically use twice the number of prescribed medication as compared to individuals who are half their age. The growth in prescribed medication also benefits from the continuing flow of new drug therapies as well as increasing participation in health care plans. New drug therapies result from greater investment and higher success rates in the research and development programmes of major pharmaceutical firms. While demographic factors help drive growth in sales volumes, the Indian drug store industry would be under pressure to reduce costs. In response, drug stores have tried to do the same by installing improved cost-reducing technologies, such as advanced point-of-sale and scanning equipment to provide them with the most up-to-date information on sales and inventory. To enhance profits, faster drug dispensing to speed up pharmacy transactions, reduce errors and improve customer satisfaction is being achieved. Moreover, drug stores are also trying to attract customers and enhance profits with higher-margin products such as convenience foods, cosmetics, etc. We seem to be following the west in such developments. Meanwhile, drug stores are also experiencing increased competition from supermarkets who are anxious to increase store traffic with pharmacy sales. Thus, we see that for a category like pharma too, generic competition is not something that stores can be immune to.

CVS – the U.S. drug chain giant

The U.S. scenario would be able to provide us with an idea to predict the nature of things to come in India. CVS Corp., Walgreens and Rite Aid are the three largest three drug chains based on sales revenue. CVS competes based on store location and convenience, customer service and satisfaction, product selection and variety, and price. It experiences active competition not only from independent and other chain drugstores, but also from health maintenance organisations, hospitals, mail order organisations, supermarkets, discount drugstores and discount general merchandisers. In addition to prescription drugs and services, CVS offers a broad selection of general merchandise, presented in a well-organised fashion, in stores that were designed to be customer-friendly, inviting and easy to shop. Merchandise categories included over-the-counter drugs (OTC), greeting cards, film and photofinishing services, cosmetics, seasonal merchandise and convenience foods. The company followed an integrated healthcare approach, bringing together industry participants such as physicians, pharmaceutical companies, managed care providers and pharmacies. The primary efforts in this area included the operation and expansion of PharmaCare, CVS's prescription-benefit-management subsidiary, and the creation of strategic alliances with healthcare partners. The company's strategy is to be the nation's most convenient and most technologically advanced healthcare retailer. Consistent with an emphasis on convenience, drive-through prescription service was offered and one-hour photo was available. This sort of a culmination of several goods in an otherwise typical drug store could be an excellent example of how for example a Health and Glow outlet could be transformed with changes in the laws in India into a health supermarket.

Indian drug retail

The drug retailers in the Indian private sector have a great role in contributing to public health. Above six lakhs drug retail outlets can play a very important role on primary health care, as they are most commonly the first source of contact. A drug cannot have its intended therapeutic effect unless it reaches consumers along with relevant information on proper use, including storage of the drug. Failure to give proper advice, suggestion and support also leads to low compliance, failure of therapy and with anti-biotic use, emergence of anti-biotic resistance. The vast majority of population prefer to visit medical stores or meet drug retailers for certain common trivial illnesses because either they find physicians are not available (especially rural areas) or escape of paying physicians fees. Drug retailers, are certainly in a position of health care dynamics, who can help general population get the most effective use out of any drug people buy, since they are the last professional to whom consumer meet before a drug is used.

The status of drug retailers in the provision of health care is far from satisfactory. It is also acknowledged that the level of drug information provided by them is insignificant. A number of recent survey studies on medical stores and community pharmacists revealed that the community pharmacists or the drug retailers in India do not do anything other than selling drugs. Public do not differentiate drug retailers from general commodity retailers (grocers). The services of qualified pharmacists as drug retailers which when implemented as per training they receive and in compliance with existing laws, could enhance the availability of right medicines for the right purposes for a majority of the Indian population.

The service angle

The increasing importance of service in the context of a drug store is evidenced by Rite Aid's RAPTOR (recognise, appreciate, praise, treat associates respectfully) and SMILE (say hello, make eye contact, identify yourself, listen carefully, express thanks) initiatives. These initiatives in the U.S. serve as a precursor to the changes that Indian drug stores also may undergo in India. The coming together of all players in the health-care market including the insurance service provider, could be a potent combination that could rewrite the rules of drug retailing. Actually, the unit could be as much a health maintenance and disease-state-management clinic as a drug store, offering all manner of diagnostic testing and screening programmes designed both to prevent and to manage illness. Imagine under one roof a customer/patient can get cholesterol and blood pressure checks, eyesight and hearing tests, bone mineral density evaluations, and prostate and thyroid monitored. Therefore, it is possible that the patient can be screened for diabetes and asthma, and taught to manage those illnesses effectively, too. Under the same health-care clinic roof, the patient can sign up for a smoking cessation effectively, too. Weight management or drug therapy consultation, join a blood pressure-monitoring group or learn about the range of durable medical equipment and diabetic and asthma products available at the store. The patient would get the results of these tests within minutes, explained to him or her by one of the full-time clinical pharmacists permanently assigned to the drug store's staff. Such a separate healthcare centre, adjacent to an open and easily accessed pharmacy could potentially offer a breadth and depth of preventive screening, testing services and great accessibility.

Some of the new developments in the drug store segment in the U.S. are bewildering. These include:

- Utilisation of robotics to dispense the 100 most frequently dispensed drugs and organisation of filled prescriptions alphabetically in a hanging fixture for speed in getting them to the patient.

- Usage of portable paging devices similar to those used by high-volume restaurants to alert the patient that her prescription is ready, even if that patient is away from the store.

- Free home delivery service.

- Private label line, one effectively positioned as a quality and value alternative to the national brands in a drug store. Given the population in India, some of these services and a concept like private label in drugs could revolutionise drug retailing.

Medicine Shoppe India

Already developments in this direction have taken place in India with the setting up of the Medicine Shoppe. Medicine Shoppe India with its referral programmes, monthly gift programmes, and programmes for expectant mothers offers a definite threat to the established traditional drug retailers. Medicine Shoppe tied up with pharmaceutical companies for sponsoring free diagnosis once a week. It tied-up with Nicholas Piramal for diabetes, with Elder for bone densitometry tests for osteoporosis, with Parke Davis for dental examination, and with Omron for examining blood pressure. In a bid to provide another value-added service, The Medicine Shoppe India and Oriental Insurance Company have joined hands to offer free Mediclaim to Medicine Shoppe customers. Now with every purchase of Rs 5,000 made at a Medicine Shoppe pharmacy a customer will get a Mediclaim policy worth Rs 5,000. These are indications of the kind of change that is to hit the drug retailing industry in the country.

Prescription discount

One of the important dimensions of drug retailing that is related to consumption of drugs for chronic diseases is the need for repeated use of a drug for a long period. This can be utilised effectively to targeted prescription discount cards. There are several such branded cards like AARP Prescription Discount Card; aClaim Rx Savings Club; Aetna Rx Savings Card; ArgusRx Preferred Prescription Discount Card; Rx Savings, distributed by Reader's Digest; and ScriptSave Premier. This can greatly help most prescribed generics as well as brands and the consumers effectively.

Electronic prescription

A major innovation slowly taking shape in the U.S. is that of electronic prescribing. Electronic prescribing, limited a few years ago to just a few dozen physicians and pharmacies in a handful of markets across the U.S., is on the verge of becoming part of every pharmacy's daily operation. In a country like India, which is the hot bed of development in the IT sector, development of such a system would be an easy task. With the spread of IT literacy, this one area can help retailers. Currently even in the U.S., E-prescribing is illegal in some states because established laws say that no third party can have access to prescription information. While the growing number of pharmacies that can accept new and refill prescriptions electronically has been a big factor in getting more physicians to explore e-prescribing, a number of other recent developments have also helped convince doctors that the technology will be an important part of their future. Prescribing errors can cause patients to suffer adverse reactions to medication. While some of those reactions occur because of mistakes made at the pharmacy, many are a result of physician errors. Adverse reactions are preventable and e-prescribing would eliminate two-thirds of preventable reactions. Moreover, integration of the patient, doctor as well as drug retailer information would have a tremendous benefit for the lawmakers in tracking citizens, doctors, pharmacists and pharmacies.

Innovations in the Indian context are required for some of the typical problems faced by retailers like –

a)   The mushrooming of pharma brands

b)   Not enough space for so many brands in the outlet and for the retailer

c)   Inventory issues, especially of some costly drugs

d)   Maintenance of an air-conditioned outlet for stocking some medicines in a situation where constant power cuts are the norm

e)   Differential tax rates across states

f)   Absence of a professional relationship between doctors, chemists and companies in the pharma business.

The consolidation of the healthcare business poses a threat to the traditional drug retailers, unless they look at innovative marketing measures to stay in the market. The need is for juxtaposing general retail management principles to drug retailing to come up with ideas for sustaining efforts to grow in pharma retailing.

The ageing of the Indian population and efforts at long-term tackling of issues related to the health of especially senior citizens in the country are coming to the fore in discussions at the future directions of government spending. The drug retail industry cannot be ignored in this scheme of things. However, these business persons, to exploit this opportunity in the future require innovative ways of tackling the current problems facing them. A market/consumer (patient) oriented approach as is being exhibited in the west could be the answer. The market is ripe for innovations and those who get to the market first with new services as a drug retailer, are the ones who will eventually succeed.

JEWELRY RETAILING

The jewelry market in India is estimated to be growing at 10% per annum. Of the total Rs. 50,000-crore Indian jewelry market, which is growing at 3-5%, the diamond studded market accounts for around Rs 9,000 crore and is growing at 20%. Of the total diamond jewelry market, only 2% is branded jewelry catered to by around 8-10 brands, which is why there is a huge potential for branded diamond jewelry in India. Gold jewelry forms the major part of the jewelry market in India.

Jewelry is a very fragmented business. There are around 2,50,000 jewelry retailers and there are many more manufacturers. Tanishq and Oyzterbay are some of the prominent national players in the serious fine jewelry segment. The others jewelry retailers are in just one city or have a limited regional presence. Acquiring a high reputation for styling and reliability and becoming an aspirational brand are prerequisites for the success of the national brand. As regards reliability, the jewelry industry has chronically lacked ethics. In the Indian context, therefore hallmarking has become a major movement in order to convince consumers about genuineness of the jewelry purchased.

Hallmarking

As per this scheme the jewelry retailer/manufacturer desirous of obtaining a license, apply to BIS for use of Standard Mark (Hallmark) on their jewelry. After registration, a Preliminary Inspection for verification of premises retailing/manufacturing, BIS Officials carry out testing of facilities and competence of testing personnel. A sample is drawn from the jewellers' retail/manufacturing premises for independent testing. Based on the satisfactory Preliminary Inspection report and test report of the sample drawn during inspection, license is granted to the jeweller.

After grant of license, the jeweller (retailer/manufacturer) has to follow a BIS approved Scheme of Testing and Inspection on a continuing basis to have confidence in the homogeneity and purity of the gold jewelry offered for hallmarking. A BIS certified jeweller (retailer/ manufacturers) has the right to register himself with any of the BIS recognised Assaying and Hallmarking Centres to get his jewelry hallmarked. BIS maintains surveillance on the certified jewellers, at a defined periodicity. Market surveillance involves collection of hallmarked gold jewelry from licensee's retail outlet/manufacturing premises and having it tested for conformity in BIS recognised Hallmarking Centre.

Deviations in degree of purity of fine metal and observance of operations not in conformance to the system may result in cancellation of BIS licence, and invoke legal proceedings for penalties under the BIS Act, Rules and Regulations. .A hallmark, consists of five components i.e. BIS Mark, the Fineness number (corresponding to given cartage), Assaying and Hallmarking Centre's Mark, Jeweller's Mark and year of Marking denoted by a code letter and decided by BIS (e.g. code letter "A" was approved by BIS for year 2000, "B" being used for the year 2001 and "C" for 2002). The marking is done either using punches or laser marking machine. The BIS hallmark, a mark of conformity widely accepted by the consumer, bestow the additional confidence to the consumer on the purity of gold jewelry. The total cost of hallmarking for a retailer who produces 5,000 pieces per year including the initial application fee, inspection fee, testing charges, annual license fee and annual minimum marking fee would work out to Rs 29,900. That means the cost of hallmarking one piece will work out to only Rs 46. The consumers are willing to pay this additional Rs 46 per piece to get a jewelry of pure quality.

Branded jewelry

Branded jewelry is close to Rs 10 bn in India and growing at around 15%. Branded jewelry as a fashion accessory still commands a small share – less than 1% – of the Rs 40,000-crore jewelry market in India, but it is growing at a healthy 20-30% annually. The urban market is shifting from heavy gold jewelry to lighter, trendier ornaments. Consumers are replacing one expensive, chunky set with several lightweight ones that would fit a variety of occasions. Inter Gold is the only jewelry company in India, which has tie-ups with the three leading jewelry organisations such as DTC (De Beers), PGI (Platinum Guild India) and WGC

(World Gold Council). Internationally, it is working closely with several of the top designers including Vera Wangs, Stefan Hafner and Roberto Coin. The major national brands in jewelry in India are Tanishq, Nakshaktra, Gilli and Asmi. Tanishq is more into gold jewelry. Branded Jewelry retailers in India face tough competition from traditional family jewellers who for generations serve families. The customisation, emotional bonding and tradition act as a strong hurdle in families switching to branded jewelry. However, the new generation of customers has taken to branded jewelry, due to effective promotion.

The U.S. market

In the U.S., Zale is one of the leading nationally branded jewelry stores. Based out of Irving, Texas, this company has stayed successful by means of realigned executive and divisional management teams, upgraded merchandising programmes, and a fully integrated "Piercing Pagoda." Piercing Pagoda has broadened Zale's range of jewelry stores for customers who appreciate quality jewelry at everyday low pricing. It revolutionised the industry in the initial years by changing the cash-only policy of jewelry retailing, choosing to offer credit to working-class customers and allowing payment in installments. Other innovations were an employee profit-sharing plan, mass advertising, commitment to sales training, and development of a corporate child-care facility. Zale opened a permanent office in Antwerp, Belgium, to buy uncut stones, a first for the retail jewelry business.

The retail jewelry environment in the U.S. is one of intense competition from many different types of retailers. Both high scale and low scale retailers are in direct competition with each other in this market. While some might consider jewelry a luxury item, to some it is a necessity. Establishments are primarily engaged in the retail sale of any combination of the lines of jewelry, such as diamonds and other precious stones mounted in precious metals rings, bracelets, and broaches; sterling and plated silverware; and watches and clocks. Wal-Mart just a few years ago was the number one in jewelry retail sales and it is not a retail jeweller! Sterling is a retail jeweller that is a subsidiary of Signet Group (U.K.). Sterling has also targeted its Jared Galleria of Jewelry superstores as its future growth vehicle. J.C. Penny along with Sears Roebuck, and Co. is also known for jewelry retailing. JC Penney has recently added jewelry to its Web offerings, beefed up its diamond inventory, and is testing some higher-end lines in platinum, 18K yellow and white gold Italian designs, and more fashionable gemstones lines like the Princess Alexandra collection for the younger, upscale consumers.

The attraction of the yellow metal is also strong in the U.S., which last year marked the 13th consecutive year of gold jewelry sales increases. The sales growth came amid political uncertainty, a weak dollar and rising gold prices. One of the interesting observations in the U.S. markets is in amount of details available in the form of data. Reports go to the extent of describing - Bracelets increased. Earring sales increased significantly, influenced by the fashion world's embrace of yellow gold hoops, dangling chandelier-style earrings and shoulder-duster drop earrings.

Jewelry.com, an e-jewelry retailer in the U.S. was instrumental in bringing key jewelry retail names together on the net, allowing a "cooperative competition" programme to be established for the inaugural Gold Month to promote gold jewelry. This convergence of manufacturers, wholesalers and retailers under the World Gold Council's media banner has benefited the whole jewelry industry and its best customers.

The jewelry retailing market in the U.S. is also largely similar to India, in terms of the maximum sales of jewelry happening only through jewelry stores. However, there is a significant difference in the use of super markets and departmental stores in the U.S. for the retailing of jewelry that is yet to happen in India.

Jewelry store related issues

To keep your jewelry inventory current with the latest fashions, there is just one important rule: Know Your Market. Learn everything you can about your customers. That means that if your clients were mostly young teens, you would need to monitor the jewelry worn by models in Teen Fashion magazines. There are tons of resources available online. A search at your favourite search engine for fashions targeted at your age group is an easy way to understanding your market.

Store design issues

One of the most important issues that any jewelry store deals with is how the store is designed. When looking at the design, a store would look at security and ambience. When looking a security the store needs to make sure it protects its property. Because jewelry stores carry many high cost items, it is important that security is an utmost priority. With the inclusion of cameras and, for some higher end stores, guards this overt presence does well to hinder theft. However, other things need to be done. Alarms on all cases are an easy way to prevent theft. Putting your most valuable pieces of jewelry in a visible place so that your employees can keep an eye on them is another way to prevent theft. In addition, a comprehensive insurance package greatly saves the jewelry retailer from the trauma of an unfortunate happening.

Ambience is a great way to sell your store and its products. A combination of the five senses allows a consumer to enjoy the experience of buying jewelry. When a store is looking at a colour, they want to look at muted tones, with blues, greens, and reds accentuating the gemstones. The use of natural light is also an important aspect of store design. Natural light enhances the customers' view of the jewelry and gives them the feeling of comfort. Sound is another way of making customers enjoy their experience. Experts suggest hidden speakers with light jazz or light classical music. This selection lets the customer relax in a store. The scent of your store can make or break a sale. Many companies now offer scents to be introduced into a store. While a scent alone does not guarantee a sale, it does guarantee that the customer does not leave immediately. Touch is one that maybe hard to do but if the store has nice velvet pads for piece showing and the cases are not greasy messes, then the store has enhanced the customers' experience. Finally, taste is hard because you cannot taste stones but a store can offer complimentary drinks and snacks that make a customer feel at home.

Characteristics of jewelry retailing

Low asset turnover is expected in jewelry retailing. Jewelry is typically durable, expensive, and infrequently purchased by most consumers. Jewelry is also a strongly differentiated product. A single jewelry store may carry over 150 different styles of watches. The consumer will choose one watch from among the entire selection. Hence, the jewelry store must maintain a large inventory to support its sales. Because the jewelry store's main asset is inventory, which has a slow rate of turnover, the typical jewelry store will show low asset turnover. Jewelry is a differentiated product where the typical buyer cannot easily assess the quality of the item being purchased. Consequently, differentiation among jewelry retailers falls along lines of intangibles such as service, quality, and reputation.

E-retailing of jewelry

Jewelry sites need to have a descriptive, visually defining web site. Efficient product viewing is essential to every retail web site; long load times shun customers away from your web site. Images and photos of products are a very big part of load time, but to be an effective online jewelry store, images and photos must be included. We will look at both effectiveness and efficiency of jewelry sites. The determination of whether a site is usable or not will be based on –

- How well the site incorporates effectiveness of describing the product

- Efficiency at which the site is viewed.

The ideal site will provide a balance between both of these usability aspects. Users visit jewelry sites for many different reasons, mostly to get information about certain jewelry. The whole idea behind a jewelry web site is to generate interest in a particular piece and maybe even a purchase. To be able to spark an interest in a customer searching through numerous sites that offer jewelry, the optimal site must offer an information-intensive website that runs as efficient as possible. Jewelry sites need a description of the product, which should include aspects such as weight, size, metals, etc. Jewelry sites need to be self-explanatory, when a user accesses the site they need to be able to tell a link from text otherwise it will waste their time and they will be looking at another jewelry site within seconds. For an effective jewelry website, one must design an online product-catalogue that describes and displays every product, efficiently. A basic design is to utilise product level pages. These include a top-level product page and a bottom-level product page.

A top-level product page is a web page that consists of a number of similar products listed. An example would be a list of platinum rings in a jewelry store. The basic design of this page would include a small image of each product with the product name and brief description. An example would be a web page on a platinum ring with one big diamond and two small ones. This type of product page would include

- An in-depth description of the product
- Several images of the product and images at different angles
- Links to larger, more detailed, images of the product

For a successful online jewelry web site, this is almost mandatory. The basic criterion for this assumption is because jewelry sites are going to sell expensive products and products, which are bought because of their looks. Simply providing the user with one medium-sized photo of the product will, most of the times not yield a purchase.

Italy's strength is in plain gold jewelry, Thailand's strength is in gemstone jewelry and China and Hong Kong are strong in diamond jewelry, while India has an edge over all these major international jewelry exporters, with a capability to offer all this jewelry, manufactured in most modern factories. This makes India a great jewelry destination. In addition, the huge population in our country makes India a lucrative retail destination for jewelry as well. The new developments reported in the print media prove a good augury for jewelry retailers in India. Fort Group, a Kolkata-based real estate promoter and developer, has planned to set up the first ever jewelry mall, 'Fort Knox' in Kolkata, to tap the sprawling gems and jewelry market.

The Rs 20 crore project, the first of its kind in eastern India, would house reputed national and international brands and non-branded jewelry. It is proposed to be a nine-storied mall for the gems and jewelry business. It will accommodate 37 shops and 40 offices for leading jewellers. Aerens Goldsouk International plans to set up 10 malls across the country to retail an entire range of jewelry in gold, silver, platinum, diamonds, semi -precious stones, watches and lifestyle accessories. The Gurgaon Gold Souk will cater to Delhi and 20 other nearby cities including Jaipur, Jalandhar, Ludhiana and Chandigarh. The second such store is likely to come up at Mumbai. This mall would give customers access to jewelry from all regions in India under one roof and also spare to the jewellers.

Higher levels of disposable income, awareness to fashion, information, and availability of various options in jewelry have made jewelry retailing a very interesting proposition for retail development. In the Indian context, rural areas have a unique affinity towards imitation jewelry. Imitation jewelry has assumed large proportions to stimulate development of fancy stores in to exclusive imitation jewelry shops. These retail outlets in the semi-urban areas have been catering to the aspirations of many consumers who cannot afford to buy luxurious jewelry. This unique trend has no parallels in the west, especially the context of jewelry retailing.

FURNITURE RETAILING

An estimated 4.5 million houses are built every year and there is a latent demand for 33 million homes in India. The housing sector is expected to grow at a fast pace driven by easy availability of finance, rising 'youth' population and declining average age at which an individual purchases a house (at 25-30 years as against 35-40 a few years ago). One's furniture made by the local carpenter is time consuming and one has no guarantee of after-sales service. Only about 10% of the public still has their furniture made by local carpenters. In addition, there are not as many skilled carpenters as 10 - 15 years ago. Moreover, no matter how skilled the carpenter is, s/he cannot equal the finish that readymade or imported furniture can give. The furniture goods sector comes next to grocery and apparel in being one of the largest retail sales goods in the world. Furniture retail in India is a Rs. 17,500 crore annual industry including both residential furniture and office furniture segments. The United States furniture industry is a very large and fragmented market. No U.S. furniture retailer has more than 3% market share. In the U.S., average stock turns in the furniture retail industry are at just 2.5 to 3.0 per year. In spite of typical 50% (or greater) gross profit margins in the U.S., the cost of inbound freight, retail display, warehousing, handling, and re-delivery make the job of furniture retailing quite difficult. The situation is no different in India. The lack of data on this front, however, makes it difficult to make an emphatic statement about furniture retailing in India.

In the U.S., Ethan Allen is a leading manufacturer and retailer of home furnishings/ furniture products. It sells a full range of furniture products through a network of more than 300 retail stores – 25% of which are corporate owned and 75% are run by exclusive franchisees. In addition to its retail presence, the company also has 21 manufacturing plants and three sawmills throughout the country. The vertical integration of its furniture design, manufacturing, and distribution operations provides the company with competitive advantages that allow it to leverage its buying power, streamline operations and shorten manufacturing lead times – all of which lead towards cost savings. In India too but for a few national players like Durian, Style Spa, the industry is dominated by local players. We however do not see such a large presence of nationally branded furniture retail outlets compared to the U.S.

Brick and mortar - purchase process

Women overwhelmingly dominate the furniture buying process both in the U.S. as well as in India. They generally initiate purchases and control 80% of all purchasing decisions. The brick and mortar-furniture-store-visitor's buying process generally starts with a predilection for the type of furniture they want to buy. General tastes are determined by media influences as well as the influence of those closest to the purchaser. In order to purchase furniture, the general offline model requires the customer to drive to a store. Interaction with salespeople will help fill what gaps the purchaser has. Salespeople should be able to lead the consumer to the best available solution at their particular stores. The offline consumer values this interaction.

Unfortunately, the bulky nature of the product makes it very difficult for a store to keep a wide product selection or a significant amount of inventory. The purchaser then makes a decision based on how well the furniture meets his or her needs. The ability to "look, touch, and feel" is another valued purchase behaviour in the offline environment. Often, consumers will need to go to several different stores in order to get the type of furniture they initially envisioned. Since this is a long-term purchase (even longer than that of a car), consumers are very selective.

The main occasion of purchase in the life of an individual in the Indian context is when one gets married – the bridegroom buys furniture himself or the parents-in-law gift the same to him. In addition, couples purchase new furniture when getting into a new house. Transfer from one city to another within an organisation or while joining a new organisation also triggers new furniture purchase depending on the number of years of working as well as the allowance/reimbursement provided by the organisation for new furnishing. In some organisations like banks, furniture is available on rent from the organisation that makes the consumer postpone the purchase, until he buys his own house for permanent living.

Nature of product and e-retailing implications

Furniture is more of an experiential product than standardised and inexpensive products like books and CDs. The greater price points on furniture as well as the long product life of furniture, combine to restrict impulse purchases and encourage extensive product research by the consumer. Consumers rate home furnishings as the second least likely item they would purchase online. Men currently comprise the majority of online users and consumers (buyers of products online) both in India as well the U.S. This means a mismatch between those who buy furniture and those who use online sources in general. In spite of this, it may be more apt to initiate and explore furniture purchases online. Although furniture consumers may be more task-oriented, storeowners should not ignore the experiential component of their experiences. This experience may provide considerable opportunity for increasing sales per transaction and greater cross-selling opportunities. For example, two of U.S.'s largest upholstered furniture manufacturers – Flexsteel and La-Z-Boy – recently partnered with an internet application service provider, Intellitek, to provide software that will allow consumers to design furniture on-line, access new fabric patterns and view accurate digital imagery of selections. Once a design is chosen, the software's retail locator will find the nearest retailer for seeing the finished piece or obtaining more information.

The use of manufacturer's brand name

The case goods (wooden furniture – initially furniture made out of wooden cases) sector within home furnishings requires a capital-intensive manufacturing process due to the customisation of products and hand finishing that is often required. There are a variety of design styles, wood options and price points within the category. In the U.S., the two largest manufacturers, La-Z-Boy and Furniture Brands International understood that furniture retailing is a marketing-driven business where store owners are able to grab market share by differentiating their brand and serving niche markets. They found that, because they own the brand, they are able to go directly to the consumer through branded retail outlets. Ethan Allen has been a pioneer in this model and others have followed. This is something that can happen in the Indian context, well-established brand names in the manufacturing industry would venture into retailing in a big way to help reap benefits of retailing. While this has happened in the case of steel furniture manufacturers like Godrej and Usha, it is yet to happen in a big way in wooden and plastic furniture segments.

Developments in the future

Two developments are similar in the U.S. and Indian furniture-retailing sector. Both these countries are facing an onslaught of cheap products/components from countries like China. At the same time, most retailers have established relationships with furniture manufacturers in China, Malaysia etc to thrive in the business. Wal-Mart, Ethan Allan and Rooms To Go (retailers in the U.S.) have all established a long-term sourcing relationship with one of the biggest Chinese pinewood goods manufacturer, Markor, Inc. Ethan Allan has even signed a long-term strategic contract with Markor where the company would not only buy large amounts of goods directly every year from Markor but would also join with Markor to exploit the furniture retailing business in China. Merger, acquisition and consolidation are the major forms of developments that one can see in the future in the highly fragmented industry. Continuing with a popular acquired brand rather than trying to attach other names to their offerings is likely to be the trend. Through allocation of fixed costs over more brands and units, acquisitions make economic sense for most acquirers.

Customer relationship management and marketing alliances have made furniture retailing a more marketing oriented business. In marketing, a widely cited example of the use of customer-specific information comes from selling a specific type of home furnishing – the nation's number one vendor of clocks is American Express, a firm with a comprehensive database on the spending patterns of higher-income families. The use of databases effectively through data mining and obtaining the right time to impact upon the consumer goes a long way in achieving success in the retail marketing of furniture. Stores also use partnerships to integrate online shopping with furniture retailing. Furniture Fan. com and Best Brands Plus, for example, have made plans for an online alliance. Furniture Fan is providing Best Brands Plus stores with a web presence designed to lead shoppers to a bricks and mortar store. Consumers' benefit from the search engine in furniture fan.com and access to large amounts of information, but many consumers make actual purchase through a neighbourhood store. The combination of customisation through the web and convenience by the help of accessible physical store location make the alliance a major hit with consumers.

International competition and new niche products

Containerised shipping has lowered international transportation costs, and compressed packaging technologies have lowered damage from shipping. In addition, consumer acceptance has been high for easily shipped "knock-down" and "ready to assemble" furniture. In addition to these developments, new segments have sprung up in the retail furniture market. Some of them that are already in vogue in the U.S. and would impact India in the not so distant future are:

a.   Furniture for home offices

b.   Customised furniture i.e. wood furniture that is unstained, allowing consumers to apply the specific finish type, colour and texture they desire

c.   Occasional tables with etched glass insignia or logos that can be changed for specific "micro" markets

   Specialised furniture like dual-purpose sleep furniture; lift chairs, video game chairs and many other furniture products today are highly specialised by function. In the future, specialised furniture products will likely grow in number and many will incorporate health functions and other concerns of an aging population. Beds, chairs and other furniture pieces, for example may increasingly provide "high tech" back support or include electronic devices to monitor, record and transmit heart rate, sleep time and other health-related information. In addition, with growth in larger homes and with increased numbers of relatively affluent consumers, demand is increasing for specialised cabinets and other furniture designed for larger bathrooms, walk-in closets and entertainment.

Environment friendliness as a niche

Green furniture: General consumer awareness of the environmental "friendliness" of products will continue to increase and manufacturers and marketers of furniture have been and are responding to this trend. For example, furniture retailing giant IKEA requires manufacturers to phase out the use of solid wood from "ancient" forests unless the Forest Stewardship Council certifies the wood. Manufacturers and marketers can be proactive in addressing this trend by incorporating more recycled raw materials and by developing more "renewable" furniture products, e.g., products with easily changed cushions, covers and drawer faces.

Changes for the Indian furniture retailer

The Indian consumer in the home furniture market is now in a situation where a deluge of options is available in terms of the material of furniture as well as its customisability. Case goods furniture retailers the traditional lot among the retailers now face an onslaught in terms of cheaper, trendier/fashionable, lighter, dismountable options. It has been observed in the U.S. too that the consumer goes only to furniture retailers, rather than to a departmental store for buying furniture. Therefore, the retailer needs to expand his outlet in order to provide variety. With the increase in variety it would be possible to also open niche furniture shops concentrating on one type of material, like say for example only cane furniture. Tax laws as well as problems of regional competition hamper branding, consolidation and establishment of a large retail network. In addition, the imported furniture effect also takes a toll on even the traditional furniture outlets. Better customisation than the conservative carpenter-constrained-customisation, and using technology at both the manufacturing and retailing end, would see the beginning of a new era of furniture retailing in India.

HOME DEPOT-A MODEL HARDWARE STORE

Home Depot was in the news recently as it was about to decide on an Indian outsourcing partner for its business processes. In this context, it would be worthwhile to look at the organisation, which is the leader in the home improvement market in the U.S. Some of the unique management practices of Home Depot represent its individual persona as a business entity. It also represents a case of an otherwise mature industry for the products transformed into a retailing success through innovative efforts and a strong business model/plan to back. The ingredients of success of Home Depot are worth emulating even in the Indian home improvement market.

Building blocks

Home Depot offers the widest selection of items in huge stores that average over 130,000 square feet. The store design, involving no frills and very high ceilings, allows the outlets to store large quantities of merchandise on store shelves. Home Depot has no warehouses or distribution centres, but stores receive direct deliveries 24 hours per day from a strictly limited number of vendors. Goods unloaded from vendor trucks are placed directly onto the selling floor using palettes. These represent a single-minded proposition offered to the customers and followed through in the activities of the company. Home Depot employs well-trained employees, many of whom are former trade's people, to provide customer service. The company appeals especially to "do-it-yourselfers," many of whom are men, as well as smaller contractors. This aspect represents the identification of the market segment very clearly. Both are attracted to Home Depot's low prices. The efforts of Home Depot thus reflect clearly the understanding of basics of retail marketing in a category.

Most retailers attempt to grow sales profitably by pursuing some combination of two generic merchandising tactics: (a) build traffic; and (b) exploit the existing installed customer base. With traffic building, the retailer attempts to grow store sales at a rapid rate while pursuing cost containment. Retailers employ aggressive loss leader pricing to bring consumers into the store and fuel a favourable price/value image that they can leverage when opening new stores that steal shares from existing competition. Home Depot, the home improvement chain successfully used this basic formula to open new stores at a fast enough pace to compensate for the diminishing sales rate increases generated by their portfolio of older (> 5 years) store locations. Home Depot revolutionised the do-it-yourself market looking across two different industries: in the past people interested in home improvements could hire contractors, at an expensive rate, or buy tools and materials from a hardware store and do the work himself. Both the solutions had weak points: the first was expensive and the second was difficult for inexperienced people. The management of Home Depot analysed the relative merits of each substitute industry and created a new type of store, offering free specialised consultancy by trained sales assistants and even lower prices than conventional hardware stores.

The power of alliances

Retailing is an established industry. In the retailing sector, food, apparel, furniture, and later home improvement are one of the oldest categories. In established industries, the industry structure long remained unchanged. For the following reasons, the innovation opportunities that do exist are most likely to exist in the "white spaces" between companies:

- Opportunities that fall within corporate boundaries have already been studied and exploited relatively well. This represents the internal efficiency achieved by the companies by concentrating on activities within the organisation.

- The industry structure inevitably lags changes in the marketplace, thus leaving white-space opportunities unexplored. Hardware stores were in operation for several years that they ignored other possibilities as consumer behaviour changed.

- Corporate boundaries and corporate orthodoxies—the deeply held beliefs of managers about the scope and capabilities of their firm—act as blinders that prevent managers from identifying opportunities outside the company's traditional business. And whereas corporate boundaries are becoming increasingly permeable by means of virtual or Internet technology, free-agent workers, and open-source movements, such boundaries still often serve as relatively rigid business demarcations. Home Depot is a good example of a company that has exploited extended innovation, exploring white-space opportunities by recombining its own assets and competencies with those of other companies. The power of alliances and the openness to join hands with product and service providers in boundary spanning activities, result in greater utilisation of a network of organisational capabilities and the synergy that comes along with it.

For instance, the retailer of home-improvement and hardware supplies has leveraged its competence in branding to establish a line of Home Depot–branded tools for young children. Home Depot is selling these toy tools through a partnership with Toys "R" Us, which contributes competence in marketing to children as well as an enormous distribution channel through its stores. This act utilises retail brand equity to develop products and then use the retail brand equity of other stores to one's advantage, but at the same time catching consumers young and reminding them of Home Depot as the brand for home improvement. Nevertheless, Home Depot's innovation extends beyond alliances in the retail industry to include alliances with the real-estate developer, an insurance company, and a provider of consumer credit.

Home Depot is helping real-estate developers in Southern California to publicize their residential developments. In return, the developers allow Home Depot to demonstrate painting techniques, window treatments, landscape design, and other projects at show homes. In another partnership, Home Depot and insurance company Allstate are collaborating to drive traffic to Home Depot stores while reducing home repair costs for Allstate. Under the arrangement, Allstate insurance adjusters encourage contractors to buy replacement materials from Home Depot stores, where prices are low. The benefits to Home Depot are significant: Allstate paid an estimated $100 million in claims for carpet damage alone in the year 2000, and Home Depot can now expect to gain a significant share of that business. Meanwhile, Home Depot customers can now receive on-the-spot approval for major home-improvement loans in Home Depot stores through an alliance between Home Depot and GE Capital Financial. Loans are available for use on products and services at any Home Depot store. Customers can charge purchases to their Home Depot loan account for a period of up to six months after their first purchase.

Vehicle of promotion

Promotion of the retail store is one of the crucial elements of the retail marketing effort. Staff with knowledge and capability in their departments (e.g. roofing, floor covers, painting, etc.) can be great supplement to external promotional efforts. Home Depot staff members can demonstrate techniques and offer advice to its key demographic consumer segment. Real-estate developers can provide settings for Home Depot staff to demonstrate wallpapering, flooring, painting, etc. A network of large warehouse-style stores with space to promote can provide promotional support to partners of these stores. Home depot promotes real estate developers in its stores, alleviating high promotional costs that developers usually face. A store of the size of Home Depot provides national brand recognition real estate developers can promote home depot to builders—a major target market for Home Depot. Home Depot's strategic assets and competencies provide a customer base with strong interest in home improvement, home maintenance, yard work, etc. Moreover, they have established relationships with builders thus making availability of show homes and homes that are still under construction. This matches with the residential real-estate developer's strategic assets and competencies.

IT initiatives

A Web based alliance between Home Depot and GE highlights the importance and benefits of supplier facing systems. The effective use of IT in this effort highlights the strong affiliation towards IT usage in business for strategic gains by both the retailer and the supplier. In its attempt to offer higher product variety, but lower inventory, Home Depot set up a strategic partnership with GE, whereby an Internet application enables GE appliances purchased at Home Depot to be delivered directly to consumers' homes from the nearest GE warehouse. This alliance helps both partners avoid any conflict that is typical in multi-channel environments. Systems integration initiatives act as the glue that holds internal, customer and supplier facing systems together. Successful e-business practice for a traditional organisation necessitates seamless flow and sharing of order and customer information throughout the value chain across all channels of operation. Home Depot has approached this problem methodically by ensuring a complete integration between its online and back office capabilities. This represents enterprise wide access to information across all the points of the value chain. This capability results in great service to consumers and helps suppliers to be effective in providing services. The use of alliances in IT is another way of strategic advantage of IT. Access to technology and marketing services (couponing etc.) helps to improve functionality of retailer websites like Home Depot. Home Depot uses Lifeminders.com to send "how to" e-mail to its consumers.

The idea and the pangs of birth

Home Depot came into fruition with a grand idea of two entrepreneurs. A huge warehouse store of 55,000 to 75,000 square feet compared to the 35,000 square feet of the largest Handy Dan store. There would be no intermediaries. Home Depot would purchase Merchandise directly from the manufacturer and would deliver directly from the manufacturer to the stores. Sales volume would be $7 to $9 million thereby allowing the stores to be profitable with gross profit margins of 29 to 31% compared to the industry norm of 42 to 47%. This would allow the new chain to be profitable at prices sharply below the traditional competitors who might do an annual volume of $3 million. The stores would stock large assortments of merchandise in large amounts and it would display the merchandise in the high ceiling warehouse store in a manner that implied bargains for the customer. In addition to the low prices, customers would be motivated to make purchases by trained sales people who would help the customer determine what they needed to make the home repair or home improvement.

While Bernie and Arthur, the two entrepreneurs were developing the plans for what became Home Depot, someone else actually opened a warehouse home improvement store, which was close to being the Home Depot model. Pat Farrah opened that store in the greater Los Angeles area in January 1978. When Bernie and Arthur discovered Farrah's store they considered buying it and going into business with Farrah. However, a closer look revealed that Farrah's business lacked adequate financial controls. It was achieving unheard of sales volume yet losing money. It had already accumulated substantial debt, so Bernie and Arthur chose not to make the purchase. They wanted Farrah to join them, so they encouraged Farrah to simply close his store and join them. Farrah went bankrupt a short time later and then went to work for what became Home Depot. His merchandising talents would turn out to be one of the secrets to Home Depot's subsequent success.

Initial hiccups

The Home Depot held its grand opening in Atlanta on June 22, 1979. The immediate response was not encouraging. A very small number of customers appeared the first day and in the weeks that followed the turnout was well below Bernie and Arthur's expectations. They attributed the slow build-up of traffic to a cultural factor. As they saw it, home improvement customers in Atlanta had established personal ties with smaller, higher price stores in Atlanta. Bernie thought a key moment occurred when J.C. Penney decided to close the Treasure Island stores that operated in the same facility as Home Depot. Penney offered unbelievably low prices as part of the going-out-of-business sale. A huge number of people came out to take advantage of the Penney sales and in the process became acquainted with Home Depot and its unbelievably low prices. Thus, an unexpected event produced the opportunity for many consumers to visit the Home Depot.

New employee practices

Unique employee practices brought in a new trend in the home improvement business. Marcus had never liked paying commissions for sales because he felt that commissions give workers the wrong incentive. Instead, Marcus and Blank trained workers to be sure that the customers get the right products for their needs, whether it is a 59-cent nut or a $59 power tool. Marcus went to the extent to say, "….the day they lay me out dead with an apple in my mouth is the day we'll pay commissions…", "…..if you pay commissions, you imply that the small customer isn't worth anything…" All company executives, including lawyers, were required to work in the stores when they first joined the company. Arthur and Bernie made it a point to work periodically in the stores throughout their careers. Home Depot used Low level of civility in terms of dealing with demanding situations combined with a deep level of support and respect in some decision-making situations as contrasting styles of dealing with employees to make work more passionate.

Customer relationship

The entrepreneurs were greatly inspired by the book - The Big Store: Inside the Crisis and Revolution at Sears, Donald R. Katz's behind-the-scenes look at Sears, Roebuck. It had a big effect on them, and for a number of years, they insisted that executives in Home Depot read the book. Each encounter with a customer was an opportunity to help the customer learn about new products and new methods, which might better, meet the customer's needs than what the customer initially planned to buy. This was not simply a method designed to induce the customer to trade up to higher margin products. Indeed, every Home Depot associate was trained to recommend less expensive ways of doing the job. The thinking was that the customer would appreciate such a helpful approach and become a trusting, loyal Home Depot customer. This was a great idea in obtaining customer loyalty. In addition, the founders answered customer queries and complaints through phone calls. This meant that employees were sure that every mistake if any of theirs would directly reach the founders. On the other hand, consumers were happy that the highest level in the hierarchy at Home Depot was involved in listening to the consumer. This act had a quite a strong qualitative impact on the consumer.

Indian hardware stores have a great example to emulate in Home Depot in serving their customers. The Home Depot story shows how the basics of business have to be stuck to in order to succeed in business, marketing and retailing. The success of Home Depot also exhibits how the best in class follow an untried path and exploit opportunities effectively. The use of IT, exploitation of the power of alliances and network and the emphasis on strong consumer relationships are aspects that are universal to contemporary businesses and have been followed effectively by Home Depot.

HOME FURNISHING RETAILING

The Indian speciality retail sector is developing in several directions. One of the areas that is developing fast is the home furnishing retail sector. Home furnishing consists of several products including home textiles like bed linens, bed over (meaning bed coverings), bed upholstery, bedding (all of the items under the sheets), fibres, floor, hygiene, miscellaneous, production, stores, table, upholstery, and window. Home textiles have become a rage in the Indian context following the western pattern, as interior decoration is becoming a popular fashion statement of the owner of the house. Moreover, the housing sector is developing, thanks to the availability of cheap loans and a tax break for housing investment. In addition, loans especially now from banks for new houses also include furnishing cost.

Developments

As the unorganised home furnishing sector is gaining momentum in the market, the organised sector, which includes established giants like Bombay Dyeing, Welspun, Portico and Kurlon among others, have made significant innovations and forays in this segment. The bed and bath domestic market is estimated at Rs 1,800 crore. It is growing at nearly 25% per annum. Just like apparel and footwear, the home linen market is moving from unbranded to branded products. In fact, more international brands are likely to enter this market. The challenge is how one creates brand consciousness in consumers' minds for home furnishings, a category which is highly commoditised and where brands do not matter much to the consumer. One of the ways to create brand awareness for home furnishing companies is to lay more emphasis on the overall shopping experience while buying these products. Retail ambience, coordinated product ranges; in-store display; point-of-purchase promotional literature on the product features as well as the company's lineage and superior in-store service are some of the initial steps that home furnishing companies need to think to be successful. The retailer has to do this in conjunction with innovative product and brand advertising and some innovative promotions. Consumers, who have seen the outside world, now want more of a western look for their homes. This brings home the fact that a kind of 'reverse buying' pattern is happening in the top echelons of the Indian market. Large retail stores like Wal-Mart, which typically represents the consumer-buying pattern in the U.S., usually buy ethnic home textiles products from India. These products are made in places like Rajasthan. Indian buyers, on the other hand, want more of a 'western' look.

Media influence

In the U.K. and elsewhere, interior decoration has become a popular television format, with advocate programmes including Changing Rooms (BBC) and Selling Houses (Channel 4). In the United States, the TLC Network airs a popular programme called Trading Spaces that has a format similar to the U.K. programme Changing Rooms. The Home & Garden Television and Discovery Home networks show many programmes on interior design. In India too, the NDTV programme "scope for improvement" and other variety channels programmes on interior decoration and home furnishing have added the media dimension of propagating the concept of home furnishing beyond furniture.

Marketers – what should they do?

The primary focus of marketers should be to get the category to evolve constantly. This evolution can happen only through customer education. Marketers can achieve it through creation of excitement in the segment bringing fashion into home textiles. A new collection each season and education to the customers about coordinating their bed sheets with their curtains etc is a way of increasing brand consciousness. If designs, colours and prints are contemporary, and the packaging and labelling are as per the highest quality standards, home furnishing companies could hope to bring in consumers. Other ways to look at awareness and increase frequency of buying and volumes is to educate customers about issues such as hygiene. Most of us are comfortable with changing our bed sheets once in two weeks. Similarly, most families use only one towel between themselves. None of us have ever realised that if the entire family uses the same towel, each member of the family is prone to infection.

A few years ago consumers never emphasised on buying branded home furnishing products. That is not the case today. Many consumers go in for branded furnishings as they feel that it signifies quality and even eventuality. However, for most consumers, branding would mean that the store would price the product higher. Therefore, for a brand to sell, it will have to tread the middle path — work on pricing and raise volumes. Unless the retailer creates the market, volumes are unlikely to grow.

Education

The home furnishings industry is a multibillion-dollar business worldwide. The retailing of home furnishings is, therefore, a significant sector in the retail industry. There are plenty of jobs available in this sector. A home furnishings merchandiser helps retailers and consumers select from broad categories of furnishings and accessories. Students in the U.S. have the liberty of specialising in home furnishing merchandising to be employed in department and furniture stores, home centres and homebuilders, as manufacturers' sales representatives or as showroom managers. Graduates also might work directly with designers and customers. The students in this specialisation are exposed to subjects like aesthetics and environment, computer-aided design, textiles, the history of furniture, kitchen and bath planning, promotion, merchandising math, consumer studies and advanced merchandising applications. In addition, these courses teach drawing skills using hand and computer methods. They learn to create and interpret floor plans, create estimates for materials and finishes, apply basic business principles, and offer excellent customer service.

Indian situation

The unorganised sector dominates the Indian market in the home décor segment. The focus for the organised sector needs to incorporate the latest fashion trends and contemporary styles in our products so that their customers can never run out of choice. An in-house design studio consisting of a team of highly qualified and experienced designers and professionals will ensure that they offer the best to their customers. The advantage of being an export house will help companies like Welspun, as they are constantly catering to the demands of the international market — in terms of trends and designs — and can thus use the expertise for Indian market. Home furnishing is emerging as the next hot destination for textile players. Exports of home textiles - bed, bath and kitchen linen - have zoomed over the past six months, after the dismantling of quotas, sparking off a fresh wave of investment in the segment.

Larger players, such as Welspun India and Abhishek Industries, are sinking big money into expanding capacities. Smaller companies, some of whom are in unrelated businesses, are also foraying into home textiles - Gangotri Textiles, KG Denim, S Kumars Nationwide, Bannari Amman Spinning, to name a few. GHCL (Gujarat Heavy Chemicals), which has a spinning division, plans to get ahead in the race by acquiring companies in the U.S. and Europe. With manufacturing facilities closing down in the west, international retailers are stepping up their sourcing of home textiles from countries such as China, India and Pakistan. Besides, home textiles appear to be a good way to scale up the value chain or diversify as is the case with companies such as KG Denim and Aarvee Denim. For fabric players, home textiles might prove to be a logical extension to their existing business.

American home furnishing retailers

Let us first look at the top home furnishing retailers in the U.S.

Bed, Bath & Beyond, Inc. (BBBY): Bed, Bath & Beyond is a nationwide chain of superstores that sells high quality domestic merchandise typically found in upscale department stores. The company sells merchandise at everyday low prices that are substantially below regular department store prices and generally comparable with or below department store sale prices. Bed, Bath & Beyond's merchandise line includes items such as bed linen, bath accessories and kitchen textiles. Its home furnishings line includes items such as cookware, dinnerware, glassware and basic housewares and it operates about 500 stores.

Linens' n Things, Inc. (LIN): Linens 'n Things, Inc. is a national large-format retailer of home textiles, house wares and home accessories. The company operates over 400 stores. Their stores provide a wide selection of brand name linens such as bedding, towels, window treatments and table linens, as well as house wares, home and decorative accessories. In 1990, LIN introduced its superstore format. This format, with an average of 35,000 gross square feet per store, resulted in the subsequent closure of most of the smaller stores.

Pier 1 Imports, Inc. (PIR): Pier 1 Imports is a speciality retailer that offers a diverse selection of products consisting of over 4,000 items imported from over 40 countries around the world. These items include a variety of furniture, decorative home furnishings, dining and kitchen goods, bath and bedding accessories and other speciality items for the home. The company operates stores under the names Pier 1 Imports, The Pier and Cargokids. It operates about 950 Pier 1 Imports and 25 Cargokids stores in the United States, 60 Pier 1 stores in Canada, and 25 stores in the United Kingdom under the name The Pier.

Williams-Sonoma (WSM): Williams-Sonoma is a speciality retailer of home furnishings. The company has stores under the names Williams-Sonoma, Pottery Barn, Pottery Barn Kids, and Hold Everything, seven direct-mail catalogues, as well as four e-commerce websites. It operates about 500 retail stores, located in 42 states, Washington, D.C. and Toronto, Canada. The average leased square footage for new and expanded stores will be approximately 10,500 leased square feet for Pottery Barn, 7,700-leased square feet for Pottery Barn Kids and 7,300-leased square feet (including two flagship stores) for Williams-Sonoma. WSM sells a selection of upscale cookware, serve ware, tools, and linens for the kitchen. *Pottery Barn* offers stylish, affordable furniture and accessories, including lamps, rugs, draperies, and oversized sofas and chairs. Hold Everything offers highly functional and appealing storage solutions.

A look at these speciality stores gives an idea of the level of saturation of the home furnishing retail market in the U.S.

Competition from formats

Target Corp (TGT): Target Corporation is a general merchandise retailer, comprised of three operating segments: Target, Mervyn's, and Marshall Fields. Target is a family-oriented discount retailer and operates approximately 1,000 Target stores in 46 states. Stores usually average 126,000 square feet and emphasize basic merchandise, including apparel, personal care products, home decorating products and automotive items. Mervyn's is a middle-market promotional department store that emphasizes name brand and private label casual apparel and home soft goods. There are 267 Mervyn's stores in 14 states across the southern and western United States. An average store comprises 75,000 square feet. Marshall Field's operates 64 department stores in eight states located in the North and Midwest. Fashion is the core of Marshall Field's product offerings. Its trend experts identify, research, and predict fashion and home trends to ensure a wide assortment of products that extend beyond home furnishings.

JC Penny one of the top departmental stores in the U.S. has very recently announced the introduction of Studio. Studio by JC Penney Home Collection is an exclusive, private brand that is available through JC Penney department stores, catalogs and jcpenney.com. The initial launch includes a complete line of bedding, bath, window coverings, area rugs, lamps, vases and decorative accessories. A studio furniture line of bedroom, living room and dining room groups, as well as tabletop and other line extensions are planned. Studio complements an existing mix of traditional furniture and accessories that are offered under the JC Penney Home Collection brand. Studio presents more options in home furnishings and addresses the decorating needs for casual, relaxed living.

Tuesday morning represents a new format competition in the speciality sector as a close out retailer. Tuesday Morning's merchandise mix includes upscale decorative accessories, rugs, lamps, books, crystal, luggage, toys, cookware, and seasonal items. Suppliers include Samsonite, Waterfield Crystal, Royal Doulton, Wedgewood China, Krups, KitchanAide and Cuisinart. Each store operates during periodic "sales events" lasting three to five weeks. Stores are closed during the traditionally slow months of January and July. Stores also close between sales events to stock new merchandise for the next event. Tuesday Morning is very precise about calculating necessary inventory, thus less than 5% of all inventory is more than a year old. This results in consumer excitement for each sales event and creates a "treasure hunt" atmosphere throughout the store. The Company buys brand-name merchandise at closeout and sells it at prices 50% to 80% below those generally charged by department stores and speciality and catalogue retailers. It does not sell seconds, irregulars or factory rejects. Tuesday Morning uses low cost effective advertising tools. Increased radio and television ads featuring Hollywood legend Lauren Bacall give Tuesday Morning national exposure to potential customers. Tuesday morning also heavily uses print advertising in local newspapers in order to acquire new customers. Their largest most effective form of advertising is their "green card" which is a low cost newsletter sent to all current customers that register with the Company's mailing list. Similar to the "green card", "E Treasures" is an email newsletter that has been gaining increasing popularity among customers. Stores now have KIOSK machines where customers can input their personal information, adding them to the mailing and email lists, serving as a quick and easy form of contacting consumers on upcoming sales. By using these methods, Tuesday Morning has kept its advertising costs low while increasing their effectiveness.

Indian home-furnishing speciality-stores and plans
Portico

Creative Mobus Fabrics Pvt. Ltd. retails a home furnishings brand Portico. Portico offers a range of bed sheets, curtains, bath towels and cushion covers through almost 300 outlets across the country. Through a licensing arrangement with Portico Homes of New York, the range for the brand will be manufactured in India and positioned at the premium end of the market. The products will be pegged at Rs. 500 onwards. Creative Mobus has simultaneously decided to enter the retail market by setting up its own chain of stores under the brand Creative Living. It has already launched its first two stores in Bangalore. Apart from selling the Portico range, the stores also stock other allied retail brands belonging to other companies. Ranging from furniture, crockery to candles, Creative Living is expected to have 15 outlets across the country in the next two years.

@ Home

Nilkamal has its exclusive stores called Nilkamal Home Ideas in as many as 20 SEC B&C towns. It is planning to set up 15 more stores in the next six months. Recently, Nilkamal also ventured into large format retail with the launch of its home solutions store @home, which has been positioned as an aspirational mid-market brand. The store offers furniture, home furnishings and accessories. Nilkamal wants to position its new home solutions store as homemakers and not a furniture store. The company has set up stores in Pune, Mumbai, and Ahmedabad, and is planning to set up 27 @home stores in the next three years, company would be looking at tie-ups with international furniture and home furnishing brands, which would be exclusively marketed through the @home stores. Also in the pipeline are setting up of full-fledged kitchen and office solutions within the @home stores in the next couple of years under the brand names @kitchen and @office respectively.

Spaces

The leading linen maker in Asia and the largest exporter of terry towel to the U.S., Welspun made its debut in domestic retailing with a home furnishing retail chain, Spaces – Home & Beyond, in Pune. Spaces offers a range of bed, bath, and kitchen and table linen, all specifically for the Indian market. The company exports its products across 32 countries. Welspun plans to expand its capacities locally, while also eyeing acquisitions and seeks to replicate its success in the export market by bringing in a new India specific brand. Apart from its own brand spaces; the company recently acquired the marketing rights of Tommy Hilfiger home furnishing products. While Spaces caters to the mid-segment, Tommy Hilfiger is targeted at the premium market. Apart from the two brands, the company is also targeting discount seekers through its factory outlets. As for the company's retail strategy, which is going to be the core of its brand-building exercise, the next three years are going to see as many as 125 stores across the country at an investment of Rs 50 crores. Of the 125, 100 would be standalone Spaces stores. Spaces outlets would be spread over an area of approximately 2,000 sq. ft. They would offer furnishings for each room of the house. Apart from furnishing items, the showrooms will also offer home décor products such as candles, curios and so on.

On the other hand, the Tommy Hilfiger collection will use the shop-in-shop format. Since the products are in the premium category, the company is initially trying out the shop-in-shop format, before investing in standalone stores. The products will be available at the Arvind flagship stores, which also have the marketing rights to sell Tommy Hilfiger casual wear in India. The company's strategy of using a mix of retail channels is a pioneering strategy in the nascent home furnishing retail market. SPACES recently launched its spring-summer collection, which featured four themes — Fusion, Tradition, Retro and Floral — in home furnishing products such as bed covers, bath robes, bedspreads, cushion covers, pillow covers, bolsters, quilts, table linens, tablemats, towels and curtains.

Bombay Dyeing

Brand leader Bombay Dyeing has already stepped up its efforts to retain leadership and market share. Meanwhile, the Rs 1,000-crore Bombay Dyeing is all set to enhance its image in the textile industry by spending lavishly on promoting its baseline 'Bring Style Home.' Plans are afoot to project Bombay Dyeing as an aspirational brand and advertising is targeted at building the mother brand of Bombay Dyeing.

Kurl-on

The Bangalore-based Kurl-on Ltd., a pioneer and leader in branded mattresses, has now decided to go beyond mattresses into retailing in home furnishings. A string of almost 50 stores under the name of 'Kurl-on Nests' is to be launched in major cities. The company is expanding its range and venturing into soft furnishings and launching bed and bath linen, curtains and towels.

Bombay Store, a well-known destination for home textiles products in Mumbai, is gradually expanding its presence in other cities. After opening a store in Bangalore and Pune some months back, the 'Store' is now moving to cities like Chennai and Hyderabad. The Mumbai-based Zeba India, which already has two home textiles stores, is planning to set up another store in the city. The New Delhi-based Maspar group is in the process of setting up a nation-wide chain of home textiles stores. Yamini is another major player in the market. Harmony is the brand of retail outlets displaying the home furnishings offerings from Reliance.

Himatsingka Seide, a leading manufacturer of silk and silk-blended fabrics, will be opening nine more furnishing stores under its retail brand 'Atmosphere' in the next three months, taking the total to 15. Besides, the company would look at shopping malls in smaller places with sizeable potential. The retail venture of the company was expected to fetch up to Rs. 15 crore in the first year. Part of the Rs 165-crore Himatsingka group, the retail venture is expected to contribute Rs. 75 crore to Rs 100 crore in the next five years. They have a range of 800 products each having different shades. The number will go up to 1,500 in the next few months. A 100 per cent EoU (export-oriented unit), Himatsingka group showed interest in the retail business as the domestic consumers were willing to pay a premium provided they got value for money. The company, which sources all its products in-house, plans to manufacture bed linen and non-silk upholstery for both Indian and export markets. 'Atmosphere' is a forward integration into retail by Himatsingka Seide through its 100% subsidary. 'Atmosphere' has positioned itself to be a luxury brand. It seeks to be the first player to have a nationwide presence in the upper end of the market. A comprehensive furnishing platform will offer its customers fabrics across various blends for the purposes of upholstery and drapes. Ninety per cent of the products in the collection have been manufactured by Himatsingka Seide, which until now had only catered to the international market.

Vijay Textiles Ltd., the home furnishings and upholstery company, is setting up a studio to let its customers have a virtual feel of the products they purchase. The studio would allow customers to see how a particular product looked in their houses or office environment. The studio would project how a particular product, in its design and colour texture, looked like when it was put up. This enables the customer to make a choice easier, better and as per their taste. Several well-known international retail houses possess such studios.

The All-India Handloom Fabrics Marketing Cooperative Society Ltd. is in the process of expanding and modernising its 'Handloom House' retail chain. The society will shortly open a 40,000 square feet Handloom House mall in Hyderabad. In addition, it will soon set up two "modern shops", one each in Lucknow and the DLF shopping complex in Gurgaon. The effort will be to enable shoppers to meet all their apparel and household furnishing needs under one roof. The store will cater to the needs of the entire family and will have refreshment facilities. With shopping increasingly becoming a family outing and even an entertainment option, the Handloom House shopping experience too needs to become more contemporary. It was in keeping with this objective that the society decided to set up the mall in Hyderabad and has subsequently gone in for more contemporary retail outlets. The society is seeking the assistance of the Kerala Government to set up similar malls in Kochi and Kozhikode.

Sabare, Siyaram, GHCL are other entities in this sector who are planning retail forays. GHCL is in advanced stage of negotiation with a company that has its own brands with presence in some global retail chains. The company plans to gain market access by acquiring these brands and eventually shifting the production base to India to cater to the global market. It is looking at branded home textile players in the developed market of the U.S. and Europe to leverage on their market reach and branding power. After acquisition, it would shift the production unit to India to benefit from the cost competitive advantage.

Seasons Furnishings is engaged in retailing of home furnishings and lifestyle products in the textile sector. SFL is presently operating through the flagship store in New Delhi and a well-established branch in Mumbai. In addition to retailing, Seasons Furnishings Limited is also catering to hotels and institutional sales. The company is one of the leading suppliers to all five star hotels in the country and to all the star hotels and motels across India. It has an in-house design studio, which delivers coordinated design schemes for the hotel industry. They supplied to the Taj Group of Hotels, Oberoi Group, ITC Welcome Group, Meridian Group, Hotel Intercontinental. The range of furnishing fabrics offered through the company owned and operated stores are in Jacquards, cottons, light weight fabrics, sheers, pure silks, chenille's and in special fabrics as well as lifestyle products to cater to elite homes and institutions. The company offers fabrics for drapes and upholstery, for home as well as for contract and hospitality. Seasons Furnishings have established two overseas outlets (at Indonesia and Dubai), which will cater to the demands from those markets.

Online retailing of home furnishing

Home furnishings feature as among products U.S. consumers buying online. This is significant, as U.S. is one country where several products have seen brisk sales online. Bombay Company and Restoration Hardware are two major U.S. home furnishing companies that offer most of their products online, while major players like Bed Bath & Beyond, Linens'nThings, and Pier One Imports offer few or none. Upscale Williams and Sonoma launched its online store and made $1.5 million in its first month of business – a good start – but only a tiny fraction of its bricks and mortars revenues.

Goodhome.com is a good ecommerce site that features a broad selection of decorative home furnishings products showcased by lifestyle, including English Country, Rustic, Coastal, Classic and Urban Contemporary. The site features high-quality Goodhome.com branded products, hand-selected by a team of professional merchandisers with more than 50 years combined experience developing merchandising strategies for The Horchow Collection (now owned by The Neiman Marcus Group), Laura Ashley, the Metropolitan Museum of Art, Williams-Sonoma, Eddie Bauer, Bloomingdale's, and Gump's. Products are arranged by individual item and within exclusively created room scenes. Each room incorporates different styles, products, functionality and budgets to provide customers with decorating ideas and inspiration to fit any personal taste and style. Everything shown in the rooms is for sale, from furniture to area rugs to artwork and accessories. Customers even have the option of purchasing all the furnishings featured in the entire room with one click. Decorative function provides the ability to change room/furniture colours. High prestige designers are available for consultation.

In the case of online consumers, ease of use of the website is necessary in the home furnishings category and it needs to be a given in their site design. Style assistance and feel are two very important categories in the decision-making process for the first time buyer and the one stop shopper. Therefore, those companies that think of selling home furnishings online need to take care of target customers carefully in deciding the features of the site.

Catalogue selling

The use of catalogues as a retail medium in the Indian context can help many established brick and mortar retailers to reach out to smaller towns. In the U.S., catalogue marketers are active in the home-furnishing segment. Coldwater Creek is a direct mail retailer of women's apparel, gifts, jewelry, home furnishings, and accessories that sells its products through direct mail catalogs, retail stores, and over the Internet. Coldwater Creek Home expands the company's product line into furniture and home accessories. Hanover Direct's catalogs and corresponding web sites offer home fashions (Domestications and The Company Store). In total, the company offers over 80,000 items through 12 speciality catalogues. Hanover Direct is presently driving its customers away from catalogues and onto its web pages. After posting all of its speciality catalogues on-line, its web-based sales increased tenfold to $8.3 million. Spiegel is an international speciality retailer that offers apparel, accessories, and home furnishings to customers through catalogs, speciality retail stores, and five Internet sites. Eddie Bauer offers outdoor-oriented apparel and home furnishings. Williams-Sonoma is a national speciality retailer of professional-style cooking and serving equipment, home furnishings, and bed and bath accessories. It markets these products through direct mail catalogues and operates over 300 retail stores nationwide. The *Chambers* catalogue offers quality linen and accessories for the bed and bath including sheets, towels, and soaps. Land End's Coming Home catalogue has offered bed and bath products for the home since 1991.

The Home-furnishing retail sector represents a vast range of products that several stores can market. The boom in this sector in both domestic and international markets has been due to the new international regime and increased disposable income in the domestic market. After garments, manufacturers in this product either should focus fully on exports or if they wish to have the domestic market share too, go ahead and set up a retail chain. The other option to enter the domestic market would be to become a private label supplier for the retail chains such as Shoppers' Stop, Westside, and Style Spa etc. Thus, retailing is an important option to pursue. The success of a speciality retail player would be driven by its ability to

- Strike a balance between export and domestic market

- Straddle various retail formats and self-owned retail outlets

- Offer the right mix of premium and mass-market offerings in its product bouquet.

Incorporating the highest standards in visual merchandising, spacious floor plan, elegant and contemporary decor and attractive displays are other components of the retail mix. Ultimately, stores can win the home furnishing retail war only by offering the ideal shopping experience to consumers.

CONSUMER ELECTRONICS RETAILING

Consumer durable retailers are one of the largest retailers in the country. One of the prominent forms of conspicuous consumption in India is that of the consumer durable. Consumer durable outlets are turning into consumer electronics stores with the increase in use of electronics in consumer goods. Consumer electronics retailing is reported to be more than Rs. 2000 crore worth business in India.

Consumer electronic retailing can consist of the following types of store/none store retailing. Retailing electronic goods via electronic home shopping, mail-order, or direct sale, retailing automotive electronic sound systems, automotive parts and accessories stores, retailing new computers, computer peripherals, and pre-packaged computer software without retailing other consumer-type electronic products or office equipment, office furniture and office supplies; or retailing these new computer products in combination with repair services—computer and software stores; retailing new computers, computer peripherals, and pre-packaged software in combination with retailing new office equipment, office furniture, and office supplies— office supplies and stationery stores; retailing new still and motion picture cameras—camera and photographic supplies stores; providing television or other electronic equipment repair services without retailing new televisions or electronic products— electronic and precision equipment repair and maintenance; retailing new electronic toys—hobby, toy, and game stores; and retailing used electronics— used merchandise stores.

Such classification, as done by the U.S. Census Bureau would be seen in smaller measure in some of the top metros in India. Consumer electronics retailers are slowly becoming gigantic super markets/departmental stores with the availability of almost all the electronic products, spread across different stores as mentioned above. One of the reasons for the above is also the way in which convergence is happening across products that facilitate information/communication along with existing consumer durables. The India launch of the refrigerator brand Tamanna by Electrolux India – a combination of the fridge, FM radio and a voice recorder is a stunning example of this churning convergence.

Lifestyle related consumption

Consumer electronic stores now have a unique responsibility of advising consumers about the fit of the product in their homes as they have transcended the barrier of products for utility/function to lifestyle products. The whole look of the store needs to be far more wide open and less cluttered, especially in the movie, music and software areas. Large posters all over the store featuring lifestyle themes and stressing how different products could entertain educate or solve problems, rather than emphasising on price or technical details is what is required to attract the consumers. Wall colours and the posters need to match the typical family or living room layouts. This provides the perfect setting for consumers to visualise the placement of products post purchase. There is also need for a small business department in the stores to cater to the needs of SOHOs. For example if the outlet has identified most of its small business customers as real estate salespeople, and therefore have a selection of packages with laptop computers, digital cameras, cellular phones and printers, in various configurations, it would greatly attract those small business customers.

Private sales events

Private sales are an in-store promotional event communicated by a direct-mail piece. They are by invitation only and typically last for one day. Marketers launch a direct-mail campaign to a highly targeted group of prospective buyers and/or a dealer's customer list. They invite prospects/customers to a timed sale event via a personalised letter, note card or postcard. Private sales are a powerful promotional tool because they generate significant revenue, turn prospects into customers, increase customer loyalty and assist retailers in creating and maintaining a customer database. Moreover, this could be the perfect platform to introduce high-end new products in your store.

Specifically, they generate increased revenue, not just on the day of the sale, but also from pre-sales and post-sales. They are also measurable, since you know what kind of traffic it produced, what your close ratio was, what your average ticket was and precisely how much you made during the event. What's more, private sales complement and supplement your traditional advertising through increased store awareness. Utilising direct mail to announce your private sale has certain advantages over other marketing media. For one thing, direct mail is targeted — it is delivered to those prospects who are your best potential customers.

Direct mail also virtually guarantees 100 % penetration of the market, assuring that your letter will get in the hands of everyone you target. In addition, despite popular belief, most people do look at their direct mail. Perhaps most important, direct mail is a more cost-effective method of targeting prospects than newspapers and/or television. Many newspapers are decreasing circulation and increasing rates, while with over 100 television channels from which to choose, it is difficult — if not expensive — to reach your target audience via video.

Thanks to human behaviour and buying psychology, attendees at private sales events tend to buy and buy big. That is because the limited time of the sale instills a sense of urgency in your customers, motivating them to buy now, and the private aspect of the sale makes those attending feel special and encourages buying. Taken together, all of these elements increase a dealer's close ratio and average ticket, so that the sale easily pays for itself while generating substantial returns.

Another important reason for running regular prospect private sales is their ability to bring new customers into your store. Many consumer electronics retailers hesitate to hold prospect-only events because of the low response rate. Nevertheless, in our constantly moving society, it is crucial for retailers to bring in new customers and private sale promotions with their targeting ability do that extremely well.

Visual Merchandising

Several empirical studies have shown that the superstore method of product display works best in consumer electronics stores, although it is far from new. Originally, it was known as "price point merchandising," or PPM. This starts with a minimum of three different models for practically every SKU in the store. The first of these models is dubbed, appropriately, the "sell" model. The one provides all the benefits a consumer can expect from the product with a fair profit for the retailer. Signage on the model is so complete that the sell piece practically sells itself to the shopper.

Alongside the sell piece in a superstore floor display is a "high-end comparison" unit. This not only has all the features of a sell model, but also some extra semi-useful bells and whistles to justify its higher price. This leaves just one model, a "low-end comparison" sample, to round out the product mix. Although it has many of the same features as the sell piece, this model has sufficiently fewer features to allow a salesperson to convince a shopper that its lower price point makes it less of a bargain.

With all three SKU models in position, the superstore salesperson is now ready to step the prospective customer through a demonstration leading to a sale. In this way, a prospect attracted by the price of one sample can easily be shown the advantages of another. Customers enter your store for a specific reason. This is where the "How may I help you?" greeting comes into play. Customers buy for the pleasure of it. Helping them achieve that goal is what makes the salesperson, working within a carefully planned display, the most important key to a sale. Thus, an understanding of the display, an evaluation of the consumer and the appropriate training of the salesperson can convert even consumer durable/electronics stores with a smaller assortment to succeed in retailing.

E-retailing in consumer durables/electronics

In the case of on line retailing of consumer products, greater explanation of complex technology products is big requirement. There is a need to take products home, test them out, and write reviews. However, the recent trend is that customers really do not care what e-tailer thinks about the products. What they care very strongly about is what the manufacturer has to say about their product. Therefore, it may a good idea to let the manufacturers talk directly to the customers. Another aspect that should be understood from an appreciation of consumer behaviour is that, consumers also want to know what other customers like themselves think about that product. So not surprisingly, customer reviews are the most popular on most e-tailer sites. Moreover, these innovators (first customers to try a product) will tell each other all kinds of hints and tips. It is actually great for accessorising, because customers will remind other customers to make sure they get the appropriate accessory.

Accessories

In many cases, despite being a small percentage of a retailer's total consumer electronic sales, accessories can account for a greater percentage of their profitability. This is the result of the typical retailer being able to generate higher net margin percentages on the sales of most consumer- electronics-accessories. Additionally, a typical retailer can see inventory turns on basic consumer electronics accessories products of between four and six times. With the onset of dramatically declining margins on televisions, audio components, DVD players and VCRs, the high gross margin contribution of accessories should only become more important. Furthermore, in many cases, required accessories will have higher retail prices than the components they connect.

Cycle counting can help ensure that accessories are in stock and on the right peg hook. Accessory products have a tendency to be the products that category managers misplace on a planogram or lose in a stock room. Store managers can tailor assortments to ensure that compatible accessory products and brands perform based upon market conditions, demographics and other factors on the selling floor and achieve compatibility in terms of technology, brand and lifestyle. Data analysis tools are available to help make this happen. With a focus on increasing the rate of attachment, retailers will see increased profits from the total sale of an item and ultimately of the entire Consumer Electronics assortment.

Increasing attachment rates is a simple strategy with a simple associated measure. Retailers can determine for every component product sold whether the outlet has sold the required accessory or accessories. To make this operational at the sales floor level, retailers can:

● Ensure that they merchandise accessories with the associated components. Implement signage that informs customers about the necessity and value of associated accessories and provide incentives for selling associated accessories.

● Create impulse sale opportunities. In this case, the strategy is to capture a sale by getting a customer to see value in an accessory product he had no predisposition to buy. Reminders that accessories at home need replacement or displays that focus on new styles and colours may stimulate these sales. To get these sales, retailers can merchandise accessories in places like cash wraps or end-caps where they can aggressively remind customers. Create lifestyle or other displays that feature the characteristics of accessories.

● Maximise upgrade sales opportunities. Many accessories exist to help improve the performance of the associated products. A good example of this practice is S-video cable sales. A retailer can use a number of tactics to help convince a customer that the step-up accessory will truly create an improvement in performance.

One approach is to create displays and point-of-purchase materials that illustrate the performance improvement and how it is achieved. Also, train and educate the staff on how the product improves performance so that a customer can understand the value of buying an accessory. Providing instruction materials is another way to convey the value of accessory upgrades to shoppers.

The increasing competition and complexity in consumer durable/electronics retailing requires strategies different compared to other retail categories. The need is to innovate on various dimensions of retail management based on consumer behaviour. The convergence of technologies and the changing lifestyles of the consumers require that retailers in this sector create experience and service as the key differentiators for the consumers. In both these differentiator levers, human capability building is paramount. Idea generation through consumers and sales persons and creative tactics to attract consumer attention are required. Private sales events and better visual merchandising are some of the few strategies that any retailer can implement. In addition, sales of accessories can be focused effectively in achieving greater profitability.

CAMERA STORES/COLOUR LABS

Speciality retailers, camera stores and digital colour labs in the country need to wake up to the realities that may strike quite early at their retailing business in camera/accessories and processing in India The digital revolution sweeping the world has brought major changes even in those involved in the manufacturing of cameras, accessories and other related equipment. Retailing in this sector needs understanding of not only technology but also the changing profile of consumers. We need to look at other opportunities/services that can be provided to the customers.

Time-starved women

A significant percentage of women in the ages 25-54 work outside the home. Although things have changed on the work front, they have not changed as much on the home front. Women are still putting in, on an average, twice as many hours a week of childcare and home care chores as their full-time working husbands. Photo retailers would find an incredible competitive advantage in offering services to save women's time. One idea is offering copies of a memory book, or family photo album that women could give as gifts to family members. An important service could be a pickup or drop-off service at the home or the office. This small gesture on the part of a local photo retailer would attract many women customers who are time starved.

In store experience – use of a gallery

Photography retailers profit from selling products and services to their customers that allow the customer to capture experiences and relive them for years. For retailers willing to change their in-store approach, there are even more business opportunities to be found, by creating their own memorable experiences inside the store. For a retailer involving in onsite photography for weddings, and other various events, a new gallery would help.

The gallery serves as a showroom for professional photography. There could be a reception desk and a presentation room. The photographers can sit down and talk to customers about their wedding or event. After the event, this place can be used to go through proofs and build an album. This therefore can be used on the front end and the back end with customers. This type of gallery arrangement can increase portrait and wedding sales. It allows retailers to highlight what they can do. When a bride comes in, she sees 12 to 15 large, framed wedding pictures. She can walk around the room to see what she might be able to get from her wedding photography. Portrait customers see what they could have for their own homes. It helps retailers, book people and gets them to make larger, framed prints. People see portraits and want something like that.

Other interesting ways of attracting customers would be to lease a small space in the gallery area to a wedding DJ. With ostentatious weddings becoming the norm in India, having him there is bringing in new customers who want entertainment for their event. At the same time, they are looking around and seeing all our jobs. If they are also looking for a photographer for their wedding or event in addition to a DJ, that gives them a reason to consider using us. Another alterative in the Internet age is that of the online exhibition. This could serve as a way to encourage customers to try new things with photography.

Custom framing

There is need to marry the gallery with custom framing, because diversification is healthy from a financial standpoint. Galleries can be a struggle, and photography is not the easiest thing to sell. There is still a market for wonderful art and the two – art and framing – fit together. People coming in to purchase art are candidates for framing, and vice versa. If they want to buy a photograph, they will have a framing need. If they come in for framing, they have a chance to see all the wonderful art on the walls. It then provide for a natural fit.

Promoting photo greeting cards

This is a unique way to survive in the digital age. Photo greeting cards can be promoted well by having templates updated regularly. In addition, customisation can do wonders. Consumers would be happy to pay a premium price for the cards. We could also promote a special package deal if customers purchase photo greeting cards along with a session at the in-store portrait studio.

Pet portraits

Another unique way of creating a niche in the market is going in for pet portraits. You may approach a pet adoption agency and offer to donate a small sum made out of every pet photograph taken on a special day. These could also be enlarged and mounted for them to use in their adoption centre. In addition, one may visit all the veterinarians in the area and when the vets learn about how the promotion would benefit, would be very enthusiastic about passing out information on your store. You may develop a reputation as a photo studio owner with dog biscuits in the studio and taking dog portraits.

Developments abroad in developing/processing

All photo processors are being forced to invest in new technology to maintain revenues abroad. The overall trend is moving towards digital capture from both digital cameras and camera phones. Consumers increasingly want to print from digital at retail, and photo retailers who do not invest will be left behind. Offering a 'prints from digital' service via an established main lab could be a good start without the need for capital investment. It is not so much in the distant future that we may have this phenomenon, taking place in India.

Retailers who are more sure of their local market needs, should make an investment in a kiosk that will provide customers with prints from digital sources in minutes, in-store, while they wait. Investment in a kiosk will also guard against obsolescence for retailers with analogue minilabs. The store can use the kiosk to enable prints from digital cameras and mobile phones, while still using an analogue lab for traditional photo processing. A kiosk, combined with the use of appropriate point of sale, creates strong in-store theatre that entices consumers to try the service and drive revenue.

Challenge of running a lab

One of the foremost challenges facing processing labs is how to get a customer to realise they can print brilliant quality photographs from digital media from a digital photo lab. We make real photographs from your digital camera, quicker, easier, and cheaper than printing at home. - This message makes the customer think a little more about the hassle of home printing. Developments in the market mean kiosks offer what consumers want: instant printing using exciting, touch-screen technology. Customers insert their digital memory card or CD, use the touch screen to select the images, and their photos are printed in seconds. Most kiosks offer an edit function, and customers can use them to print photos from their camera-enabled mobile phones via Bluetooth or Infrared in a matter of seconds.

An increasing number of households in the developed world have digital cameras, and the market is rapidly expanding. Combined with the accelerated growth in camera phone technologies, there is an ever-increasing need to provide solutions for customers. With serious print revenue generation associated with selling a large number of prints, a minilab's speed of processing means larger orders can be despatched far quicker than waiting for prints to be processed from a stand-alone unit. This, in turn, means that the outlet can deal with larger print orders in a short space of time, being uploaded to the minilab using the kiosk in a matter of minutes. Compare this to a customer using a stand-alone kiosk processing - say 30 prints - and you get a major usage issue, as any other customer wanting to use the kiosk may have to face a long wait in a queue, leading to customer dissatisfaction and lost business. Kiosks will continue to have a major impact on digital print revenue as the market continues to expand.

Camera phone adoption is expected to follow similar trends to those of digital cameras, quickly being adopted by technology-oriented individuals before moving into the mass market, where the demand for prints is expected to grow. Retailers have the ability to be ahead of the camera-phone printing curve by investing early in technology that allows easy printing of such pictures.

Product challenges for retailers

In the Indian context, we are yet to see the advent of single use cameras in a big way. They have however hit a roadblock in terms of the usage in Europe as there are strict regulations about how to deal with the waste generated by single use cameras. One-time-use cameras (OTUC) have typically been used to fill the gap for a camera left at home or to take advantage of some non-predictable picture event. If camera phones become ubiquitous, this may lower the need for – and cause a decrease in – OTUC sales. Similarly, lower-end digital cameras may need to be marketed differently if camera phones with similar mega pixel capabilities spread into the mass market.

The single-use camera market is also feeling less pressure from the uptake of digital cameras, as consumers are still happy to use a single-use camera for picture-taking occasions where they do not want to risk taking a more expensive digital camera. Camera phones will eventually affect the single-use camera category, the logic being consumers always have their phone to hand, ready for any picture-taking occasion.

While 35mm cameras are still popular among consumers, more and more consumers are opting for digital versions of both cameras and camcorders. To follow this trend, retailers must adapt your marketing and business plans to this changing environment. Determine which demographics are purchasing or at least evaluating digital technology in your own market to determine a proper marketing strategy. International trends show increasing adoption of digital cameras by young parents and women, as well as a shift towards older individuals, becoming the primary digital still camera users. It would be useful to offer cameras/camcorders of different types for those who are not planning to buy digital versions. It would be important to train your sales staff in the new features of digital cameras/camcorders and teaching consumers about the features and benefits. Moreover, it would be necessary to offer training on how to use digital cameras and how to make prints from a digital camera, particularly on how easy it is to make prints at your store. This ensures that competition from home printing option is taken care. There is a need to train your customers to come to your store for all their support, service, and other digital needs.

Digital camera sales have had a modest effect on camera stores (increased sales of equipment, decreased sales of supplies and used equipment) and a dramatic effect on labs. Stores that relied upon film sales and processing as their primary profit source will disappear unless they get the digital religion quickly. Even the ones that did (do) are going to struggle a bit against online discounting and at-home printing. Camera stores that have large used departments are sitting on film equipment that devalues itself daily. Labs are even more affected. Those that are located in high-traffic areas and tout the transition from one-hour processing to one-minute printing have a good shot with the proper marketing and pricing. Those out-of-the-way labs that relied upon pros and advanced amateurs shooting film have a bigger barrier to break, though they have a chance with custom and event work; likewise, those labs that catered to other parties (grocery stores, drugstores, etc.) are going to find the going gets rough, as all they will eventually have left is disposable camera development.

In the developed world, all types of retail stores that deal with photographic equipment/services like Camera/Video Store: with/without on-site minilab, Retail Minilab, Mail Order Lab, Wholesale/Captive Lab, Portrait Studio, Commercial Studio, Camera Repair Firm except for the Digital Imaging Firm are facing the onslaught of conversion of market to the digital mode.

Major slump in growth rates have been witnessed abroad especially in Japan, U.S.A. and Europe in disposable-camera sales, film sales, processing sales, film rolls and disposable cameras sold per location, Point-and-Shoot camera sales and SLR camera sales. These may have a repercussion in countries like India where this would mean enlarging the base of those who would be wooed into photography through cheap cameras. At the same, time with international giants in this industry operating in India, the digital revolution may strike faster making this prediction redundant. The major impact would be on retailers who are both marketers of equipments/ processors of film rolls.

AUTO ACCESSORIES RETAILING

The Indian auto accessories retail market is a fragmented and unorganised market, mainly concentrated in the four metros. The industry's product mix can be broken down into three areas: Replacement parts, maintenance items, and accessories. Replacement parts typically include both new and rebuilt parts used in repairing vehicles (alternators, water pumps, batteries, brake pads, etc.). Maintenance items are used to maintain performance and aesthetics of vehicles (motor oil, fuses, other fluids, car wash and wax formulas, etc.). Accessory items are the more discretionary, personal preference items. These include floor mats, air fresheners, seat covers, etc.

There are two segments that one can delineate in the auto accessories retail segment - The Do-It-Yourself (DIY) market and the Do-It-For-Me (DIFM) segment. The Do-It-Yourself (DIY) market comprises of individuals performing routine maintenance on their vehicles.

These consumers purchase replacement parts, lubricants, and other ancillary products from aftermarket parts retailers. The most common types of maintenance performed by this segment are basic in nature (oil changes, batteries, radiator flushes, etc.). The Do-It-For-Me segment (DIFM) is also important for the industry. This segment caters to the needs of professional installers, mechanics, and garages performing maintenance for individual consumers. These customers are usually less price sensitive than individuals and they usually pass through costs to the end consumer. The margins in the DIFM market are a bit tighter due to competition among suppliers. The DIY segment in India is still in a very nascent stage.

Car Audio

One of the conspicuous products that have gained prominence in the automotive after markets retail market is the car audio. The Indian car audio market is estimated at Rs 600 crore, majority of which is dominated by unorganised players and the grey market. The remaining market faces competition from major brand names like Kenwood, Blaupunkt, and Sony among others. Bose Corporation has exclusive arrangement with Mercedes Benz, Porsche and Audi for car audio systems. 80% turnover of Blaupunkt International, a wholly owned subsidiary of Bosch Group, comes from its tie-up with automobile companies. In contrast, in its Indian operations a very large portion of its turnover is from sales to retail customers and a small share that comes from its tie-up with automobile makers such as Tata Motors, Hyundai Motors India, Ford India and Mahindra&Mahindra. This indicates the level of focus needed in the auto accessories retail market in India. Blaupunkt's new retail strategy aims at providing a platform for customers to experience the car entertainment systems and will display the entire range of Blaupunkt products such as head units, speakers, amplifiers, and other accessories as well as car entertainment modules such as DVD players, screens, and surround sound systems.

IT accessories

A country that boasts of being the information technology super power of the world has little presence in the IT-based application in the automobile retail sector. In developed countries, electronic maps play a key role in the development of advanced in-car infotainment technology, particularly in the application of navigation systems. Their functions have been limited to monitoring and anti-theft. Competition has been focused on audio players and low-cost devices for safety and security purposes. The gradual penetration into cars of a range of new technologies, including video players, LCD displays, navigation, telematics, and hands-free telephony is set to open up new areas of competition even as it creates considerable growth opportunities. Navigation, rear seat entertainment (RSE), telephony and telematics segments are the segments that have a future. The technology stores catering mainly to computer users soon could well get into speciality retailing with these products.

The U.S. market and learning

Automotive parts retail industry in the U.S. was born with the mass production of automobiles. The industry, previously dominated by mom-and-pop auto parts stores and service stations continues to evolve to this day. Chains such as AutoZone and Advance Auto Parts began building out retail networks within target markets in the 1970's. Today, big players in the market continue to penetrate markets once dominated by independent stores. The dominant chains in the industry are Advance Auto Parts, AutoZone, CSK Auto, Pep Boys Manny Moe and Jack, and O'Reillys. Advance Auto Parts. Typical retail store holds between 16,500 and 26,500 stock keeping units (SKUs) with an additional 100,000 SKUs available for next day delivery in most locations. In addition to the accessory items, most stores also provide an assortment of candy, sodas, and other snacks at the check out counter. Most of the chains offer parts under their own private label. AutoZone is well known for this with over 50% of revenues coming from private labels (Duralast and Valucraft).

Background on major players

Advance Auto Parts is the second largest retailer of auto-parts and accessories in the U.S. The company operates over 2,500 parts stores primarily in the Southeast, Northeast, and Mid-Atlantic states. Its stores operate under the Advance Discount Parts, Discount Auto Parts, and Western Auto brand names. Retailing auto parts, therefore, has saturated to the level of developing formats. Advance Auto Parts have innovative programmes to maintain customer relationship. For example, it has a consumer education programme that includes in-store kiosks with brochures covering safety, reliability, performance, and appearance tips for automobiles. In addition, the company distributes a monthly circular focused on seasonal car care topics. Advance Auto Parts also offers brand name products to differentiate themselves from the rest. They claim that their brand name and high quality parts set them above the rest.

AutoZone is the largest retailer of aftermarket auto parts in the North America. The company currently operates a chain of just under 3,500 stores in the United States and Mexico. The company also sells some parts on the Internet through its website, autozone.com. Its customers can be broken down into three separate groups: DIY, DIFM, and diagnostic. The diagnostic segment sells ALLDATA automotive diagnostic and repair software to the commercial segment and to DIY customers. AutoZone felt that if they priced hardware and oil on a penetration basis it would bring customers in. Once inside, the customers would buy many of the higher priced items. This factor allows AutoZone to keep their profit margin up since both pricing methods are used. Autozone uses different free services such as free battery testing, charging, tool loans, fluid recycling, and a nationwide warranty. These are different promotional techniques used to attain a competitive advantage. Location is perhaps one of the biggest factors in retail competition. Auto Zone, for example, positioned themselves predominantly in the Eastern portion of the United States. Another company that uses online customer service is AutoZone. In 1996, AutoZone introduced their online web site, which allows customer to register warranties, order parts, locate stores, and get maintenance and repair information.

The O.Reilly family founded O' Reilly Automotive in 1957. It operates primarily in the mid-western and southwestern United States. The company has over 1100 stores total. Its stores are located in Texas, Oklahoma, Missouri, Kansas, Iowa, Arkansas, Louisiana, Nebraska, and Illinois. The highest concentration of stores is in Texas where 380 stores are located. The company also distributes parts to independent auto parts stores via its subsidiary, Ozark Automotive Distributors. O'Reilly's price strategy is one of a low price guarantee advertisement. Once inside the prices seemed very competitive with surrounding competitors. For the most part, O'Reilly seemed to stand behind their low price guarantee O'Reilly carries their own motor oil. O'Reilly offers a web based service called "Part locator." This service allows customer to identify the make and model of their vehicle in order to find the correct parts needed for their vehicle and create a shopping list including prices. While O'Reilly does not currently have online ordering capabilities, customer can take the shopping list to there nearest O'Reilly Auto Parts Store.

Nature of differentiation

Promotion is a major key to successful differentiation. One of the top five competitors, O'Reilly, sponsors many tractor pulls and stock car races. Consumers can see their logos on many different trucks and cars. This is a tremendous promotion opportunity. Pep Boys Auto Parts is centralised in the southern half of the United States with the exception of Washington, Minnesota, and New England. Each company uses a different approach toward location issues. Another way that retail companies seek to differentiate themselves is through offering different products.

Most large retail sectors try to tailor to customers needs through offering different products. TBC does just that. TBC offers product warranties, which are nationally backed, on all of their tires. In addition, TBC offers brand name tires that are nationally recognized. These are just a few ways the companies differentiate themselves. Another way the companies of this sector set themselves out is through specialisation. Retailers can accomplish specialisation through unique products and services. An example of specialisation through product is TBC, who only sells tyres. Most of the companies in this sector sell tyres but very few specialise in tyres. This sets TBC apart from its competition. Pep Boys sets themselves apart through specialised service. Among the top competitors in this industry, they are the only ones that provide personal customer service. Pep Boys not only sells parts to its customers they also install parts and perform a wide range of services on customer vehicles. Most of the top competitors also specialise by carrying their own brand name products. For example, another way these companies try to gain market share is through distribution which is indirectly related to market share.

Most companies operate their own distribution centres to decrease consumer prices. The lower you can get your price, better your competitive advantage. TBC for example uses more than two hundred distributors throughout the U.S.A., Mexico, and Canada. These distribution centres help to keep up their competitive advantage. O'Reilly also uses five strategically placed distribution centres. another feature that improves market share, is the basic store design.

Innovative products for retail

Ready-to-use like 50/50 pre-diluted anti-freeze & coolant, a global Extended Life Anti-freeze & Coolant that can be used in all automobiles and light trucks worldwide regardless of make, model, year or original antifreeze color, premium performance spark plug, Do-It-Yourself bed liner kit, wiper blades featuring state-of-the-art rubber technology and an exclusive wear indicator - The wear indicator provides the consumer with an easy way to remind them to replace their blades, comprehensive windshield wash programme, lightly scented formula of auto air fresheners made specifically to eliminate odours inside of car interiors, auto dry carwash system that delivers significantly better car wash results in less time, with no need to hand dry. The list of such products in retail merchandising is long, typically in developed countries as there is constant need to attract consumers to the store with new offerings. In India, as we reach a sizeable population of four wheelers in the market such innovative products may also be available in the market.

The use of Internet

AutoByTel, AutoWeb, GreenLight.com – are examples of successful auto retailing on the net. Where the Internet has made a tremendous impact is in the information gathering process. Recent studies in U.S. indicate that more than 60% of car buyers do at least some of their research on the Web. Popular sites include Edmunds for new and used pricing and comparative model data, and Kelly Blue Book for insight on their trade-in value. Internet shoppers using Autobytel saved about 2% on the price of a new car over traditional car buyers (although they get less for their trade-in vehicles). E-retailing has allowed dealers to maintain a more consistent dialog with people throughout the life of their ownership experience. This has resulted in etailing initiatives being extended to where people routinely schedule service and repair appointments on the Web and gets reminders that it has time. This has created value addition through Net based services for the brick and mortar retailers and thereby dealer loyalty. Internet therefore has converted transactions into relationships in the context of automotive retailing. The penetration of Internet in India would allow for such relationships.

The Japanese way

Japanese "car life" retailer Autobacs are much larger than other auto parts retailers in the United States are. Its Super Autobacs stores are up to 55,000 square feet. The square footage includes space for the sales floor and the service and maintenance area. By comparison, the average U.S., auto parts store is about 6,500 square feet. The only retailer that comes close to Autobacs' size is Pep Boys, where the stores average about 11,500 square feet, carry more than 80 brands and 10,000 products. In addition to staple products such as oil, tires, and engine parts, Autobacs in its outlets feature a full line of car stereos and security systems. It also carries a wide array of what Autobacs calls "car lifestyle" products, such as custom bumpers, car magazines and books and merchandise like sunglasses and novelty products. Moreover, like some of its U.S., competitors, such as Pep Boys, Autobacs prides itself on high quality service. The store has a 15-bay pit service area in the store that offers standard maintenance and specialized services such as car customization and installation of car audio systems. The store also has a cafe viewing area on the second floor where customers can watch mechanics work on their car. Customers can be attracted to the store in these new ways.

Future product categories

Stylish accessories and premium items would increasingly become a focus for automotive product retailers. This is due to a shrinking market for do-it-yourself repair and maintenance basics such as oil filters and spark plugs. With this ongoing trend, shifting more money to service providers, retailers need to rely more and more on impulse items to drive store sales. The future merchandise trends in the automotive channel may stray increasingly from core categories. Hot revenue growth areas in future would include mobile entertainment, and cell phone accessories. Mobile video systems and global positioning devices are two potential new segments. Many retailers in the U.S. attribute their success to new categories and better merchandising. Fashion and convenience accessories would gain in popularity. Among the future trends would be an emphasis on performance or tuner market products, premium car-care items, accessories targeting females and truck owners, and chemicals geared toward high-mileage vehicles. In motor oil and lubricants, new items focused on synthetic oil blends, tuner products, and formulations for older vehicles. Products for "all makes" and longer-life products, with a lifetime use guarantee could become common.

In accessories, fashion could take centre stage, with products targeting women getting more attention. Coordinating items such as steering wheel and seatbelt covers, floor mats, and visor organisers are appearing in dramatic colours could be an imminent trend. Decorative accent lighting could be another strong growth category, with colour-changing LED lights making their way into a growing array of vehicle parts and accessories such as stereo speakers, license plate covers, trailer hitches, and exhaust tips. Convenience, safety, and security items are other popular categories. Power inverters could boom with the proliferation of mobile electronics products, along with car coolers that plug into a cigarette lighter.

The auto accessories retailing field is a product and service marketing driven field. A constant look at new and innovative products would go a long way in reducing the wear out effect of consumers visiting a store. As consumers use new gadgets along with automobiles and as product complexity increases with the bundling of many features and benefits, new services by retailers in the auto accessories segment would become important. In India, as ownership of automobiles increases and the need to differentiate through accessories is stepped up the retail market in this segment which is currently in a nascent stage would indeed grow rapidly.

LUXURY RETAILING

Luxury brands and luxury retailing survive in the world because of five major forms of perceived value that any prospective consumer sees in products or services, namely:

1. Shoppers view consumption of prestige brands as a signal of status and wealth, and whose price, expensive by normal standards, enhances the value of such a signal (perceived conspicuous value). Thorstein Veblen many years ago suggested that people use conspicuous consumption to signal wealth and, by inference power and status. Thus, the utility of prestige products may be to display wealth and power and one could consider that highly visible prestige brands would dominate the conspicuous segment of the consumers

2. If virtually everyone owns a particular brand, it is by definition not prestigious (perceived unique value) – The Snob Effect

3. The role-playing aspects and the social value of prestige brands can be instrumental in the decision to buy (perceived social value) – The Bandwagon Effect

4. For a brand, which satisfies an emotional desire such as a prestige brand, a product's subjective intangible benefits such as aesthetic appeal, is clearly determining the brand selection (perceived hedonic value) – The Hedonic Effect

5. Prestige is derived partly from the technical superiority and the extreme care that takes place during the production process. For instance, a Rolex Sea-dweller works 1,220 meters under water and is handcrafted (perceived quality value)–The Perfectionism Effect

Thus, interpretation and recognition of what is luxury may vary for different people, depending on their socioeconomic background. Translated into marketing terms, consumers develop prestige meanings for brands based upon interactions with people (e.g., aspired and/ or peer reference group), object properties (e.g., best quality), and hedonic values (e.g., sensory beauty). Such interactions occur at personal and societal levels. Thus, luxury retailers have a tough task in hand to identify potential consumers. Examples of luxury brands and retailers are Louis Vuitton, Porsche, Kenzo, Cartier, Ferrari, Fred, Moet & Chandon, Chanel, Dunhill, Hermes, Christian Dior, Mercedes-Benz, Gucci, Rolex, Versace, Ralph Lauren, Tiffany, Patek Philippe, Mont-Blanc, Lalique, Gianfranco Ferragamo, etc.

Indian consumers on the whole are becoming more affluent and have more money to spend. They have the inclination to spend it on luxuries that give them pleasure. Therefore, there is a very strong market out there for luxury. However, luxury consumers are spending their money differently. The big increase in terms of overall luxury spending is in the experiential range and that means travel, fine dining, entertainment, spa, beauty, home landscaping and home services. Psychographic aspect of luxury is that consumers feel entitled to spend money on luxuries - things that make them feel good. This comes out of the feeling that they have worked hard to achieve the level of financial and worldly success that they have. They look at luxuries as rewards and benefits of their hard work. Old-luxury attributes of quality and being the best of the best are no longer the definitions of a luxury product. The consumer is the arbiter of luxury - they say what luxury is and what is not and it does not necessarily have anything to do with how much the product costs or what brand it is. The ideas of status and conspicuous consumption are ending. This therefore entails greater pressure on luxury retailers.

The common belief that high-income consumers buy high-end products in every instance may not be true. An American study finds that in many product categories, luxury consumers (defined as those with yearly household incomes of $150,000 or more) frequently "trade down." Even in the product categories where prestige counts the most, luxury consumers do not always pay for the best. For example, about 30% of luxury consumers in a survey said that they always or usually select the most luxurious option when buying electronics. 21% participants said the same thing for automobiles; 20% for fragrance and cosmetics; 18% for jewelry; 17% for watches and 21% for travel. In other product categories, such as linen and bedding, furniture, apparel, dining and home services, 15% respondents or fewer said they always choose the most luxurious option. It shows that luxury retailing also needs to be tailored to the product and service offered.

The country of origin effect

Country-specific factors are inextricably linked with brand power and heritage and, hence, gaining a foothold in the country known best for a particular line of products, is of paramount importance. Access to local artisans, local raw materials, and the ability to tap into the local knowledge base are crucial aspects of building a reputation in this business. Although this means that the costs of labour are often prohibitive given the low volumes manufactured, it is an essential element of defining brand reputation. Italy, for example, is widely believed to be the leader in the manufacture of leather goods. It is home to some of the best leather design houses, best manufacturers of leather processing equipment, and some of the best leather retailing outlets. Complemented by the burgeoning fashion clothing business in Milan, the leather industry in Florence is able to develop synergistic advantages. Over the years, the Italian customer has developed a very sophisticated awareness of leather fashion products. Therefore, to compete successfully in this region, companies have to strive hard to attract Italian customers, who were demanding and knowledgeable. Firms such as Bottega Veneta, Salvatore Ferragamo, and Tod's were a few of the Italian companies at the forefront in leather goods. Thus, the "Made in Italy" label is considered an important element that discerning customers worldwide insisted upon, when buying luxury leather goods.

France is widely seen as the hotbed of creativity in the ready-to-wear-fashion business. Tracing its lineage to the French court at Versailles and the pomp and circumstance that surrounded French royalty, the country had given birth to some of the most well reputed design houses. The leading perfumeries and cosmetic goods companies traced similar roots. The legendary flower fields of the Province region provided much of the critical raw materials that these industries required. France dominated the wine business that was built on locational advantages, such as access to fertile land, and winemaking heritage. Winemaking had been part of the culture for a very long period and helped put regions such as Burgundy and the Loire valley on the oenophile's map. The support of the French government and the careful control of the industry through the appellation system also helped the wineries gain a foothold in world markets.

Switzerland has built a global reputation for its jewelry and watches. Many of the leading firms that compete in these segments traced their heritage to the master artisans and jewellers who fled religious persecution in France and settled around Geneva to establish the traditions of Swiss artisanship. Over time, quality and precision have become synonymous with Switzerland. While each of the major design houses had originated through a focus on a distinct set of products that were rooted in local craftsmanship, they had since branched out through cross-border acquisitions to build empires spanning wines and champagnes, apparel, watches, and jewelry. The quintessential global luxury product company was a result of such aggressive expansion. In the new globalised world however, country of origin effects are fast diminishing and presence of the brand in maximum no of countries is an indicator of the luxury nature of the product. Moreover, WTO regulations on country of origin as well as the global value chain for the production and marketing of products and services make the concept of country of origin less relevant.

The major world players

The major competitors in the luxury goods industry, LVMH, Gucci, Richemont, Bulgari, and Hermès, control about 20% of worldwide industry sales. All of these firms compete in multiple product lines and multiple geographic markets. LVMH and Bulgari dominate the Asia-Pacific region, while Richemont and Hermès were strong contenders in Europe. Gucci is a well-entrenched player in both Europe and North America. It has been building a strong presence in Japan as well.

LVMH is one of the greatest players in the luxury retail arena of the world. The vertical integration strategy of LVMH came to fruition when the selective retailing arm was established.

This division managed LVMH investments in Sephora, DFS Galleria, and Miami Cruise line Services. DFS Galleria with 150 duty-free and general merchandise stores is one of the world's largest travel retailers. Miami Cruise line Services (MCS) offers retail services on board cruise ships and has a majority of the world's major cruise lines (over 100 ships) as its customers. LVMH acquired La Samaritane, the prestigious Paris department store. The company also entered the retailing end of the made-to-order tailoring business with the acquisition of Thomas Pink, the legendary Mayfair tailoring house that had a worldwide reputation for excellence in shirts. Thomas Pink has retail outlets in the United States as well. LVMH has also a minority position in the 200-year-old U.K. fashion retailer, Asprey & Garrard that has global aspirations of its own.

China is a new destination for LVMH. Vuitton has stores in major Chinese cities; including a new global store in Beijing. Vuitton is one of the few luxury brands to be present in first-, second- and third-tier Chinese cities. It has followed unique promotional forms in China. Vuitton created an exhibit about the brand's history that travelled to five cities during 1997 and 1998. Then, in 1998, Vuitton sponsored a classic car race from Dalian to Beijing.

Nordstrom is a major luxury retailer in the U.S.. It has four main competitors: Federated Department Stores, May Department Stores, Saks, and Neiman Marcus. Nordstrom's attracts a broader base of customers by having a more diverse selection of merchandise. For example, they have their women's clothing divided up by brand and price range. Clothing for women in there 20's to 40's is divided into three sections Savy, the most expensive, TBD, and Brass Plum that is the least expensive. This gives a competitive advantage because it markets to all customers while still maintaining the luxury retail experience. Over the past few years, the fashion industry has been struggling due to uneasiness in the American market. Consumer spending has decreased dramatically because shoppers are spending money on more long-term stable investments like homes, education, and savings. Consumers are not willing to splurge on high-end jeans and designer purses. Therefore, Saks is struggling to maintain customer loyalty during such difficult times. Nordstrom has a competitive advantage over Saks and Neiman's because they target a broader customer base. Nordstrom offers the feel of a luxury retail store while continuing to sell affordable and high-end exclusive clothing and accessories. Therefore, when buying trends change they continue to stay in the market and offer retail to all different members of a family in all different economic situations.

Luxury retail consumer

The business in Asia and therefore as in India is about display — who am I and what do I have and what do I want you to know about me by wearing it and using it? There is a need to have a high-performance experience with special and unique products when dealing with these kinds of customers. There is a need to provide a service that is unique to each individual and help that consumer find the products that are right for him or her. Indulgence factor plays a role here, but we need to find and define what that means for each customer. One of the terms no longer applicable to the luxury market is "exclusivity." Instead, retailers should think individuality and specialness. The other aspect is aspirational value. There is no one consumer shopping one way within a particular demographic or psychographic segment. There are choices available to the consumer today and she/he is taking them.

The major issue facing retailers is how do we make it fun for the shopper? When people travel — they shop. They like to go to new places and find new things that they do not find at home and new experiences. There is a lot of shopping that goes on in tourist areas — almost all first-class hotels have some sort of boutique environment in them. Also, a force to be recognised, are shopping environments that are shifting into lifestyle centres with a heavy emphasis on bringing in entertainment and restaurants and a totality of experience. The excitement and appreciation of these products' uniqueness is shared with customers as part of the retail experience. Thus, the luxury retail consumer needs to be treated to a luxury retail experience rather than the product or the service only. As the notion of luxury changes, marketers of high-end products are wrestling with the challenge of maintaining brand exclusivity while reaping higher benefits. It is, therefore, much more difficult to conjure up a consistent picture of luxury living.

Indian context

The number of Indian households with an income of $100,000 or more and purchases of $9,000 on designer goods is growing and experts expect the segment to grow at 15% each year. With the arrival of luxury retailers, wealthy Indians will become increasingly aware of the value of designer brands. Tata International, the largest Indian leather exporter, has tied up with Lloyd, a leading German footwear maker whose shoes will retail in Indian showrooms in a range stretching from Rs. 9,000 to Rs. 45,000 a pair for men. The women's range starts from Rs. 8, 000. Lloyd GmbH plans to hawk its top-of-the-line footwear through multi-brand luxury retail outlets and by the year-end will introduce an exclusive Lloyd store in Delhi. They said that the size of the premium market in the country is to the tune of Rs. 500 to Rs. 600 crore. Lloyd is a well-established lifestyle brand part of the Ara group that sells close to 14 million pairs of shoes a year.

In a clear indication of global luxury retail kicking in, the $1.28-billion (e1.09 billion) high-end ready-to-wear German clothing major Hugo Boss has decided to set shop in the country. The store will retail top-of-the-line Hugo Boss Black Label for men, which is business-oriented urban wear. The base price for a suit will begin approximately at Rs 35,000. There are no plans, as of now, to introduce the range for women or the Orange and Green labels. Alternatively, even Hugo the casual wear portfolio that has taken the world by storm. The reasons are clear. The company has a market presence in 108 countries, with a strong presence in Japan and China. BOSS already has a customer base among Indians, who currently buy our collections in shops outside the country. Now we are bringing the market to the consumer. At the same time, we will be building up the consumer base within India. Hugo Boss will not be the first luxury brand to dig into the country's blooming market for high-end lifestyle products, in particular clothes. Ermenegildo Zegna, Louis Vuitton and Escada already have stores in place in Delhi and Mumbai. BOSS is one of the few non-Italian labels that have succeeded in growing its market. Instead of taking on the competition, it joined them. The brand is known to use the finest virgin wool, cashmere, and cashmere mixtures from the leading Italian weavers Carlo Barbera, Loro Piana, Torello Viera, not to mention rivals in the ready-to-wear segment Cerruti and Zegna.

Canali's flagship store is to set shop at India's oldest running five star hotel — The Taj Mahal Palace & Towers, Mumbai — besides a host of others like Armani, Cartier, Bvlgari, Rolex, Gucci, Louis Vuitton to Prada to name a few. The entry of these brands at the Taj Palace means is that the heritage wing of the hotel will add as much as 5,000 sq ft of new retail space. At present, the Taj Mumbai has a total retail space of 25,000 sq ft. According to market reports, there are close to 23 people in the reckoning for the new space, which commands a rate of Rs 750-1,000 per sq. ft. All the new retailers will be on a three to six year licensee or franchisee arrangement. While the Palace wing will define the super luxury shopping experience, the Towers wing will retain the small shop formats with existing retailers for now, though it will be given the look, feel and unified character in keeping with the new positioning and retail strategy. For the Palace wing, the focus is to build an experience comparable to London's Bond Street, or Chimes in Singapore, where there has been an adaptive reuse of space. Unlike Europe, the U.S. or even South East Asia, India has failed to create public spaces like Champs Elysee or a Bond Street.

Christian Dior has opened its first store in India. The luxury goods brand's store in New Delhi offers Indian consumers the haute couture from $1,000 handbags to $400 sunglasses. Luxury retailers like Louis Vuitton, Chanel, Cartier, Fendi, Bulgari and Dolce & Gabbana already have outlets in India, and others like Gucci and Valentino are following their example. Western luxury retailers are more welcome in the country now that the Indian government has amended certain legislation pertaining to foreign ownership of a single-brand. The government allowed single-brand retailers to own up to 51% of an outlet in India. Christian Dior, however, had already chosen for a franchise before the changes were put into play.

Luxury retail through the net

E-retailing for luxury products is yet to take off, even in developed countries. There is a sense of insecurity about high-end online purchases. Furthermore, prices of high-end items must be lowered to sell online. This is because consumers think 'If I can get everything else online at a discount, why shouldn't I get a discount on fine art online too?' Online luxury retailers often have a hard time translating their brands and the look and feel of their luxury shops that connote exclusivity, extravagance, excessive wealth, and entertainment into a web-site that the masses will see.

Guild.com is a good example of a type of an e-luxury retailer. It uses database company Abacus to fine-tune its mailing list. Guild.com compares its typical customer profile with Abacus's database, which includes mailing lists from the likes of William Sonoma and the Museum of Modern Art. Using a set of about 125 attributes, Abacus searches the database for the most likely customers for Guild.com. This fine-tuning of its mailing list enables Guild.com to decrease catalogue circulation. Having high quality photos on the site is a key sales driver, so Guild.com takes special care with this. Guild.com requires artists to provide excellent photos of their work. Additionally, the site has a full-time photo artist devoted to making photos look compelling, from meticulous scanning to colour correction. Guild.com works with a Web analytics company called FireClick that provides in-depth data on how shoppers use the site, including complete lists of how each user navigates through the site. Guild.com uses this data, for example, to change how the main page for its paintings section is presented. Depending on what category of painting is most clicked upon, the site will rearrange the page's top four supporting graphics to promote this.

Luxury brick-and-mortar retailers such as Neiman Marcus in the U.S. are approaching e-commerce and have upgraded their site from brochure ware to an e-commerce offering. One reason that these stores should quickly pump some money into their no frills e-commerce sites is because of the fierce competition they are facing from pure plays that are specifically targeting the rich. For instance, jet setters can log on for Isabella Fiore bags from Ashford.com or chat real-time about diamonds with a customer-service rep on Mondera.com. In addition to opening up their wallets and improving their cyberspace stores, luxury brick-and-mortars also stop snubbing proven e-commerce marketing techniques such as affiliate programmes and e-mail.

Luxury goods manufacturers must constantly balance sales volume against the risk of diminishing the prestige of their brands. Another challenge is consumers' desire to have increasingly personalised products. Distribution channels are, therefore, a major consideration for luxury-brand marketers. Luxury retailing, thus, gains prominence. In the case of say luxury cosmetics, marketers are defined by not only innovation and the quality of the products, but also on an interesting shopping experience. Luxury-brand growth increasingly is tied to licensing. The new growth platform is all about licensing brands from big multibillion companies and launching products. The goal is not to build brands, but to build categories. Hummer has a fragrance, Burberry licenses leather goods, and Coach is now a lifestyle brand. Coach has licensed everything from home furnishings to watches to shoes. It is not just a handbag company. Companies are no longer limited by the abilities of their companies to create a luxury category. As categories, increase under a single brand, retailing becomes a viable proposition.

Shifting income and demographics have placed tremendous spending power in the hands of young people. The number of young people who have the financial ability to buy luxury goods is astounding. Counterfeit and knockoff products remain troublesome for luxury businesses. High-end manufacturers are struggling to strike a balance between exclusivity and driving volume sales in this period of shifting definitions of what a luxury lifestyle means. Marketers should strive to find ways to dominate the "emotional space" in their category. Holding firm to the high ground of exclusivity may not be an option. If a luxury brand is purist and does not go for mass commercialisation, it risks someone else taking the brand and doing the same. To draw the middle market up into luxury price brands, marketers need to make sure their products are credible. Even if unsophisticated buyers cannot tell the difference between the high-end products and a lower quality substitute, they will take their cue from knowledgeable shoppers who can tell the difference. If it is not credible to an expert, it is not aspirational to the novice. Thus, shop, retail and shopping experience is key to luxury brands and therefore the greater chance of luxury retailing becoming prominent. Even if a brand reaches out to a broader market, managers must still protect the essence of their luxury product. It is really about how you maintain the image and how you create accessible price points so that people can get a piece of what you are offering. The future of luxury is very bright. More markets are opening up, and developing countries like Russia, China and India represent huge new markets. Even in developed nations there will always be opportunity, because people never stop wanting to learn new things. A key characteristic of luxury brands is that they serve to educate people.

Selected References

Abernathy F, Dunlop J, Hammond J, Weil D, 2000, "Retailing and Supply Chains in the Information Age", *Technology and Society*, 22, 5-31.

Abrams, E., M. Sefton, and A. Yavas, An Experimental Comparison of Two Search Models, *Economic Theory*, Vol. 16 (2000), pp. 735-749.

Affecting the Performance of Individual Chain Store Units: An Empirical Analysis. *Journal of Retailing* 59, 22-39.

Alba, Joseph W. and J. Wesley Hutchinson (1987), "Dimensions of Consumer Expertise," *Journal of Consumer Research*, 13 (March), 411-454.

Allen, F. and A. M. Santomero (1997), "The Theory of Financial Intermediation," *Journal and Semantics, 3: Speech acts* (pp. 41-58), New York, Academic Press.

Anderson, Cynthia E., David J. Burns and Jane S. Reid (2003), "The Next Evolutionary Step for Regional Shopping Malls," *Journal of Shopping Center Research*, 10(2), 27-59.

Andrews, R. L., A. Ainslie and I. S. Currim (2002), "An Empirical Comparison of Logit Choice Models with Discrete versus Continuous Representations of Heterogeneity," *Journal of Marketing Research*, 39, 4, 479-487.

Andrews, R. L., A. Ansari and I. S. Currim (2002), "Hierarchical Bayes versus Finite Mixture Conjoint Analysis Models: A Comparison of Fit, Prediction and Partworth Recovery," *Journal of Marketing Research*, 39, 1, 87-98.

Arnold, S. J., T. H. Oum and D. J. Tigert (1983), "Determining Attributes in Retail Patronage: Seasonal, Temporal, Regional, and International Comparisons," *Journal of Marketing Research*, 20 (May), 149-157.

Bailey T.C., Gatrell A.C. (1995), Interactive Spatial Data Analysis, Longman, Essex.

Baker, Julie, A. Parasuraman, Dhruv Grewal and Glen B. Voss (2002), "The Influence of Multiple Store Environment Cues on Perceived Merchandise Values and Patronage Intentions," *Journal of Marketing*, 66(2), 120-141.

Banerjee, B. and D. Kovenock, Localized and Non-localized Competition in the Presence of Consumer Lock-in, Advanced in Applied Microeconomics, (1999) 8, pp. 45-70.

Barsalou, Lawrence W. (1985), "Ideals, Central Tendency, and Frequency of Instantiation as Determinants of Graded Structure in Categories," *Journal of Experimental Psychology: Learning, Memory, and Cognition*, 11 (October), 629- 654.

Basuroy, S., M. K. Mantrala and R. G. Walters (2001), "The Impact of Category Management on Retailer Prices and Performance: Theory and Evidence," *Journal of Marketing*, 65, 4, 16-32.

Baumol, William J., and Edward A. Ide (1956), "Variety in Retailing," *Management Science*, 3 (1), 93-101.

Bawa, Kapil, Jane T. Landwehr, and Aradhna Krishna (1989), "Consumer Response to Retailers' Marketing Environments: An Analysis of Coffee Purchase Data," *Journal of Retailing*, 65 (4), 471-95.

Baye, M.R., R. Gatti, P. Kattuman, and J. Morgan, 2005, Estimating Firm-Level Demand at a Price Comparison Site: Accounting for Shoppers and the Number of Competitors, Working Paper.

Baye, Michael R. and John Morgan, Information Gatekeepers on the Internet and the Competitiveness of Homogeneous Product Markets, *American Economic Review* (2001), 91(3), pp. 454-474.

Baye, Michael R. and John Morgan, Price Dispersion in the Lab and on the Internet: Theory and Evidence, *RAND Journal of Economics*, (2004), 35(3), pp. 449-66.

Baye, Michael R., John Morgan, and Patrick Scholten, Price Dispersion in the Small and in the Large: Evidence from an Internet Price Comparison Site, *Journal of Industrial Economics* (2004), 52(4), pp. 463-96.

Bell, David E 1994, *Harvard Note on Retail Economics #9-595-006*, Harvard Business School Press, Boston, MA.

Bergen, Mark, Shantanu Dutta, and Steven M. Shugan (1996), "Branded Variants: A Retail Perspective," *Journal of Marketing Research*, 23 (February), 9-19.

Berry, Leonard L., Lewis P. Carbone and Stephan H. Haeckel (2002), "Managing the Total Customer Experience," *MIT Sloan Management Review*, 43(3), 85-89.

Bettman, James R. and Michel A. Zins (1979), "Information Format and Choice Task Effects in Decision Making," *Journal of Consumer Research*, 6 (September), 141-153.

Bettman, James R., Eric J. Johnson, and John W. Payne (1990), "A Componential Analysis of Cognitive Effort in Choice," *Organizational Behavior and Human Decision Processes*, 45 (1), 111-139.

Bihun, Y. 2000, "On the Home Front," Timber & Wood Products International 393(6373), 44-46, Boxwell, R.J., Jr. 1994, *"Benchmarking for Competitive Advantage,"* McGraw-Hill, New York.

Boatwright, Peter, Sanjay Dhar, and Peter Rossi (2001), "Explaining the Variation in Price and Promotion Sensitivities - It's More than Demographics," GSIA working paper, Carnegie Mellon University.

Bowlby, Rachel (1997), "Supermarket Futures," in Pasi Falk and Colin Campbell eds, The Shopping Experience, London, Sage, pp. 92-110.

Brandenburger, A.M. and B.J. Nalebuff, 1998, "Co-opetition," Doubleday, New York.

Briesch, Richard A., Lakshman Krishnamurthi, Tridib Mazumdar and S.P. Raj (1997), "A Comparative Analysis of Reference Price Models," *Journal of Consumer Research*, 24 (Sep), 202-214.

Broniarczyk, Susan M., Wayne D. Hoyer, and Leigh McAlister (1998), "Consumers' Perceptions of the Assortment Offered in a Grocery Category: The Impact of Item Reduction," *Journal of Marketing Research*, 35 (May), 166-176.

Brucks, Merrie (1985), "The Effects of Product Class Knowledge on Information Search Behavior," *Journal of Consumer Research*, 12 (June), 1-16.

Buchanan,L., Carolyn Simmons, Barbara Bickart (1999), "Brand Equity Dilution: Retailer Display and Context Brand Effects," *Journal of Marketing Research*, August, 345-355.

Bullard, S.H, "The Geography of U.S. Homefurnishings Sales," Furniture World, 120(5), 28-33, Bullard, S.H. and B.J. Seldon, 1993, "Substitution Among Capital, Labor, and Raw Materials in Upholstered Household Furniture Manufacturing."

Bullard, S.H. 1989, "Furniture Manufacturing and Marketing in the 'American Economic Transition'," Res. Report 14, Mississippi Forest Products Utilization Laboratory, Mississippi State, Mississippi.

Caillaud, B. and B. Jullien, Chicken and Egg: Competition Among Intermediation Service Providers, *RAND Journal of Economics*, 34 (2003), 309-328.

Caillaud, B. and B. Jullien, Competing Cybermediaries, *European Economic Review*, 45 (2002), pp. 797-808.

Campbell, Margaret C. and Ronald C. Goodstein (2001), "The moderating effect of perceived risk on consumers' evaluations of product incongruity: Preference for the norm," *Journal of Consumer Research*, 28 (Dec), 439-449.

Campbell, Margaret C. and Ronald C. Goodstein (2002), "The Attenuating Effect of Risk on Consumers' Evaluations of Moderatel Incongruent Stimuli," University of Colorado, Boulder Working Paper.

Campo, K., E. Gijsbrechts, T. Goossens and A. Verhetsel (2000), "The impact of location factors on the attractiveness and optimal space shares of product categories," *International Journal of Research in Marketing*, 17(4), 255-279.

Cason, T. and D. Friedman, Buyer Search and Price Dispersion: A Laboratory Study, *Journal of Economic Theory*, 112 (2003), pp. 232-260.

Chen, J. and P. Scholten, Price Dispersion, Product Characteristics and Firms Behaviors: Stylized Facts from Shopper.com, Advances in Applied Microeconomics (2003), pp. 143-164.

Chevalier, J. and A. Goolsbee, Measuring Prices and Price Competition Online: Amazon and Barnes and Noble, Quantitative Marketing and Economics (2003), 1(2), pp. 203-222.

Chintagunta, P. K. (2002), "Investigating Category Pricing Behavior at a Retail Chain," *Journal of Marketing Research*, 39, 2, 141-154.

Chintagunta, P. K. 1993, Investigating purchase incidence, brand choice and purchase quantity decisions of households, *Marketing Science*. 12(2), 184–208.

Chintagunta, P. K., J. P. Dube and V. Singh (2003), "Balancing Profitability and Customer Welfare in a Supermarket Chain," *Quantitative Marketing and Economics*, 1, 1, 111-147.

Chintagunta, Pradeep (2002), "Endogeneity and Heterogeneity in a Probit Demand Model: Estimation Using Aggregate Data," *Marketing Science*, forthcoming.

Clarke-Hill, C.M. (1991), "Habitat-Mothercare plc", in Clarke-Hill, C.M. and Glaister, K. (Eds), Cases in Strategic Management, Pitman, London.

Clemente, Peter State of the Net: *The New Frontier*, McGraw-Hill, 1997.

Crewe L, 2000, "Geographies of retailing and consumption", *Progress in Human Geography*, 24, 275-290.

Crewe L, 2001, "The beseiged body: geographies of retailing and consumption", Progress in Human Geography, 25, 629-640.

Currah A, 2002, "Behind the webstore: the organizational and spatial evolution of multi-channel retailing in Toronto", *Environment and Planning*, A, 34, 1411-1441.

Currah A, 2003, "The virtual geographies of retail display", *Journal of Consumer Culture*, 3, 5-37.

Daily Telegraph (1994), "Conran's Habitat seeks Chapter 11", 11 January.

Dawson J, 2000, "Retailing at century end: some challenges for management and research", *International Review of Retail, Distribution and Consumer Research,* 10, 119-148.

Dekimpe, Marnik G. and Dominique M. Hanssens, 1999, Sustained Spending and Persistent Reponse: A New Look at Long-Term Marketing Profitability, *Journal of Marketing Research,* vol. 36, 397-412.

Desrochers, D.M., G.T. Gundlach, A.A. Foer 2003, Analysis of Antitrust Challenges to Category Captain Arrangements, *Journal of Public Policy & Marketing,* Vol. 22, No. 2, (Fall), 201-215.

Dick, Alan S. and Basu, Kunal (1994), "Customer Loyalty: Towards an Integrated Framework", *Journal of the Academy of Marketing Science,* 22, 2, 99-113.

Dodds, William B., Monroe, Kent B., & Grewal, Dhruv (1991), Effects of price, brand, and store information on buyers' product evaluations, *Journal of Marketing Research,* 28, 307–319.

Dodge M, 2001, "Finding the Source of Amazon.com: Examining the Store with the *'Earth's Biggest Selection' in Worlds of E-Commerce: economic, geographical and social dimensions* Eds T Leinbach and S Brunn (Wiley, Chichester), pp. 167-180.

Drèze, Xavier, Stephen J. Hoch and Mary E. Purk (1994), "Shelf Management and Space Elasticity," *Journal of Retailing,* 70 (4), 301-26.

Duany, Andres and Elizabeth Plater-Zyberk and Jeff Speck, Suburban Nation: The Rise of Sprawl and the Decline of the American Dream, North Point Press, New York, 2000.

East, Robert, Harris, Patricia, Willson, Gill and Hammond, Kathy (1995), "Correlates of First-Brand Loyalty", *Journal of Marketing Management,* 11, 5, 487-497.

East, Robert, Harris, Patricia, Willson, Gill and Lomax, Wendy (1995), "Loyalty to *Supermarkets",* International Review of Retail, Distribution and Consumer Research, 5, 1, 99-109.

East, Robert, Lomax, Wendy, Willson, Gill and Harris, Patricia (1994), "Decision Making and Habit in Shopping Times", *European Journal of Marketing,* 28, 4, 56-71.

Economist Intelligence Unit (EIU) (1993), "Company Profile No. 5 ± IKEA", *Retail Business Quarterly Trade Review,* No. 25, March.

Eisenhardt, Kathleen M. 1988, Agency – and Institutional – Theory Explanations: The Case of Retail Sales Compensation, *Academy of Management Journal,* 31, 488-511.

Ellison, Glenn and Sara Fisher Ellison, .Lessons about Markets from the Internet, *Journal of Economic Perspectives,* (2005) 19(2), pp. 139-158.

Elmuti, D., & Kathawala, Y. (1998), Outsourcing to gain a competitive advantage, *Industrial Management,* 40(3), 20-25.

Fitzsimons, Gavan J. (2000), "Consumer Response to Stockouts," *Journal of Consumer Research,* 27 (September), 249-266.

Food Marketing Institute (1997), "Home Shopping Programs: A Strategic Guide," prepared by Robert E. Linneman and Patrick J. Kirschling, Department of Food Marketing, Saint Joseph's University.

Forest, Stephanie A. (1999), "A Penney Saved," *Business Week,* March 29, pp. 64-66.

Fredriksson, Cecilia (1997), "The Making of a Swedish Department Store Culture," in Pasi Falk and Colin Campbell eds, The Shopping Experience, London, Sage, pp. 111-135.

Frei, F. X. and Harker, P. T. (1996), "Measuring the Efficiency of Service Delivery Processes: With Application to Retail Banking," Operations Group Working Paper, 96-04, Simon School of Business, University of Rochester.

Frook, John Evan, "Linking the Supply Chain with the Cash Register," Internet World, April 6, 1998.

Gallanis, Peter (2000), "Sears rolls out pilot program to test in-store innovations," *DSN Retailing Today*, Vol. 39, (September 20, No. 18), pp. 1, 113.

Garbarino, Ellen C., & Edell, Julie A, (1997), Cognitive effort, affect, and choice, *Journal of Consumer Research*, 24, 147–158.

Gay, C, & Essinger, J. (2000), *Inside outsourcing*, Naperville, IL, Nicholas Brealey.

Gielens, K. and M. Dekimpe, 2001, Do International Entry Decisions of Retail Chains Matter in the Long Run? *International Journal of Research in Marketing*, 18, 235-259.

Gijsbrechts, Els, Campo, Katia, and Tom Goossens, 2003, The Impact of Store Flyers on Store Traffic and Store Sales: A Geo-Marketing Approach, *Journal of Retailing*, 79 1-16.

Girishankar, Saroja, "Virtual Markets Create New Roles for Distributors," Internet World, April 6, 1998.

Godek, John, J. Frank Yates and Seigyoung Auh (2001), "Evalution of Customized Products: The Effects of Assortment and Control," University of Michigan Working Paper.

Goodstein, Ronald C. (1993), "Category-Based Applications and Extensions in Advertising: Motivating More Extensive Processing," *Journal of Consumer Research*, 20 (June), 87-99.

Greaver, M. (1999), *Strategic outsourcing*, New York: American Management Association.

Grice, H. P. (1975), "Logic and Conversation," In P. Cole & J. L. Morgan (Eds.), *Syntax*.

Grocery Manufacturers of America, Category Management, Joint Industry Project on Efficient Consumer Response, 1994.

Guiltinan, Joseph P. and Gregory T. Gundlach (1996), "Aggressive and Predatory Pricing: A Framework for Analysis," *Journal of Marketing*, 60, (3, Summer), 87.

Gupta, Sunil (1988), "The Impact of Sales Promotions on When, What, and How Much to Buy," *Journal of Marketing Research*, 25 (Nov), 342-355.

Gupta, Sunil (1988), "Impact of Sales Promotions on When, What, and How Much to Buy," *Journal of Marketing Research*, 25 (Nov), 342-55.

Hagerty, James R, "A Free Spirit Energizes Home Depot," *The Wall Street Journal*, April 11, 2000, p. B1, B4.

Heath, Timothy B. and Subimal C. Chatterjee (1995), "Asymmetric Decoy Effects on Lower-quality Versus Higher-quality Brands: Meta-analytic and Experimental Evidence," *Journal of Consumer Research*, 22, (3), 268-284.

Henisz, Witold J. 2000, "The Institutional Environment for Multinational Investment", *Journal of Law, Economics and Organization* 16, (2), 343-363.

Herman, C.Peter and Deborah Mack (1975), "Restrained and Unrestrained Eating," *Journal of Personality*, 43 (December), 647-660.

Hetherton, Marion and Barbara J. Rolls (1996), "Sensory-Specific Satiety: Theoretical Frameworks and Central Characteristics," in E. D. Capaldi (Ed.) *Why We Eat What We Eat: The Psychology of Eating*, pp. 267-290, Washington, D.C., American Psychological Association.

Ho, T., J. Chong, 2000, A parsimonious model of SKU choice, Working paper 99-020, Marketing Department, University of Pennsylvania, Philadelphia, PA.

Hoch, Stephen J., and Shumeet Banerji (1993), "When Do Private Labels Succeed?," *Sloan Management Review*, 34 (Summer), 57-68.

Hoch, Stephen J., Eric T. Bradlow and Brian Wansink (2000), "Rejoinder to 'The Variety of an Assortment'," *Marketing Science*, 21(3), 342-346.

Hoch, Stephen J., Xavier Drèze & Mary E. Purk (1994), "EDLP, Hi-Lo, and Margin Arithmetic," *Journal of Marketing*, 58 (October), 16-29.

Hoch, Stephen, Eric T. Bradlow and Brian Wansink (1999), "The Variety of an Assortment," *Marketing Science* 18 (4), 527-546.

Hoch, Steven. "Effective category management depends on the role of the category", *Journal of Retailing*, Babson College, Summer 2001, Volume 77, issue 2.

Hogarth-Scott, S. and Parkinson, S.T., "Retailer supplier relationships in the food channel", *International Journal of Retail & Distribution Management*, Vol. 21, No. 8, 1993, pp. 11-18.

Hosgood, Christopher (1999), "Doing the Shops' at Christmas: Women, Men and the Department Store in England, 1880-1914," in Geoffrey Crossick and Serge Jaumain eds.

Hsee, Christoper K. and France LeClerc (1998), "Will Products Look More Attractive When Presented Separately or Together?" *Journal of Consumer Research*, 25 (September), 175-186.

Huffman, Cynthia and Barbara E. Kahn (1998), "Variety for Sale: Mass Customization or Mass Confusion," *Journal of Retailing*, Winter 1998, Vol. 74 (4), 491-513.

Huffman, Cynthia and Michael J. Houston (1993), "Goal-oriented Experiences and the Development of Knowledge," *Journal of Consumer Research*, 20 (September), 190-217.

Hummels, D., Rapoport, D. and Yi, K.-M. (2001), "The Nature and Growth of Vertical Specialization in World Trade", *Journal of International Economics*, 54, 75–96.

Hunter, L.W. (1997), "Transforming retail banking: Inclusion and segmentation in service work," Working Paper, Wharton Financial Institutions Center, The Wharton School (Philadelphia, PA).

Hursh, Steven R., Thomas G. Raslear, David Shurtleff, Richard Bauman, and Laurence Simmons (1988), "A Cost-Benefit Analysis of Demand for Food," *Journal of the Experimental Analysis of Behavior*, 50 (November), 419-440.

Hutchinson, J. Wesley, Kalyan Raman and Murali K. Mantrala (1994), "Finding Choice Alternatives in Memory: Probability Models of Brand Name Recall," *Journal of Marketing Research*, 31(4), 441-462.

Hutchsinson, J. Wesley (1983), "Expertise and the Structure of Free Recall," Advances in Consumer Research, (10), 585-589.

Ibrahim, Faishal and Chye Wee Ng (2002), "Determinants of Entertaining Shopping Experiences and Their Link to Consumer Behavior: Case Studies of Shopping Centres in Singapore," *Journal of Retail and Leisure Property*, 2(4), 338-357.

Inman, J. Jeffrey (2001), "The Role of Sensory Specific Satiety in Attribute level Variety.

International Journal of Retail and Distribution Management, 29, 266-273.

Isen, Alice M., Thomas E. Shalker, Margaret S. Clark, Lynn Karp (1978), "Affect, Accessibility of Material in Memory and Behavior: A Cognitive Loop?" *Journal of Personality and Social Psychology*, 20 (January): 203-53.

Iyengar, Sheena S. and Mark R. Lepper (2000), "When Choice is Demotivating: Can one Desire too much of a Good Thing?" *Journal of Personality and Social Psychology*, 79 (December) 995-1006.

Iyer, G. and P. B. Seetharaman (2003), "To Price Discriminate or Not: Product Choice and the Selection Bias Problem," *Quantitative Marketing and Economics*, 1, 2, 155-178.

Jain, Dipak and Siddhartha S. Singh (2002), "Customer Lifetime Value Research: A Review and Future Directions," *Journal of Interactive Marketing*, 16(2), 34-46.

Jain, Dipak C. and Naufel J. Vilcassim (1991), "Investigating Household Purchase Timing Decisions: A Conditional Hazard Function Approach", *Marketing Science*, 10, 1, (Winter) 1-23.

Janiszewski, Chris (1998), "The Influence of Display Characteristics on Visual Exploratory Search Behavior," *Journal of Consumer Research*, Dec, 290-301.

Javalgi, R. & Moberg, C.R. (1997), Service Loyalty: Implications for Service Providers, *The Journal of Services Marketing*, 11, pp. 165-179.

Johnson, Eric J. and John W. Payne (1985), "Effort and Accuracy in Choice," *Management Science*, 31 (April), 395-414.

Johnson, Eric J., and J. Edward Russo (1984), "Product Familiarity and Learning New Information," *Journal of Consumer Research*, 11(June), 542-550.

Kahn, B. E. 1999, Variety: From the consumer's perspective. T. Ho, C. Tang, eds, *Research Advances in Product Variety Management*, Kluwer Academic Publishers, New York.

Kahn, B.E., B. Wansink, 2004, The Influence of Assortment Structure on Perceived Variety and Consumption Quantities, *Journal of Consumer Research*, Vol.30, 519-533.

Kahn, Barbara E. (1995), "Consumer Variety-Seeking among Goods and Services," *Journal of Retailing and Consumer Services*, 2 (3), 139-148.

Kahn, Barbara E. and Brian Wansink (2002), "Impact of Perceived Variety on Consumption Quantity," The Wharton School, University of Pennsylvania working paper.

Kahn, Barbara E. and Donald R. Lehmann (1991), "Modeling Choice among Assortments," *Journal of Retailing*, 67 (3), 274-299.

Kahn, Barbara E. and Leigh McAlister (1997), *Grocery Revolution: The New Focus on the Consumer*, Reading, MA, Addison-Wesley.

Kahneman, Daniel (1973), *Attention and effort*, Englewood Cliffs, NJ, Prentice Hall.

Keah C. R. K. & R. B. Handfield(1998),"Supply Chain Management, Supplier Performance and firm Performance,"*International Journal of Purchasing and Materials Management*, pp. 2-9.

Kinley, Tammy, Youn-Kyung Kim, and Judith Forney (2003), "Tourist-Destination Shopping Centers: An Importance-Performance Analysis of Attributes," *Journal of Shopping Center Research*, 10(2), 51-72.

Kivetz, Ran and Itamar Simonson (2002), "Earning the Right to Indulge: Effort as a Determinant of Customer Preferences towards Frequency Program Rewards," *Journal of Marketing Research*, 39 (May).

Kleinmuntz, Don and David Schkade (1994), "Information Displays and Choice Processes: Differential Effects of Organization, Form, and Sequence," *Organization Behavior and Human Decision Processes*, March 57 (3), 319-337.

Knee, Chirstopher (2002), "Learning from Experience: Five Challenges for Retailers," *International Journal of Retail and Distribution*, 30(11/12), 518-531.

Kooijman, Dion (2002), "A Third Revolution in Retail? The Dutch Approach to Leisure and Urban Entertainment," *Journal of Retail and Leisure Property*, 2-3 (August), 214-229.

Lafontaine, Francine and Kathryn L. Shaw (1998), "Franchising Growth and Franchisor Entry and Exit in the US Market: Myth and Reality," *Journal of Business Venturing*, 13, 95- 112.

Lal, Rajiv and Ram Rao (1997), "Supermarket Competition: The Case of Every Day Low Pricing," *Marketing Science*, 16(no.1), 60-80.

Larkin, Jill H., John McDermott, Dorothea P. Simon and Herbert A. Simon (1980), "Models of Competence in Solving Physics Problems," *Cognitive Science*, 4 (October-December), 291-308.

Lee, H., K. So, C. Tang, 2000, The value of information sharing in a two-level supply chain, *Management Science*, 46(5), 626–643.

Lemm, J.J. 2000, Household Furniture. U.S. Industry and Trade Outlook 2000, (Part of Section 38), *USDC International Trade Administration*, McGraw-Hill, New York.

Licata, Jane W., Abhijit Biswas and Balaji C. Krishnan (1998), "Ambiguity and Exaggeration in Price Promotion: Perceptions of the Elder and Nonelder Consumer," *Journal of Consumer Affairs*, 32 (Summer), 56-81.

Loken, Barbara and James Ward (1990), "Alternative Approaches to Understanding the Determinants of Typicality," *Journal of Consumer Research*, 17 (September), 111-126.

Lusch, Robert F. and Ray R. Serpkenci, 1990, Personal Differences, Job Tension, Job Outcomes and Store Performance: A Study of Retail Store Managers, *Journal of Marketing*, 54, 85-102.

Mangleburg, Tamara F., Patricia M. Doney and Terry Bristol (2004), "Shopping with Friends and Teens' Susceptibility to Peer Influence," *Journal of Retailing*, 80(2), 101-116.

Marcus, Bernie and Arthur Blank with Bob Andelman, Built from Scratch, New York, Random House, 1999.

Margolies, J.M.(1995),Best Practiecs in Retailing:The Grocery Industry and ECR, Chain Store Age, 71, pp. 92-94.

Marsh, P. (2001), "A Sharp Sense of the Limits to Outsourcing", *The Financial Times,* 31st July, 10.

McAfee, Preston R., Competitive Solutions, Princeton University Press, 2002.

McGoldrick, Peter J. and Andre, Elisabeth (1997), "Consumer Misbehavior: Promiscuity or Loyalty in Grocery Shopping", *Journal of Retailing and Consumer Services*, 4, 2, 73-81.

Mclaren, J. (2000), "Globalization and Vertical Structure", *American Economic Review*, 90, 1239–1254.

Mejia, L.C. and J.D. Benjamin (2002), "What do we Know about Determinants of Shopping Center Sales?" *Journal of Real Estate Literature*, 10(1), 3-26.

Meyers-Levy, Joan and Alice M. Tybout (1989), "Schema Congruity as a Basis for Product Evaluation," *Journal of Consumer Research*, 16 (June), 39-54.

Michon, Richard, Jean-Charles Chebat and L.W. Turley (2005), "Mall Atmospherics: The Interaction Effects of the Mall Environment on Shopping Behavior," *Journal of Business Research*, 58, 576-583.

Montgomery, A. L. (2004), "The Implementation Challenge of Pricing Decision Support Systems for Retail Managers," Working Paper, Carnegie-Mellon University.

Morse, Dan, "A Hardware Chain Struggles to Adjust to a New Blueprint," *The Wall Street Journal*, January 17, 2003, pp. A1, A6.

Morton, Fiona Scott, Florian Zettelmeyer, Jorge Silva-Risso, Internet Car Retailing, *Journal of Industrial Economics*, 49 (4), 2001, pp. 501-519.

Mudgil, V. (2003, September 1), Future of retail technology, *Retail World*, 56, 18-19.

Nelson, Kristi, "Category & space management connect," Consumer Goods Technology, March 2000.

Nestle, Marion (2002), *Food Politics: How the Food Industry Influences Nutrition and Health,* Berkeley, CA, University of California Press.

Oliver, Richard L. (1999), "Whence Consumer loyalty?," *Journal of Marketing*, 63 (Special Issue), 33-44.

Ooi, L. T. and C.F. Sirmans (2004), "The Wealth Effects of Land Acquisition," *Journal of Real Estate Finance and Economics*, 29(3), 277-294.

Orme, Bryan, (2002), "Conjoint Analysis has Value," *Marketing Research*, Winter, 46-47.

Ozanne, Julie L., Merrie Brucks and Dhruv Grewal (1992), "A Study of Information Search Behavior During the Categorization of New Products," *Journal of Consumer Research*, 18 (March), 452-463.

Pan, Yigang and Donald R. Lehmann (1993), "The Influence of New Brand Entry on Subjective Brand Judgments," *Journal of Consumer Research*, 20, 76-86.

Pascual, Aixa, "Tyding Up at Home Depot," *Business Week*, November 26, 2001, pp. 102-104.

Pramataris, K.C., Papakiriakopoulos, D., Motsios, T. & Doukidis, G.I. (2000), "A Multidimensional Approach to Product Advertisement in the Virtual Retail environment". In Proceedings of European Conference on Information Systems (ECIS 2000), 3-5 July 2000, Vienna, Austria.

Pramataris, K.C., Vrechopoulos, A.P. & Doukidis G.I., (2000), "The transformation of the promotion mix in the virtual retail environment: An initial framework and comparative study", *Journal of New Product Development and Innovation Management*, Special issue on retail, June/July 2000.

Raghubir, Priya and Aradhna Krishna (1999), "Vital dimensions in volume perception: Can the eye fool the stomach?" *Journal of Marketing Research*, 36 (August), 313-326.

Raju, Jagmohan S., Raj K. Sethuraman and Sanjay K. Dhar (1995), "The Introduction and Performance of Store Brands," *Management Science*, 41(June), 957-78.

Ratner, Rebecca K. and Barbara E. Kahn (2002), "Private vs. Public Consumption: The Impact of Impression Management on Variety Seeking," *Journal of Consumer Research*, (September).

Ratner, Rebecca. K., Barbara E. Kahn and Daniel Kahneman (1999), "Choosing Less-Preferred Experiences for the Sake of Variety," *Journal of Consumer Research*, 26 (June), 1-15.

Ratneshwar, S and Shocker, Allan D (1991), "Substitution in use and the role of usage context in product category structures," *Journal of Marketing Research*, Vol 28(3), August 281-295.

Rayner, Hollie A. and Leonard H. Epstein (2001), "Dietary Variety, Energy Regulation and Obesity," *Psychological Bulletin*, 127, (3), 325-341.

Rolls, Barbara J. (1986), "Sensory-specific Satiety," *Nutrition Reviews*, 44, 3, 93-101.

Rolls, Barbara J., Edward A. Rowe, Edmund T. Rolls, Breda Kindston, Angela Megson and Rachel Gunary (1981), *Variety in a Meal Enhances Food Intake in Man, Physiology & Behavior*, 26 (February), 215-221.

Rossi, Peter E., Greg Allenby and J. Kim (2000), "Modeling Consumer Demand for Variety." Working paper, University of Chicago.

Roth, A.V. and M. V. D. Velde (1992), *World class banking: Benchmarking the strategies of retail banking leaders*, Chicago, IL, Center for Banking Excellence, Bank Administration Institute.

Roush, Chris, Inside Home Depot, New York, McGraw-Hill, 1999.

Russo, J. Edward and Barbara Ann Dosher (1983), "Strategies for Multiattribute Binary Choice," *Journal of Experimental Psychology: Learning, Memory, and Cognition*, (October), 676-696.

Russo, Jay E. (1977), "The Value of Unit Price Information," *Journal of Marketing Research*, 14 (May), 193-201.

Saran, C. (2003), Gartner advises firms to consider alternative offshore IT locations. *Computer Weekly*, 5.

Schuler, A., R. Taylor and P. Araman, 2001, Competitiveness of U.S. Wood Furniture Manufacturers: Lessons Learned from the Softwood Moulding Industry, *Forest Products Journal*, 51(7/8),14-29.

Schwarz, Norbert (1996), *Cognition and Communication: Judgmental Biases, Research Methods and the Logic of Conversation*, Mahwah, New Jersey, Lawrence Erlbaum Associates, Publishers.

Schwarz, Norbert (1998), "Warmer and More Social: Recent Developments in Cognitive Social Psychology," *Annual Rev. Sociology*, 24 (1), 239-64.

Schwarz, Norbert and Gerald L. Clore (1983), "Mood, Misattribution and Judgments of Well-Being: Informative and Directive Functions of Affective States," *Journal of Personality and Social Psychology*, 24 (September), 161-99.

Seetharaman, P. B., S. Chib, A. Ainslie, P. Boatwright, T. Chan, S. Gupta, N. Mehta, V. R. Rao and A. Strijnev (2005), "Models of Multicategory Choice Behavior," Marketing Letters.

Shankar, V. and R. N. Bolton (2004), "An Empirical Analysis of Determinants of Retailer Pricing Strategy," *Marketing Science*, 23, 1, 28-49.

Shannon, Claude E. (1948), "A Mathematical Theory of Communication," *Bell System Technical Journal*, 27 (July), 379-423.

Shannon, Claude E. and Warren Weaver (1949), "Information Theory," Champaign, IL, University of Illinois Press.

Shanteau, James (1992), "How much Information Does an Expert Use? Is it Relevant?" *Acta Psychologica*, 81(1992), 75-86.

Sharp, Byron and Anne Sharp (1997), "Loyalty Programs and their Impact on Repeat- Purchase Loyalty Patterns," *International Journal of Research in Marketing*, 14 (5), 473-486.

Shaw, S.A., "Competitiveness, relationships and the Strathclyde University food project", *Journal of Marketing Management*, Vol. 10, 1994, pp. 391-407.

Shaw, S.A., Harris, N. and Carter, S., "The UK tomato industry: Market intelligence and producer co-ordination", *British Food Journal*, Vol. 95, No. 10, 1993, pp. 1-17.

Simonson, Itamar (1990), "The Effect of Purchase Quantity and Timing on Variety- Seeking Behavior," *Journal of Marketing Research*, 27(May), 150-162.

Simonson, Itamar, Stephen Nowlis and Katherine Lemon (1993), "The Effect of Local Consideration Sets on Global Choice Between Lower Price and Higher Quality," *Marketing Science*, 12 (Fall), 357-378.

Sivakumar, K. and S. P. Raj (1997), "Quality Tier Competition: How Price Change Influences Brand Choice and Category Choice," *Journal of Marketing*, 61(3, July), 71-84.

Smith, M. D., The Impact of Shopbots on ElectronicMarkets, *Journal of the Academy of Marketing Science*, 30 (2002), pp. 446-454.

Solomon, Michael R. (2002), *Consumer Behavior: Buying, Having and Being*, Upper Saddle River, NJ, Prentice Hall.

Spiggle, Susan (1987), "Grocery Shopping Lists: What Do Consumers Write?" *Advances in Consumer Research*, Vol. 14, Melanie Wallendorf and Paul F. Anderson, Eds., Provo, UT, Association for Consumer Research, 241-245

Stayman, Douglas M., Dana L. Alden and Karen H. Smith (1992), "Some Effects of Schematic Processing on Consumer Expectations and Disconfirmation Judgments," *Journal of Consumer Research*, 19 (September), 240-255.

Steiner, R.L. 2001, Category Management - A Pervasive, New Vertical/Horizontal Format, Antitrust, 15 (Spring), 77-81.

Sujan, Mita (1985), "Consumer Knowledge: Effects on Evaluation Strategies Mediating Consumer Judgments," *Journal of Consumer Research*, 12 (June), 16-31.

Sujan, Mita and James R. Bettman (1989), "The Effects of Brand Positioning Strategies on Consumer's Brand and Category Perceptions: Some Insights from Schema Research," *Journal of Marketing Research*, 26 (4), 454-467.

Terborg, James R. and Gerardo R. Ungson, 1985, Group-Administered Bonus Pay and Retail Store Performance: A Two-Year Study of Management Compensation, *Journal of Retailing*, 61, 63-77.

Terhune, Chad, "Home Depot Founder Blank Quits Board to Clear Path for Current CEO Nardelli," *The Wall Street Journal*, February 22, 2001, p. B10.

Thibodeaux, A. 2001, Upholstered Manufacturers Upgrade Websites to Lure Internet-savvy Consumers, Modern Woodworking, 15(7), 24-26.

Thomas, Jacquelyn (2001), "A Methodology for Linking Customer Acquisition to Customer Retention," *Journal of Marketing Research*, 38 (May), 262-268.

Thorndyke, Perry W. and Barbara Hayes-Roth (1979), "The Use of Schemata in the Acquisition and Transfer of Knowledge," *Cognitive Psychology*, 11 (January), 82-106.

Toivanen, Otto and Michael Waterson, 2000, Empirical Research on Discrete Choice Game Theory Models of Entry: An Illustration, *European Economic Review*, 44, 985-992.

Van Herpen, Erica and Rik Pieters (2002), "Assortment Variety: Attribute-versus Product-Based," *Marketing Science*.

Verhoef, Peter C. (2001), "Analyzing Customer Relationships: Linking Relational Constructs and Marketing Instruments to Consumer Behavior," Doctoral Dissertation, Erasmus University Rotterdam.

Vilcassim, N. J. and P. K. Chintagunta (1995), "Investigating Retailer Product Category Pricing from Household Scanner Panel Data," *Journal of Retailing*, 71, 2, 103-128.

Wang, Shuguang, Ricardo Gomez-Insausti, Marco Biasiotto, Pina Barbiero and Bruce McNally (2000), "A Comparative Analysis of Entertainment Cross-Shopping in a Power Node and a Regional Mall," *Journal of Shopping Center Research*, 7(1), 59-84.

Wansink, Brian (1996), "Can Package Size Accelerate Usage Volume?" *Journal of Marketing*, 60 (July), 1-14.

Ward, Michael R and Michael J. Lee, Internet Shopping, Consumer Search and Product Branding, *Journal of Product and Brand Management*, (2000), 9(1), pp. 6-18.

Webb-Pressler, Margaret, "Moving merchandise (around)", Washington Post, February 3, 2002.

Weber, Renee and Jennifer Crocker (1983), "Cognitive Processes in the Revision of Stereotypic Beliefs," *Journal of Personality and Social Psychology*, 45 (November), 961-977.

Wesley, Scarlett and Melody LeHew (2002), "Tourist-Oriented Shopping Centers:Investigating Customers' Evaluation of Attribute Importance," *Journal of Shopping Center Research*, 9(Fall/Winter), 31-52.

Whiteoak P., "The realities of quick response in the grocery sector", *International Journal of Retail & Distribution Management*, 1993, Vol. 21, No. 8, 1993, pp. 3-10.

Wilder, Clinton, "Distributors get their own Shot at Web Sales," Information Week, September 8, 1997.

Williamson, P.J., "Supplier strategy and customer responsiveness: Managing the links", *Journal of Business Strategy*, Summer, 1991, pp. 75-89.

Wolfe, Harry B, 1968, A Model for Control of Style Merchandise, *Industrial Management Review*, 9 69-82.

Wright, Peter D. and Frederic Barbour (1977), "Phased Decision Strategies: Sequels to an Initial Screeening," *North Holland TIMS Studies in the Management Science*, Eds. Martin K. Starr and Milan Zeleny, Amsterdam, North Holland.

Yoo, C., Park, J. & MacInnis, D.J., (1998), Eþects of store characteristics and in-store emotional experiences on store attitude, *Journal of Business Research*, 42, pp. 253-263.

Young, Michael E. and Edward A. Wasserman (2001), "Entropy and Variability Discrimination," *Journal of Experimental Psychology: Learning, Memory and Cognition*, 27 (1), 278-293.

Zacharias, John and Victor Schinazi (2003), "The Impact of an Entertainment Retrofit on the Performance of a Shopping Center," *Journal of Shopping Center Research*, 10(1), 29-44.

Zenor, M. J. (1994), "The Profit Benefits of Category Management," *Journal of Marketing Research*, 31, 2, 202-213.

Zou, Shaoming and S. Tamer Cavusgil, 2002, "The GMS: A broad conceptualization of global marketing strategy and its effect on firm performance," *Journal of International Marketing*, 66, October, 40-66.

Index